PORTFOLIO
WHAT I DID NOT LEARN IN B-SCHOOL

Rajeev Agarwal is the founder and the chief executive officer of MAQ Software. Prior to founding MAQ Software in 2000, he worked at Microsoft Corporation, Redmond, for nearly seven years in various product management groups.

MAQ Software has been listed as one of the fastest-growing companies in the US eight times—a rare achievement.

Rajeev holds a BTech degree in mechanical engineering from IIT Kharagpur, a master's in engineering from Iowa State University and an MBA from the University of Michigan Business School, Ann Arbor.

He runs a non-profit organization, Foundation for Excellence, which provides science and mathematics education facilities to girls in rural India.

Rajeev lives in Bellevue, Washington, with his wife, Arpita, and their two children.

Share your success stories at www.MBAbook.in. You can contact the author at rajeev@maqsoftware.net.

ADVANCE PRAISE FOR THE BOOK

'Advances in the software industry continue to accelerate at an astonishing pace. India has been at the forefront in helping companies worldwide implement software-driven innovations. With exciting advances in artificial intelligence, cloud and mobile computing, the industry needs to yet again adapt quickly. More than ever, managers will play a critical role in developing and adopting new technologies. This book is an excellent guide full of useful insights for managers looking to stay ahead. Highly recommended!'

C.P. GURNANI, managing director and chief executive officer, Tech Mahindra

'This engaging book will make a big difference to managers. The chapters are so clear that even a person who is not into reading will be tempted to read the book.'

S.V. NATHAN, chief talent officer, Deloitte India

'This book takes the reader through a roller-coaster ride of a manager's life, from hiring, retaining and motivating teams, to managing time effectively while at the same time growing as an individual. The book demystifies this process with an assured touch and genuine sensitivity.'

ARJUN MALHOTRA, co-founder, HCL Technologies

'*What I Did Not Learn in B-school* is very practical and addresses real issues in our businesses. All managers should read it to set realistic expectations for themselves and their teams.'

SUNIL GOYAL, chief operating officer, Sopra Steria Group

'To build and scale a company, an entrepreneur needs to build a strong culture that is backed by a stronger set of management practices. Rajeev does a fabulous job of providing useful tools in this book for entrepreneurs to use and keep in mind as they build teams and leaders. Using his personal experiences and observations, Rajeev has addressed critical issues without the usual buzzwords and complexity. I strongly recommend this book for every leader.'

S. SOMASEGAR, **managing director,**
Madrona Venture Group

'Great leaders ask powerful questions. I cannot help but comment that the style of this book by Rajeev is like that of a great leader. He leads and draws you in through a series of questions. Most chapter names are in the form of questions and the answers are varied as well as contextual. Finally, Rajeev reflects on issues we constantly battle as we often lead with personal leadership styles, which may vary. I agree with Rajeev that leaders who build lasting organizations deeply focus on institution-building, constant learning and relearning, with a focus on both the customer and the competition, on long-term and short-term goals, on extraction and exploration, strategy and execution, alignment and autonomy, intuitive insights and structured thinking, etc. These are the issues one faces day in and day out, whether running a large corporation or a lean start-up. I thoroughly enjoyed this roller-coaster ride into the world of management practices.'

R. MUKUNDAN, **managing director and chief**
executive officer, Tata Chemicals

'This authentic and inspiring book will help many young managers advance in their careers. Many leadership development departments will use this book to supplement their own training programmes. A must-read for new managers to develop skills and to gain an additional perspective on life in management.'

ANKUR PRAKASH, vice-president of New Growth and
Emerging Markets, Wipro

'Revenue growth and more importantly, sustained business growth is difficult and requires exceptional leadership. In order to scale up a business, it is critical that the leadership team grows and develops. Using his experience of building a sustained growth company, the author shares insightful and important management practices that are supported by relevant research. To dominate their markets, business leaders should share this book with their management teams. A great contribution to the entrepreneurial community!'

BRIAN BRAULT, global chairman,
Entrepreneur's Organization

'This book will help new and aspiring managers develop the skills necessary to reach their full potential. The author has an approachable style and offers practical guidance that I think readers of all levels of experience will appreciate.'

NEEL MAHAPATRO, corporate vice-president,
Microsoft Corporation

'In my work with thousands of companies worldwide, very few scale up to any significant size. One practice that is essential across successful scale-up companies is that they grow their leadership teams at multiple levels. This book is a great resource for growing leadership teams in sustained growth companies. As a Gazelles growth company, MAQ Software has implemented key management techniques explained in the book. I highly recommend *What I Did Not Learn in B-school* to industry leaders.'

Verne Harnish, founder and CEO of Gazelles, Inc. and bestselling author of *Scaling Up: How a Few Companies Make It . . . and Why the Rest Don't*

'We shared the author's first book, *What I Did Not Learn at IIT*, with our new engineers. It helped them easily integrate into our company. I look forward to sharing the next book, *What I Did Not Learn in B-school*, with our team leads and managers. I am certain that the insights in this book will help our teams improve project execution and management.'

Vipul Kulshrestha, co-founder and head of India operations, Optimus Information

'This is a jewel of a book for aspiring executives. Rajeev intertwines his personal experiences with a deep insight into the workings of organizations, and provides a practical guide to life within an organization. I wish I had had this book to read when I graduated with an MBA almost three decades ago. It would have given me an invaluable blueprint for my professional life.'

Siddharth (Sid) Pai, management consultant and technology expert

'Having evaluated thousands of engineers for the industry, we found that just a bit of counselling takes them much further in their career. This book should be a required read for MBA programmes. For MBA graduates, this book will act as a mentor and provide them with useful tools. A great resource!'

Aseem Marwaha, director, eLitmus Evaluation

'Managers play a critical role in the success of companies. For companies to win, significant investment in training and growth of managers is needed. This book will help new managers develop a perspective on their organization, their role and their teams. I strongly recommend managers to review this book to gain valuable insights.'

RAVI VENKATESAN, philanthropist, mentor and author of the bestselling *Conquering the Chaos: Win in India, Win Everywhere*

WHAT I DID **NOT** LEARN IN **B-School**

INSIGHTS FOR NEW MANAGERS

RAJEEV AGARWAL

Foreword by Arjun Malhotra

**PORTFOLIO
PENGUIN**

An imprint of Penguin Random House

PORTFOLIO

USA | Canada | UK | Ireland | Australia
New Zealand | India | South Africa | China

Portfolio is part of the Penguin Random House group of companies
whose addresses can be found at global.penguinrandomhouse.com

Published by Penguin Random House India Pvt. Ltd
7th Floor, Infinity Tower C, DLF Cyber City,
Gurgaon 122 002, Haryana, India

Penguin
Random House
India

First published in Portfolio by Penguin Random House India 2017

ISBN 9780143440079

Typeset in Sabon by Manipal Digital Systems, Manipal
Printed at Thomson Press India Ltd, New Delhi

www.penguin.co.in

'The art of war does not require complicated manoeuvres; the simplest are the best and common sense is fundamental. From which one might wonder how it is generals make blunders; it is because they try to be clever.'

—Napoleon Bonaparte

Contents

Foreword

In conversations with fellow managers, one remark surfaces over and over again: 'Nothing prepares you for your first day on your first job.' Whether you've earned your MBA degree from an Ivy League business school or from one of the top trinity of Indian Institutes of Management (IIMs), or you chose to skip an MBA programme altogether, it has no bearing on your level of preparedness for your career. The place, the people, the demands and the nuances of a workplace are all strange new elements you must gradually decipher.

When my co-founders and I created HCL, we were role-playing as managers. We were all between twenty-five and thirty years old, each with just a few years of work experience. Recruiting the right people for our start-up was one of our biggest challenges. Initially, we experimented with lateral recruitment from outside. We experienced 100 per cent failure.

After some brainstorming, we changed our approach. We developed unique recruitment methodologies and training modules—our own differentiated strategy to win. To persuade sharp minds to join our company, we offered *adventure*—of being pioneers and opening up a completely new market.

Armed with this strategy, we recruited from the best engineering and management schools. We aimed for the sharpest, brightest minds in India. As managers, we had to sell our dream of adventure to convince top-tier graduates to come on-board. We pursued candidates who fit our profiles and work culture, and would help us achieve fast growth.

Our strategy worked. We recruited a team of sharp young minds and in 1981 we launched the HCL System-2.[1] We realized a dream that year. Little did we know that we also created the foundation of a $100-billion industry that would contribute to more than 7.7 per cent of India's GDP in times to come!

HCL's impact on the country's now-flourishing IT industry shows what can happen when an employer empowers its workforce through good management. Empowerment can not only strengthen an organization but also help create an industry. Many of the young people who worked for HCL in its early years went on to become highly effective managers, founders, chairmen, CEOs, presidents and thought leaders in their own rights. As managers, we truly and passionately empowered these employees to chart their own courses.

Fostering our company culture did not happen overnight. Training was integral to our success. We adopted the mantra 'train hard and fight easy'. A critical success factor for HCL's decades-long position as number one in the industry was the quality of our talent and our training programme. We built a cadre of loyal, diehard, persuasive people with a high achievement need.

Cultivating a successful recruitment, motivation and mentoring strategy is a key part of any organization's success. You don't learn this in business school, but you do through real-life business and personal challenges. Even after earning a business degree, entering a managerial role for the first time is truly an intellectual, attitudinal and emotional transition.

The world of companies, organizations, departments, functions and expectations can be bewildering. That is precisely why this book is so necessary today. It shows new managers how to think more clearly, and shows them the path to a fulfilling career, with or without an MBA. This book is by a hands-on manager and successful entrepreneur who generously shares his wealth of experience and insight with lucidity and a distinctive style.

Rajeev takes the reader through the roller-coaster ride of a manager's life, from hiring, retaining and motivating teams to effectively managing time, while growing as an individual. I have often felt that too many promising team members get so caught up in the minutiae of daily life that they forget they have a mind that needs nourishment, a brain that is craving to grow. Rajeev shows young professionals not only how to be an effective manager, but also how to grow into an inspiring leader. A good leader attracts great minds and builds awe-inspiring companies. Rajeev demystifies this process with an assured touch and genuine sensitivity.

As students in the Indian Institute of Technology, Kharagpur, neither Rajeev nor I knew where life would take us. For me, it is very satisfying to see my fellow alumnus emerge as a thought leader and a teacher. This is how he is making a difference.

Arjun Malhotra
Co-founder, HCL Technologies

Preface

'If there's a book that you want to read, but it hasn't been written yet, then you must write it.'

—Toni Morrison
Winner, Nobel Prize in Literature

Why did I write this book?

In 2005, I spoke at a weekly meeting with our managers to share my vision and growth prospects for our company, MAQ Software. Most of the participants were first-time managers. Their experience ranged from a few months to a few years. While I had experience as a manager, I was still learning how to run a growing company. All of us were responsible for ensuring strong software delivery from our engineering teams.

During this meeting, I focused on understanding some of the challenges our young supervisors faced. Many of them were barely older than the engineers they supervised. One manager had an especially tough job.

He led a team that tested a website used in 172 countries and in forty-two languages. The engineers on the test team manually ran test cases to meet urgent (and increasingly shorter) deadlines set by the website's marketing team.

As we brainstormed, the manager asked, 'How do I become a better manager?'

I did not have a prepared answer. I said I would get back to him, but never did. His question, however, stayed with me for years. I researched textbooks and business books that addressed the concerns of new managers in the context of growing companies and our industry. I studied industry leaders. I observed effective managers at our company and in customer organizations. I attended numerous management training sessions and conferences.

I marvelled at how teams led by good managers consistently performed well, without any friction, while other teams struggled with seemingly simple projects. I tried to understand how some autocratic managers helped their company outperform the competition, but the same managers would not last beyond a few months in a different company. I tried to understand how a thriving performer in one company failed to meet minimum performance standards in our company.

Eventually, I found that great managers share three qualities:

- **A focus on execution:** They are actively involved in the details and follow-through. Not all micromanagement or attention to detail is bad.

- **An emphasis on teaching:** To teach, these managers continuously learn.
- **An acute awareness of their strengths and social style:** With self-knowledge, they are better prepared to communicate with other personality styles and are better able to manage others.

Managers who possess these qualities are satisfied personally, appreciated by their teams and are valuable to their companies.

My research also broadened my view of managers' impact on the national economy. Great managers improve their team's productivity, leading to greater company profits and increased employee wages. In this way, improved management practices offer an opportunity to better the quality of life in India and lift the nation's economy.

Achieving one's potential as a manager, however, can be challenging and requires serious personal commitment. Management in India faces many obstacles. Limited market size (due to low per capita income) and stifling regulations have made it difficult to do business in India. On the plus side, the Indian economy has opened to global trade and competition for the past twenty-five years. Our management practices are improving. But there still remains a large gap between management practices in India and those in other countries. This management gap contributes to the nation's economic underperformance.

India's economic underperformance is notable when we compare its per capita income in the recent decades with China's. According to the World Bank, China's per

xx   Preface

capita income increased from $375 in 1990 to $7925 in 2015, rising nearly twenty-one times in twenty-five years. For India, per capita income increased from $316 in 1990 to $1582 in 2015, an increase of just under five times in twenty-five years. Reflecting on this gap, an average person in China is currently nearly five times better off than an average person in India. What is more important, if China's story were to mirror the economic history of South Korea[1] and Japan—both of which went through similar periods of rapid economic growth—its per capita income may rise even faster in the next twenty-five years[2].

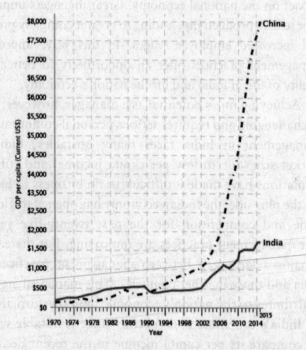

Figure 0.1: GDP Per Capita (China and India, 1970–2015)

While there are many factors that contributed to China's astounding growth, managers—both in the government and in the private sector—undoubtedly played a crucial role in transforming the country. These entrepreneurial managers in China learned how to invent, sell, market, produce, recruit, motivate and even work with Party officials. The managers had to produce extremely high-quality goods and services at a low cost. It can be argued that China produces subpar goods, but keep in mind that high-quality products such as iPhones are manufactured in China.

Today, managers in India have a unique opportunity to transform the country's economy. Yes, there are difficult realities to negotiate. But we can choose to view these realities as either burdens or strengths. That would depend on our mindset.

Those with a *negative* mindset will say . . .

- 'We are a democracy; how will we get ahead with so many competing viewpoints?'
- 'We have twenty-six languages; how can we communicate efficiently?'
- 'We have a large population; how can we support them all?'
- 'We don't have the infrastructure to support business!'

Those with a *positive* mindset will say . . .

- 'We have well-established private sector and public-sector companies.'

- 'We use English, which allows us to communicate globally.'
- 'We have a young population that has many years to contribute to the country's growth.'
- 'We have technologies that allow us to access information and communicate with just our cell phones.'

Regarding the last point, today we have access to new technologies that were not available, and certainly not affordable, in China twenty-five years ago. Compared with what Chinese managers went through, our job is easier. Information about global developments is easily available to us from the Internet. Access to capital through the global markets is easier than it used to be in the past. Advances in software and technology allow us to adopt new techniques more quickly and cheaply.

As we look forward, today's India is in a better position than China was a quarter of a century ago. India can and should be able to increase the average annual income per person (per capita income) from ₹1,00,000 (approx. $1582) to ₹5,00,000 (approx. $7925) in less than twenty-five years.

For India to reach the per capita income level of today's China, management graduates will need to play a large role in transforming the economy. Instead of lamenting India's low per capita income, let us turn our low income into the advantage of being a low-cost economy.

Some companies engage in *jugaad*, a so-called uniquely Indian management innovation. Jugaad often results in shortcuts or compromises in quality, safety or proper procedures. While ingenuity is a virtue, I do not believe in shortcuts or compromises. It takes a long time to build good organizational practices that can allow us to grow in a sustained manner.

Managers play a great role in every economy. I am awed by great managers who build great companies. They inspire their team members to accomplish the impossible. Some world-famous managers began as engineers. Before Jack Welch transformed General Electric (GE) as its CEO, he was an engineering manager.

This book, written from a manager's point of view, almost certainly carries some of my biases and prejudices. To provide a broader perspective, I have also shared the lessons I learned about management from leading thinkers.

I have organized this book into twelve chapters, each of which represents a question that has come up repeatedly in my years as a manager. It is my hope that many ambitious engineers and managers will benefit from the discussions in the book. I hope it helps them broaden their perspective on business and life. I am certain many readers will contribute enormously to the economic success of their enterprises. Perhaps you will be the next manager to transform your department, your enterprise and even the economy.

1

Do You Need an MBA to Be a Great Manager?

'Success in management requires learning as fast as the world is changing.'

—WARREN BENNIS

'I don't have an MBA. Is this holding me back?' Employees often ask me this question. Many feel stuck in their jobs. They think they have nowhere to go if they don't enter the management track. Often, they believe that becoming a manager requires an MBA.

In my experience, one doesn't need an MBA to become a manager. Nor does earning an MBA guarantee success as a manager. The degree only holds value when students have entered and graduated from MBA programmes with the right mindset.

When I was pursuing my MBA nearly twenty years ago, there was constant discussion on the value of such a degree. Our dean commented that this was a cyclical debate; every few years the same discussion took place.

Since my graduation, new MBA programmes have produced hundreds of thousands of additional graduates. In India, more than 3,00,000 MBA students, from over 3000 MBA programmes, graduate annually.[1] In contrast, the US produces approximately 1,00,000 MBA graduates every year.[2]

Is it worth it for so many people in India to get an MBA?

Attending a top-tier MBA school in India typically results in two years of lost wages and work experience, and expenses of over ₹20,00,000. Many experts say the degree is not worth this investment. 'Over the past decade or fifteen years the MBA has gone from a must-have to a nice-to-have,' Michael Goodman, Managing Partner at Long Ridge Partners, told the *Wall Street Journal*.[3]

In his book, *Managers Not MBAs*, leading management authority Henry Mintzberg stirred some controversy about the value of an MBA. He states that MBA programmes are not only a huge expense, but also a waste of time and resources for students and the industry. Mintzberg contends that MBA students do not gain relevant skills that can be applied at their jobs. Conventional MBA programmes, he writes, 'Train the wrong people in the wrong ways with the wrong consequences.'[4]

Given the debate, students are realizing that an MBA degree is not necessary. They can acquire relevant skills with specialized one- or two-year master's programmes. In addition, there are online courses offering the same resources that MBA programmes do, and are even customized according to a person's career needs.

The observations of Goodman and Mintzberg came to life for me when I joined Microsoft Corporation in 1993. At the time, Mike Maples Sr was president of the products group. Maples was a fatherly figure. He had an MBA from Harvard Business School and nearly thirty years of experience at IBM before he joined Microsoft. He oversaw product development and product marketing for the entire company.

As part of a one-week product-manager boot camp, he spoke to the twenty MBAs, including me, hired that year. One of the attendees asked him a question related to the idea of fast-tracking employees holding an MBA or degrees from well-known universities. Without a second thought, Maples explained that one's degree allowed one to put one's foot in the door at Microsoft. Beyond that, education and grades did not matter. In his view, what determined promotions and salary increases in any company was on-the-job performance.

Almost every company has senior managers who have never attended formal MBA programmes. These individuals are so driven that they can use the company itself as a university. They gather the knowledge and skills needed for their promotion and continued success.

Most companies are lucky to have them, with or without an MBA.

For new hires this reality isn't always clear. During my first week at the University of Michigan MBA programme, a recent alumnus addressed all 420 first-year students. He cautioned that many of us would end up working for managers who didn't have MBAs.

At the time, his statement was puzzling. As it turned out, at my post-MBA job none of my direct supervisors had MBAs. All had risen through the ranks in the company and were very effective in their roles.

Given that most companies are trying to compete in very tough markets, they need to promote and reward their top performers. Markets react to results, not to degrees or college brands. It does not make sense to reward unproductive employees simply because they attended prestigious colleges ten years ago.

As a result, most companies fill managerial positions with a mix of recent MBA graduates and internal promotees. Depending on the pace of the industry, the ratio of external hires may vary from 10 per cent to 30 per cent in the mid-level pool. In many companies, internal hires continue to dominate on account of their knowledge of the company and the industry, and their proven track record.

If you look at CEOs of tech companies, you will find that many do not have MBAs. The same applies to these companies' leadership teams. Appendix C has a list of key technology companies and the educational qualifications of their CEOs or managing directors.

Expectation vs Reality

On Monday, 28 June 1993, I joined Microsoft Corporation as an associate product manager for the Visual C++ marketing team. This was my dream job at a dream company because I am passionate about software. At the time, Microsoft employed about 13,500 worldwide, and was growing quickly. Like millions of others, I loved Microsoft products, including Windows 3.1 and Word for Windows 2.0.

After the initial orientation, I met my hiring manager for lunch, which was customary. My manager asked me, 'What are your areas of interest? What would you like to work on?' Being an ambitious MBA graduate, I told him I would like to work on 'corporate strategy'. My manager was puzzled, but tried to be polite. He asked, 'So, you want to work on product planning?'

The phrase 'product planning' in a traditional MBA career would have appeared to sell my degree short. I ended up working with the cost accounting team (called the finance team) and a programme manager to help evaluate a business case for Visual C++ for a 32-bit compiler for an upcoming enterprise operating system aimed at the Japanese market. Once the 'strategy' decision was made by the technical project manager (not by me), the product would be released in the market.

This was my first introduction to how a new hire's expectations of the workplace might differ from the reality—but it was not the last.

In addition to my input for the project, there were many other factors involved in product planning—feedback from a Japanese subsidiary, the company's larger corporate goals, and availability of engineers. The experience was incredibly valuable but not what I, coming out of my MBA programme, had expected it to be.

In those days corporate strategy was all the rage in MBA programmes. Most large companies had corporate strategy departments staffed by bright MBAs from top business schools. Apart from the leading management consulting firms, corporate strategy departments of companies were considered among the most prestigious places to work in. I assumed that these departments made the maximum impact on the company and had the most exposure to top management.

At that time, however, Microsoft did not have an elaborate corporate strategy department. Product features and product release timelines reflected the company strategy. By deciding on product plans, Microsoft was in effect deciding which markets or customers to pursue. My expectation of joining the company and making an immediate difference needed a quick reality check.

After leaving Microsoft in early 2000 to start my own company, I found that even when I was in charge of a team, my expectations were not always in sync with reality. I often had to deal with contradictions in management theory when I put it into practice. For example, one leading management expert would advise companies to diversify while another would suggest that a company should specialize.

Over the years, I needed to sort through these dilemmas and contradictions in management. The list below includes a few of the difficult choices every company has faced, or will face, over the years:

- Focus or diversify?
- Market share or profits?
- Hire specialists or employ generalists?
- Bet the entire company or minimize risks?
- Learn by experimenting or avoid costly mistakes?
- Reduce costs or invest in raising employee morale?
- Hoard cash or return cash to investors?
- Take loans or avoid debt?
- Focus on the big picture or pay attention to detail?
- Go public to raise capital or use internally generated funds?
- Fire people fast or never lay people off?
- Acquire companies or grow organically?
- Avoid micromanagement or pay attention to detail?
- Innovate or avoid mistakes?
- Downsize or prepare for growth?
- Empower individuals or make sure they follow corporate rules?
- Keep overheads low or provide lots of perks?

If you pose these questions to ten different managers, you are likely get ten different responses, and none of them would be wrong. As I gradually learned, a manager's answers depend on the state of the economy, the stage of a company's growth, and the timing of the question itself.

An answer that is successful for one company may not be successful for another. In this book, I hope to share my business experiences to help MBA graduates develop perspective which they can use to formulate their own answers through their career.

An MBA Does Not Guarantee Success

I went into the Michigan MBA programme with high expectations. In 1988, *Business Week* published its first-ever MBA rankings based on feedback from company recruiters. In the past, most MBA rankings were built on input from students and academic research by professors. *Business Week*'s ranking methodology distinguished its list from other MBA lists by emphasizing recruitment statistics. The magazine observed that recruiters are the 'customers' of MBA programmes—recruiters use MBA rankings as a major component of their hiring criteria. Journalist John Byrne (formerly an executive editor at *Business Week*) ushered in the updated ranking methodology. The magazine listed the Michigan MBA programme as one of the top six in the US. MBA recruiters ranked Michigan even higher.[5] As someone who was thinking about going to business school in a few years, Michigan's ranking made me feel confident that earning my MBA there would help me get a great job someday.

A year before, while applying for MBA admission, I had read another *Business Week* story. It mentioned how recruiters were aggressively courting recent MBAs. I relied solely on business magazines to assess career prospects.

I assumed that the MBA economy would remain vibrant forever—or at least until after I graduated.

At the time, I was living in Webster City, Iowa, a town with a population of 7200. I did not know anyone who was attending or had graduated from top MBA programmes in the US. There was no LinkedIn, email or Facebook that I could use to contact anyone. Based on what I read in business magazines and newspapers, I assumed that an MBA from the University of Michigan would immediately expand my career options. The opportunity cost of leaving a full-time job as well as the additional expense of a two-year programme were great financial burdens. I did not fully understand what an important investment the tuition and expenses that came with the degree would turn out to be in my own future.

On 28 August 1991, I joined the MBA programme at the University of Michigan. We were welcomed by Dean B. Joseph White. I remember the two things he had said. Firstly that we were the brightest class that ever entered Michigan, and secondly that 'finding a job was the student's responsibility', and not his. Dean White assured us that he would do his best to provide us a great education and recruitment resources. Finding a job, however, was our job!

The irony of searching for a job so soon was that I had just left a job with a good company the previous week. Many of my classmates had at least three to four years of work experience prior to joining the MBA programme. Dean White's welcome speech was unsettling to me, as it probably was to most of my fellow students. Graduation, and the job after graduation, seemed far away (two years from that point). I had joined the programme for higher education, but the job search began right from the day I started class.

In the MBA recruitment game, I was a difficult graduate to place. Given my advanced engineering education and experience in a manufacturing company, I had too much of the 'baggage' that came with having an engineering mindset. For cost accounting jobs (such as corporate controller)—which were called 'finance jobs'—I was not suitable because it was assumed that I talked and thought like an engineer. Put another way, I did not look or talk like a traditional fast-moving consumer goods (FMCG) marketer. FMCG jobs were out for me.

A logical choice for me was to go after jobs in my previous field, the major appliance industry. I applied to Whirlpool, a company that was actively recruiting Michigan MBA students. Unfortunately, I did not make the cut. I visited my previous employer, Frigidaire, in search of a corporate marketing job. I had a good meeting with the vice-president of the marketing team. Unfortunately (or fortunately, in retrospect), my previous employer didn't offer me a job.

The top two US automotive companies, Ford and General Motors, were big recruiters on campus. The third major automaker, Chrysler, had recently emerged from bankruptcy and was not hiring. I was interviewed for a cost accounting job with Ford. My interviewer was a Michigan MBA alumnus who also had a mechanical engineering degree. *Okay, this is it*, I thought. My hopes were high that

I'd land a cost accounting (or 'finance') job with Ford, so when I received a rejection letter from the company, I was devastated. That was my ideal job, in a dream company. Shortly afterwards, I received a rejection letter from IBM for a financial analyst's position. It was beginning to feel as if I would graduate without a job, a terrifying prospect.

Towards the end of my MBA programme, I was still unemployed. I had applied to at least 500 companies. My morale was at an all-time low. It was the middle of a cold Michigan winter. I would often work on job applications till late into the night. In those days, there was no email or Internet. To apply for jobs, I had to find the fax numbers of companies by going to the career centre or the library. Sending faxes meant costly long-distance phone charges. I didn't own a dedicated fax machine, so I would use my Gateway computer with a fax card. It was tedious and time-consuming. The fax software did not always work. The faxes were not always completely sent. Each cover letter had to be personalized and, of course, free of mistakes. I had to wait for a confirmation that each fax did go through. If a transmission failed, I had to try again.

I was not having any luck with traditional employers. The last recruiters to come to campus were from the high-tech industry. This industry was changing and growing rapidly. They could not forecast their manpower needs even a year in advance. Because I was still unemployed, I had to apply to them. But as I interacted with the recruiters I began to realize that the high-tech industry was actually a very good fit for my skill set.

How does my story relate to this book? If I had access to a book like this while pursuing my MBA, I would have had additional perspective and direction. In the coming years, the workplace for MBA graduates will change in ways we cannot imagine. With rapid acceleration and continuous innovations in the IT industry, MBA graduates will be working in industries and applying for jobs that have not even been invented yet. Uncertainty is the norm, meaning we must be prepared to adapt to constant change. This is something I wish I had understood at the start of my career. Fortunately, you can begin yours armed with the benefit of my hindsight.

Why Do Companies Hire MBAs?

In Silicon Valley, it is common to hear that to get a management job you don't need an MBA. You just need to be a techie.[6] Many people claim that unless you go to a Tier-1 MBA programme, your MBA is useless. However, after the finance and consulting industries, the technology industry is the third largest employer of MBA graduates.[7]

There are many reasons companies hire new MBA graduates. First, most companies do not have enough future 'vice-president material' within their organizations. Most CEOs want intelligent, aggressive, articulate, hardworking and broadly educated managers with a team-player mentality, who can eventually lead the business. Great MBA programmes do an excellent job of identifying high-potential people from a very large, highly qualified pool of applicants. In my interactions with IIMs and their graduates, I find that many of the leading management institutes provide a rigorous education to their students.

Companies often supplement their management teams with young MBA graduates who have great potential. In the context of the current Indian educational system, most engineering graduates, with their narrow engineering education, could use an additional two years of MBA education to gain maturity, exposure to the liberal arts subjects, teamwork skills and communication skills.

Finally, most organizations have a strong need for management support jobs. These activities include recruiting new engineers, training new employees, streamlining processes, customer and sales support, and even boosting the morale of the team. An engineer may not have the experience, perspective or skills to drive some of these initiatives, but an engineer with an MBA might.

Why Do We Hire MBAs?

Given my reservations about the value of an MBA, you might wonder why we have hired many MBA graduates at MAQ Software since the company's founding. Both our founders hold MBA degrees and technical undergraduate degrees. In 2000, one of the first directors who joined our company held an MBA from IIM, Kolkata. In the last seventeen years, we have hired more than 250 MBA graduates. Many of them have thrived and are working successfully, while others left to pursue opportunities outside the company.

Many students ask the question that is the title of this section. When I visit business schools, students routinely ask me, 'Why do you hire MBAs at your company? What will an MBA graduate do in an engineering company?'

We hire them because we need smart people with the capacity to lead their peers. Top business schools screen for intelligence to ensure that the candidates are able to complete their academic programmes. When reviewing candidates, they look for evidence of demonstrated leadership in their formal work experience and extracurricular activities. Hiring MBAs is a shortcut in vetting job candidates.

The fact that someone has earned an MBA also signals persistence—a quality we seek in all of our hires. MBA students must persevere through rigorous formal training for two years. MBA curricula expose students to a wide array of functional topics, such as accounting, corporate finance, marketing, strategy, operations, and organizational behaviour. These highly intelligent, driven students must rise to the challenges of academically rigorous programmes to graduate with high marks. They must compete with other equally intelligent and successful students for high grades, internships and potential jobs. To stay competitive, motivated students must study seven days a week. Due to a rigorous curriculum and competition from peers, many Tier-1 MBA graduates have developed skills that employers find attractive. By successfully completing demanding programmes, these students have accelerated their learning, gained maturity and developed disciplined behaviours.

If a student can meet the challenges of an MBA programme, we know they will be able to thrive in our workplace—which, while demanding, is a cakewalk compared with what their education demanded of them. Most companies cannot ask even high-potential employees to put in seven-day workweeks for two years.

Beyond that, we know that someone with an MBA has received training we are not set up to provide. My company, for instance, isn't organized to train employees in a wide-ranging set of functional topics such as accounting and organizational behaviour. Corporate training programmes are not structured that way. Although only 20 per cent of MBA coursework is immediately relevant to any mid-level functional job in any industry, that education is still better than what most corporate training programmes provide.

Even when companies do offer corporate training, it has historically been limited to a small group of high-potential employees. A few decades ago, for instance, the Tata Group used the highly selective Tata Administrative Services (TAS) programme, which was designed to fill gaps in the company's management ranks. TAS, a fast-track programme, recruited fewer than 100 people every year to supplement the ranks of the Tata Group's divisional managers. In those days, Tier-1 MBA programmes admitted a very limited number of students (maybe 500 seats across all three IIMs).

Fast forward to today, and Google runs a similar Associate Product Manager programme for graduates to induct high-potential candidates into the company.

Only sixteen to twenty recruits are taken in annually; they broaden the company's talent pool. Once these students join Google, they are assigned developmental projects to help them grow as general managers. The goal is to develop these managers' skills so that they are able to run significant businesses someday.

Another reason our company likes to hire MBA graduates is that two years of education can fill the gaps in the new hires' maturity, discipline, and business education. In my experience, many MBA graduates are highly talented, driven and intelligent. At least in India, most MBA graduates hold undergraduate degrees in technical fields. At engineering colleges, there is usually little focus on people management and organizational skills. Many new engineering graduates also lack the maturity to understand organizational and business issues due to their inexperience and limited exposure. We have seen first-hand how an MBA education has helped many talented individuals develop additional skills.

Did *My* MBA Help Me?

Why did I pursue an MBA even though I had undergraduate and master's degrees in engineering? I chose to enter an MBA programme to broaden my education beyond engineering. During my engineering education and work experience, I had little exposure to general business skills. I lacked many managerial skills. In addition, I had changed my industry, from appliance manufacturing to a software-related field, which was growing rapidly.

People often ask me how my MBA degree helped me over the years. Was an MBA really necessary to run a company? I think my formal education gave me confidence. I was no longer intimidated by the management 'buzzwords' of the month. Additionally, it exposed me to broad functional areas such as accounting, marketing, operations and organizational behaviour.

Of the positives I gained from my MBA education, which of the two—being no longer intimidated by buzzwords, or functional skills—was more useful? I consider the first one more useful; it helped me stay the course while we patiently developed MAQ Software.

The Effective Executive is a classic book on management written by Peter Drucker, the father of modern management.[8] Drucker emphasizes that effective executives make decisions. A decision is, simply put, a judgement. Most of us have to make management decisions without complete, accurate or timely data. In the absence of perfect information, our decisions are a choice between 'almost right' and 'probably wrong'. As in life, in business too we are looking for that *slight edge* in arriving at a better decision without perfect information. In my experience, my formal education provided me with that *slight edge* in improving my decisions. In other words, if I had to choose between two versions of myself, one with an MBA and one without it, all else being equal, I would rely on my MBA when it came to decision-making.

Leaving a full-time job and securing a loan to finance my higher education for an uncertain future was stressful at the time. Nearly twenty-five years ago, one of my elders told me that education never goes to waste. Even today, that advice has stayed with me. In the pre-Internet days, with limited alternative means to advance my learning, I am glad I attended a formal programme to fill the gaps in my knowledge and skills.

When Should One Get an MBA?

We have discussed the value of an MBA from an employer's perspective. What about the employee's point of view?

One of the questions my employees routinely ask me is, 'When should I get my MBA?' In my view, you should get an MBA when you are mentally and emotionally ready for it. One of my family friends has a son who completed an engineering degree about seven years ago. He was an average student. My friend asked me if his son should get an MBA, and if so, from where.

In this case, the answer to when he should get his MBA was, 'Not yet'. Based on the young man's past academic background, motivation and behaviours, he could have earned an admission somewhere. However, he was still very young and didn't have the maturity or capability to understand what the professors would be talking about. My friend would just be sending his son to another school to spend two years to get an MBA, but there would be few opportunities waiting for him on the other side. This problem is very common in many households. In India, the problem is compounded because many families spend their entire savings on their unprepared graduate so that he or she may earn an MBA degree.

Instead, I advise every new graduate to accept a job—any job, at any pay—and gain work experience. Any job from which one can get fired teaches one valuable life lessons, helping one gain maturity.

Management education in India is evolving to meet the aspirations of a large and youthful population. In addition to traditional two-year, full-time MBA programmes, there are evening and weekend-only programmes for working professionals in big cities. Experienced professionals can join one-year, full-time MBA programmes (PGPX) offered by the leading IIMs and the Indian School of Business (ISB). With advances in technology and communication, distance learning programmes too are becoming an option for a large number of people.

Some experts believe that we need specialized MBA programmes, tailored to where the students are, career-wise. Professor Mintzberg argues that instead of recruiting MBAs, companies should select their key performers and send them to MBA programmes to enhance their management skills. He suggests a master's programme for practising mid-career managers with at least six to ten years of experience. For candidates without any experience, Mintzberg suggests a very specialized master's programme in business designed for a specific job function in a specific industry. Such a programme would allow students to learn in depth what is relevant to them currently.[9]

In the US, many business schools have for years been offering evening and weekend programmes to cater to working professionals. These MBA programmes (which are not funded by the broader government-funded universities) bring significant revenue and are profit generators for the business schools.

In India, many Tier-2 and Tier-3 MBA programmes take this approach, perhaps influenced by a need to improve their graduates' employment prospects. They offer courses designed for the needs of knowledge process outsourcing (KPO) companies in specific industries, such as insurance or banking.

The general trend is that a US or European multinational corporation (MNC) decides to create a 500-person KPO centre in India staffed by local analysts. It hires anyone who is willing to relocate to one of the metros—Hyderabad, Delhi, Chandigarh, etc. To fill their entry-level needs, many KPO companies arrange with MBA colleges to provide them very specific courses and training. Many companies have benefited by hiring graduates from these customized programmes.

Chapter Summary

Key Points

- An MBA will not:
  o Guarantee you success; companies reward top performers, not degrees.
  o Guarantee you a job.

- o   Teach you how every business is managed; each company is unique.
- An MBA will:
  - o   Expose you to a broad array of subjects.
  - o   Show companies that you have potential in a managerial role.
  - o   Demonstrate your leadership and perseverance.
  - o   Provide you, if you are an engineer, confidence in the business world that you might not otherwise have had.
- MBA studies are more useful after a few years of work experience. We learn, develop perspective, and gain maturity with every job, regardless of the pay or level.

2

Navigating Our Strange World of Organizations

'A group of people get together and exist as an institution that we call a company so they are able to accomplish something collectively that they could not accomplish separately—they make a contribution to society, a phrase which sounds trite but is fundamental.'

—DAVID PACKARD
Co-founder of Hewlett Packard

Barely a few months after joining the University of Michigan MBA programme, my classmates and I were scurrying to secure our first-year summer internships. I did not expect to be looking for a job just two months after leaving my position at Frigidaire. Now I had to prepare my resume and start searching for a summer job.

Internships were critical, particularly for those of us who wanted to shift industries or change our functional roles (e.g., from engineering to accounting or from finance to marketing).

When I was pursuing my MBA, many students wanted to change industries or jobs. Students who worked in finance wanted to shift to marketing. Those who had worked in marketing wanted to shift to finance. We were playing musical chairs. The grass always looked greener on the other side. Because I had only worked in engineering roles, I was confused. I didn't know whether to focus on marketing, finance, operations, or IT.

As an engineer, I had worked with numbers and equations. Finance jobs required number crunching and mathematical skills, so I thought I should focus on finance. I figured if I worked in finance within the manufacturing sector, I could also use my mechanical engineering background.

Although companies sent recruiters to my business school, securing an internship or job was challenging for students. The Gulf War had started, and the economy was entering a recession. Intense competition in the job market made summer internships difficult to obtain.

Researching a company as a future employee was not easy. The world of companies was confusing and unclear. The Internet did not exist, so company presentations were a significant resource for students in their job research. Beyond the presentations, our sources were limited to newspaper and media coverage, such as *Wall Street Journal* reports. There were also company annual reports available in the library, and the occasional book on an individual company.

The pressures many MBA students face in finding a job after graduation are not very different today. Their confusion about their career choices mirrors what I felt many years ago. At MAQ Software, we have recruited many graduates from leading management programmes in India. Some of these MBA graduates are now running the company. Others accepted our offer only as a hedge against graduating without a job. Some employees in the latter group left our company as soon as they found another position elsewhere.

Based on my interactions with MBA graduates, at least 50 per cent leave their first job within two years. Their frenzy to secure jobs and the companies' drive to recruit in large numbers create an unusual dynamic on campus. At the leading institutes, desirable candidates have at least two job offers within three days of a major career fair. Many candidates accept their job offer within a day of receiving it, without even visiting their new employer or learning much about the company. In the past, many graduates did not have any work experience, so employers mainly hired them for their potential (not fit with the company).

Compounding the problems of finding the right job is the reality that all successful companies have their own peculiar way of working, which new graduates may find strange. These peculiarities arise from the age of the company, the type of organization, and to some extent, the industry dynamic. During my career, as I shifted from the major appliance industry to the software products industry and later to the software services industry, I had to adjust my mindset. When I was working for Frigidaire in the relatively stable appliance industry, follow-up meetings were held after a gap of one month. When I joined Microsoft two years later, I learned that the company held follow-up meetings the next week. In today's software services industry, follow-up meetings are held the next day at the latest. Next week or next month is too late. Throughout my career, I had to get used to a faster and faster pace of work, adjusting my time frames from months to weeks, then from days to right now. Not all of us can (or want to) handle this accelerating pace of work.

Over the years, I have thought about what we could do to help our new MBA graduates adjust to the pace of the software services industry. I reflected on my own MBA days. Like many of my classmates, I wanted a job in a 'great company'. I had no idea what I meant by 'great company'. To identify a company that would be a great place for me to work, I needed to learn about the size, age and organizational structures of the companies I had shortlisted. These factors play a critical role in determining the quality of a workplace in a particular industry. Here is a guide on how to evaluate these factors.

Size of the Company

Based on my assessment of the process of recruitment at MBA campuses, most graduates end up working for companies that employ more than 10,000 employees.

Small companies usually do not feature in the list of recruiters at these campuses. When they do, they hire in minuscule numbers.

You seldom see start-ups at recruitment events; they can't compete with big corporations in this area. When we hired our first MBA (an IIM-Kolkata graduate), we were a start-up. We had only five employees. There was no organizational chart. There were no job descriptions. There was no accounting or HR department. The new graduate could not request a team of ten trained programmers to help him develop anything.

As the newly hired MBA graduate helped grow the company, he established the much-needed procedures and processes, which everyone followed. We did not know how to develop procedures or processes. Today, a new graduate in our company will find a very different environment.

Given that students are likely to encounter the larger firms recruiting on campus, it is important to understand how a firm's operations vary with size. As a company grows, there are formal written procedures for everyone to follow. The procedures standardize company operations and offer a roadmap for new employees to resolve issues. I have seen these processes and procedures become burdensome and generate protests from the long-term employees. As new employees enter the company, however, they find that the detailed procedures make it easier for them to understand how the company works.

With a larger-sized firm, job roles can become more specialized. This affects the employee's opportunities within the company. A larger restaurant with ten cooks can afford a chef who prepares only Chinese dishes. A restaurant with only two cooks cannot afford one of them to be cooking just one particular type of dish.

Similarly, in the early years of our company, one person handled accounting, human resources and office administration. As our company grew, we could separate these three functions into different roles. Early on, we could not afford specialized software engineers. Now we have separate teams that focus on specific technologies, such as cloud technologies or mobile devices.

The unfortunate disadvantages of job specialization are an increased need for coordination, higher complexity, and communication problems. Modern software tools, including email and workflow tools, help alleviate some of these challenges. Nonetheless, if you work in a larger firm in a more specialized role, you may find that more of your time is spent on coordination than you would like.

Companies of every size have their own unique benefits and challenges for the new recruit. The irony is, most companies want to be what they are not. Most small companies want to act and be recognized as large companies. We were no different. Large companies, on the other hand, want to be nimble and flexible like small companies.

Age of Company

As companies age, they formalize their behaviour and routines. Managers gain experience, and may publish procedure manuals. A clearer, role-based hierarchy develops, replacing the person-based hierarchies found in new companies. These routines result in predictable results and help remove uncertainty in the employee's mind. Unfortunately, strict policies and procedures that do not adapt to changes in the external environment may hinder companies in other ways.

Over the last twenty-five years, I have seen many large companies, such as Compaq, Netscape and Kingfisher Airlines, disappear. Some of them were well-respected household names. For every large company that faded away, probably another 10,000 disappeared without my notice.

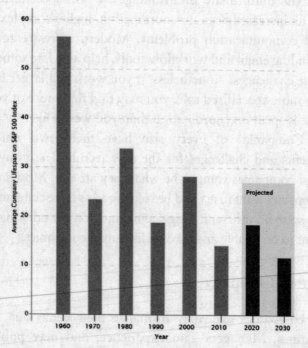

Figure 2.1: Average company lifespan on S&P 500 Index

According to an Innosight study of almost a century's worth of market data, corporations in the S&P 500 of 1958 lasted in the index for sixty-one years, on average. By 1980, the average tenure of survival on the list had shrunk to about twenty-five years. Today, the tenure stands at just eighteen years, based on seven-year rolling averages.

In the past, many of us could think of joining one company and building a lifelong career around that company. Unfortunately, such options are no longer guaranteed.[1]

Structure of Organization

When I was completing my MBA, I was very focused on acquiring functional skills in marketing, operations, and finance to ensure that I could get a job after graduating. But I could not comprehend the strange world of organizations that lay ahead of me.

It was only later that I came across the work of Henry Mintzberg. His book, *Mintzberg on Management: Inside our Strange World of Organizations*, helped me understand how organizations function and how to find one that was the best fit for me. I believe it will help you too.

In *Mintzberg on Management*, Mintzberg outlines several types of organizations that exist in the world of business. Typically, organizations within these categories have similar structures, ages, dynamics and standards.

In my experience, I found the following four organization types to be the most relevant:

1. Entrepreneurial
2. Project-based (innovative) aka adhocracies
3. Machine
4. Division-based (diversified)

Multiple organization types may exist in one company. A software company's R&D department may operate as an adhocracy. The same firm's distribution department may be a machine organization. When evaluating potential employers, it is often valuable to look not just at the company's overall structure, but also at the organization types that their individual departments constitute.

The Entrepreneurial Organization

This is the first relevant organization type as described by Mintzberg. These are its features:

1. **It is managed by a single person** (who may be the founder, owner or the chief executive). Entrepreneurial organizations are run by strong, sometimes visionary and sometimes autocratic leaders. Many of these leaders are energized by a sense of mission, which their followers find motivating. A single person takes all key decisions in such an organization. Critics of entrepreneurial organizations dislike them for their centralization of both power and decision-making.

Our current Prime Minister Narendra Modi's approach to leadership demonstrates traits of an entrepreneurial organization in the context of the central government.

Entrepreneurial companies often have an edge over their competitors, for whom decision-making involves more people and takes place very slowly. Leading management firm Bain & Company showed this to be true in its research of over 100 companies in its database. Many of the companies were publicly traded, so they shared a lot of information publicly with their investors.

Bain broadly divided the companies into two groups. The first group comprised companies where the founding team was actively involved in running the business. The founder wasn't necessarily the CEO. Bain calls these firms 'insurgents' because they are upending their industries on behalf of their customers. The second group was made up of large incumbent companies with tremendous industry experience and market power in their field.

Bain also reviewed research published by three management professors at Purdue University.[2] The research from both the company survey and the Purdue professors concluded that companies with a 'founder's mentality' consistently outperform other firms.

Entrepreneurial organizations have always been around, have always had a huge influence on the overall economy, and continue to do so. Newly styled entrepreneurial businesses that cater to customers' unmet needs continue to spring up. Just think of companies such as Flipkart, Facebook, Paytm, Amazon and Microsoft. It was only when they became popular that we realized we needed them.

2. **It operates in niche areas that can be served profitably by the organization.** The organization's markets may not be large enough for existing companies or may be protected niches that are not available to larger companies. Over time, the profit pool becomes substantial enough to attract big companies into these markets. One of the reasons big companies often acquire small companies is to enter an emerging niche market.

   Our company currently focuses on the sales and marketing analytics niche within the IT services industry. Previously, large IT services players focused on larger opportunities in financial services, enterprise resource planning (ERP), and infrastructure. The sales and marketing niche is growing, and big IT services companies are beginning to enter the market.

3. **It is simple enough to be understood and run by a single person.** The key manager does not venture into a new business area unless he is personally familiar and comfortable with the new opportunity.

4. **It has centralized decision-making and approvals by the founder.** As recently as in 2008, the CEO of the third largest IT services company in India personally approved any expense over US $5000, a small sum of money for a company of that size.

5. **It has no limit to growth.** There are many examples of entrepreneurial organizations in India that have grown to a large size in the span of just one generation. Some prominent examples across many industries include:
   - WIPRO under the leadership of Azim Premji
   - Vedanta Group under the leadership of Anil Agarwal
   - Essel Group under the leadership of Subhash Chandra
   - Adani Group under the leadership of Gautam Adani

6. **It generally does not reach any meaningful size.** While there is no limit to the size an Entrepreneurial Organization can grow to, most founders simply do not possess the ambition, capability or stamina to build a multibillion-dollar corporation.

7. **Its fluid organizational structure responds quickly to changing market conditions.** In my experience, many new employees complain about the ambiguity and lack of structure in entrepreneurial organizations. Markets change so rapidly for these companies that it's unlikely that any structure they adopt will last beyond even ninety days. For many individuals, this structural ambiguity is unsettling, which causes some workers to seek more structured roles elsewhere.

8. **Its chief executive personally supervises key personnel and usually has many direct reports.** During my years at Microsoft, many technical leaders had direct communication with the CEO without involving

management layers. Over time, the CEO learned to include the managers concerned in his emails. Still, he continued strong one-on-one discussions and relationships with hundreds of key technical personnel. To the chagrin of their managers, entrepreneurial CEOs tend to operate as if they have seventy-two direct reports and often approach anyone in the organization without going through the formal management chain.

9. **It tends to employ people who are results-oriented.** These organizations have little room for slippage when it comes to meeting goals, and they hire accordingly. They run lean. They have limited time to protect their niche from competitors. This contrasts with the approach at companies that hire 'time- and effort-oriented' employees who think, 'I put in my forty hours and I did what I was told to do. Now it is someone else's job to solve the customer's problem.'

10. **Besides the publicly known chief executive, there is always a second person who may not be visible to outsiders but handles a critical operational part of the company.** For example, former Apple CEO Steve Jobs had Tim Cook, who set up incredible supply chains to bring Apple products to the market. At a smaller construction services company, the owner who sells projects is supported by a key person who procures raw materials at low costs and manages supplier payments.

As Peter Drucker has mentioned, every company requires three roles: a thinker, a production manager and a salesperson. Usually, in a business of any significant size, the active entrepreneur performs two of the three roles (but not all three). While not well known or celebrated externally, a second person provides crucial support to the organization in one of the three areas.

11. **Its key management team members have been associated with the leader for many years.** Over time, they understand each other's strengths and weaknesses. Key management team members also exhibit a strong bond with the leader.

12. **Most of its information, power and decision-making being centralized with the chief executive, he is directly involved in key decisions.** The result is that there is little room for politics in the company. If the founder decides to locate the company office close to his residence (as is the case with one of the largest IT services companies in India), it can be argued that the decision was based on operational convenience, not politics.

13. **Decisions and promotions are based on *results* as opposed to seniority.** Many small companies have limited room for error. Mistakes in smaller companies can be fatal. Larger companies can use their cash reserves or their high market share as a cushion to absorb their mistakes and to treat the mistakes as learning opportunities.

14. **In contrast to diversified or machine organizations, it tends to hire creators with an abundance mindset.** Large organizations typically control the activities

of their managers through tight budgets, creating an environment of scarcity (the zero-sum game). If marketing is given additional funds from the budget, manufacturing may not be able to buy new equipment. Entrepreneurial organizations have limited need to control their managers' activities through formal budgets. In MBA language, if we see a positive net-present-value (NPV) project, we get it done. Unfortunately, positive NPV projects are few and far between for most companies.

15. **Founder-led organizations are vulnerable and carry risks.** First, if the chief executive is unwell or dies, the entire organization is at risk. Second, depending on the mindset and the capability of the entrepreneur, the company may not be ready to handle a change in external market conditions driven by new technologies, clients or suppliers. Third, the growth of the company is limited by the ability of the senior management team to learn about new opportunities (driven by technology, geographies, or business models). Many entrepreneurs fail to transition to new technologies or business models, resulting in the company's slow and certain death (e.g., RIM Blackberry). In the Western economies, nearly 50 per cent of new ventures do not last beyond their first five years. (Due to a large unorganized business sector in India, it is difficult to gather comparable numbers for new-venture failures here.) My sense is that many small companies go in and out of business

all the time but we don't have any formal record of this.

Finally, the longevity of a company depends on how the chief executive responds to crises. An incorrect handling of a crisis may end the company itself. The founder must have the foresight to stay ahead of the curve and keep the business on the cutting edge.

16. **Its talent supply is always less than what is needed to support high growth.** At one of my previous employers, the team always had one less person (n-1) than was required to complete the work. Part of the understaffing may have been by design, since it allowed members to assemble smaller teams and communicate and collaborate more efficiently. Another reason may have been that the company had hired nearly everyone who could be hired. By contrast, teams at large incumbent companies are overstaffed (n+1). For every task, there are multiple employees qualified and available to do the work, resulting in turf wars and duplication of effort.

Project-based (Innovative) Organizations aka Adhocracies

For most of the last twenty-five years, I've worked in project-based organizations. Mintzberg calls these organizations *adhocracies*. These organizations come in two variations: those that develop innovative solutions for internal projects (*administrative*) and those that produce solutions for external projects (*operating*). Both administrative and operating adhocracies require professional support teams, which Mintzberg calls the 'professional bureaucracy'.

Administrative Adhocracies

Administrative adhocracies work on *internal* projects to produce the next great innovative product or service for the company. These are typically younger technology companies working on projects in a race against time or on an impossible technical challenge.

During my tenure at Microsoft in the mid-1990s, I was a part of three different project teams established to deliver what were innovative products at the time: (1) Visual C++, which replaced C++ 6.0; (2) Windows NT, which eventually replaced older network operating systems, including NetWare; and (3) Microsoft Exchange, which replaced Microsoft Mail and Lotus cc: Mail. These projects (software product releases) were of various durations, from eighteen months to four years. Over the years, I have seen project cycles in all industries shrink from years to months.

Once the new software was released and the project ended, the project teams disintegrated. Depending on the market acceptance of the software product, a small percentage of the team might choose to work on the next release of the project. These team reorganizations allowed a new leader to take charge and assemble a team with a new and refined goal.

Professional Bureaucracy in Administrative Adhocracies

Administrative adhocracies come with infrastructure that isn't usually found in a start-up. At Microsoft, for instance, our projects used established processes, automated tools, and a machine-like structure to carry out software development innovations. Specifically, our software projects were supported by external infrastructure teams that provided brand marketing, early test customers, legal copyright, accounting, software-built management tools, and necessary server infrastructure.

Microsoft sales and marketing groups ran like separate machine organizations, distributing and selling the product to the distribution channel, which included large account resellers, software distributors and system integrators. The sales and marketing machine changed its product focus every quarter to maximize sales.

As products age, the established base of customers (users) increases, and the professional bureaucracy becomes more capable of maintaining the status quo. These support teams protect the interests and concerns of an installed base of customers. As a result, innovation slows down and creates opportunities for new organizations within or outside the company. The creative destruction cycle continues.

Operating Adhocracies

MAQ Software is an operating adhocracy. Operating adhocracies (also known as external project organizations) work on *external* projects, developing innovative solutions for customers. The adhocracy structure is used by consulting companies like ours, and by advertising agencies and firms that provide specialized services for hire. The specialization may result from unique technical skills (the latest software programming or machine-learning techniques), knowledge of specific markets (e.g., how to market a new product in Mexico), or purely the ability to staff a project for the customer.

Professional Bureaucracy in Operating Adhocracies

Our company's professional bureaucracy consists of *specialists* who provide visual user interfaces, engineering processes, security, privacy, project set-up, testing, and deployment expertise. These specialists support our core team of software engineers.

Instead of keeping our specialists in a separate organization, they join the project team as a shared resource. The supervisors (or managers) are part of the project team, along with software developers and specialists. The project teams are small and usually limited to five to ten individuals who cater to the customers' unmet needs (or, as Amazon's Jeff Bezos put it, teams small enough for 'two pizzas' to feed them). With improvements in communication technologies, some specialists are freelancers and may not even be employed by the external project-based organizations.

As software teams become a larger part of most companies, Agile team structures are becoming increasingly common. As Mintzberg explains, a manager's role is to coordinate activities and be actively involved in the actual work (as opposed to giving orders from a private office). Open-office floor plans are becoming the norm, to improve coordination and communication between all team members, including managers.

Specialized development teams and quick communication, however, are not always sufficient to combat the volatile world of consulting. Many consulting organizations only last a few years. Our company faces the same dangers that doom these short-lived consulting businesses: potential loss of a major client, inability to learn technologies fast enough, and inability to transition into another organization type as the company grows.

Characteristics of Project-based Organizations

Both internal and external adhocracies share certain characteristics. As Mintzberg spotlights, we observe the following ten patterns in a typical external project-based organization:

1. **Strategy is defined by the external environment, not internally.** When new MBA graduates join our company, one of their first questions to me is, 'What is

our company strategy?' That question used to be very unsettling, since I didn't have a fancy strategic framework. Like most project-based organizations, our company aligns itself with the changing computing industry. Over the last fifteen years, our focus has changed multiple times. In early 2000, it shifted from client/server computing to Internet- and intranet-based applications. Next, we turned to company knowledge management applications using SharePoint. The next computing wave involved data-driven applications, including use of Big Data platforms. Now, we are transitioning yet again, this time to cloud and mobile computing. None of these transitions were driven by us internally. We merely took advantage of changes in the external environment.

One of the largest public relations firms in the US shares a similar story. For nearly twenty years, it worked with newspapers and trade publications to help clients present their stories. With the advent of Facebook, Twitter, blogs and social media platforms, the firm changed its focus to support these platforms. The PR agency's senior management adjusted the firm's strategy to keep pace with changes in the external environment. Many other agencies did not survive the shift to social media because they fell behind the trend.

The advertising industry was also impacted when print advertising's value fell in favour of Google AdWords. As advertising companies (typically organized as external project-based organizations) shifted to new Internet media, many traditional firms disappeared.

2. **Great ideas and innovation can happen anywhere in the organization, not just at the top.** All team members in our organization are constantly searching for ways to innovate. Our teams use a new and innovative practice or tool almost every day. These innovations simplify work and increase the speed of software development. As a result, project-based organizations are a great place for creative experts at all levels.

3. **Power in these organizations comes from expertise and not from the organizational chart.** Respect is earned through knowledge and contributions, not through titles.

4. **Top managers must spend a lot of time monitoring projects to avoid missing deadlines, to ensure consistent quality, and to avoid running over budget.** All three situations are common issues at any company. With the move towards Agile engineering techniques that include software delivered daily to customers, we avoid surprises related to missed deadlines or low quality (e.g., 'This is not what I ordered'). For new and custom-developed software, budget issues are resolved by following a team-capacity model as opposed to a set price for a fixed set of features.

5. **The traditional organizational chart is not relevant; it is virtually meaningless.** For the first five years of our company's existence, when we employed fewer than fifty people, we could easily manage daily operations. Everyone reported to two people. As more

employees joined the company, however, the lack of a formal top-down structure created a lot of anxiety and operational challenges. Change happens very rapidly. Today, it is not uncommon for our employees to realize on Friday that they will work on a new project starting Monday. Sometimes, the change may include a new reporting relationship with a mentor or supervisor.

As a result, we must publish a new organizational chart every week to account for frequent shuffling of projects and people. With online tools, it is easy to update organizational charts automatically. Still, shuffling people from one team to another quickly created problems related to performance management and human resources. Programmers did not like the team changes, since they had just developed a working relationship with their previous team members. After a while, we decided to provide managers with fixed teams that adapted to handle frequent new projects.

6. **As managers, we spend significant energy on matching team members to available projects.** Because many of our projects are of three to six months' duration, we must move engineers to new project assignments almost every quarter. Senior managers review our team assignments every Monday morning to ensure that the right engineers are assigned to the projects where we need their expertise.

For most project-based consulting organizations, senior managers are always scrambling to match manpower demand with project availability. Because most of the year is 'feast or famine', the number of active projects fluctuates wildly, from one extreme to the other. There is never a balance. Frequently, we do not have enough work to keep everyone busy. At other times, we have too many projects and not enough trained engineers.

For example, in December, many of our projects come to an end as it is the close of the year. Some projects come to a logical end while others are not funded for the next calendar year. As a result, in January, we may be overstaffed by 30 per cent. We have no real work for the team members who are now surplus. By April, new projects start and we are suddenly understaffed by 35 per cent. This mismatch in demand and available capacity is a common occurrence in project-based organizations.

Almost every six months, our senior delivery managers and recruitment teams implore the sales team to provide a predictable and stable flow of work for the next twelve to eighteen months. Despite our best intentions and best efforts, we have never been able to forecast our staffing needs accurately. Just when we thought we had enough engineers, a project gets extended unexpectedly because of a last-minute change in requirements or due to newly discovered errors or bugs. We again scramble to fill the requirements for additional team members by utilizing Just-in-Time hiring or by using three-month contract resources.

As with manufacturing companies, there is a recurring tension or mismatch between the sales and manufacturing departments in our company. When product sales are high (due to high customer demand), the manufacturing department does not have the capacity to fill the orders quickly enough. When the manufacturing team has the capacity to build products, sales are not always high.

7. **Software upgrades in the underlying systems create additional work and need for new teams.** Not many brand new applications are developed for clients that are Fortune 500 companies. Most of the application development work done for them results from re-engineering of existing processes or computer technology. For example, when technology changes from a client-server application programming model to an Internet-based model, engineers have to learn new technologies. Many have spent three to five years working on client-server technologies. Suddenly, a new twenty-two-year-old college graduate joins the team, and now both the experienced engineer and the new graduate are almost at the same technical level.

Every few years, there is a shift to a new technology platform. Whenever this happens, many of our engineers resist the change. After all, they have years of experience in the soon-to-be-obsolete technology.

As managers, we have to break through this resistance. For our company to stay relevant in the marketplace, we need to be experts in the new technologies. We remind the engineers that they will be more valuable to the company and the industry if they expand their knowledge by learning the new technologies. In addition to their existing experience with old client-server computing, they will also know Internet programming models. Currently, we are transitioning our engineering team to new cloud and artificial intelligence technologies as that would be to our advantage, resulting in lower operating costs for our clients. We must learn new cloud-based development and operations (DevOps) techniques and learn how to execute projects faster.

8. **When we do not have enough work to keep our engineers busy, senior managers generate internal projects that almost always do not receive enough follow-through attention.** There is a temptation to use one's extra engineering capacity to create software products for general consumer use. My assessment of the largest project-based consulting companies indicates that most of them earn very limited revenue from selling internally developed products. If our experience is any indication, internal and external project-based organizations require different mindsets. External project-based organizations are not set up to develop products efficiently. Developing and marketing innovative products is a high-risk business for us.

One reason is that consulting companies do not have the marketing expertise or investments to support the products they develop. More likely than not, as soon as a 'billable' project comes along, the team will be reassigned to work on an immediate-revenue-producing opportunity.

9. **External project-based organizations are exciting for many creative software engineers.** They offer a variety of different projects, demand new skills and are challenging assignments. The frequent change in project assignments, however, creates anxiety for some engineers. In modern firms, project timelines are getting shorter and more demanding. There is usually not enough time to master ever-changing technology or to learn at a comfortable and easy pace (i.e., slowly).

10. **In external project-based organizations, ambiguity is a way of life.** During my MBA programme, I took a class on industrial marketing (business-to-business marketing, as it is now called) taught by Professor Robert Johnson. I believe his grey hair was a result of decades of sales and marketing experience prior to his becoming an adjunct professor. Our MBA classroom consisted of about sixty students, of whom only about 20 per cent were engineers. The rest of the students did not have technical backgrounds. In one of the class discussions, the professor empathized with the engineers. He said, 'You engineers are all right and can make good managers. However, you need to learn how to deal with *ambiguity*.'

He was correct. Many engineers and managers are uncomfortable with ambiguity. All of my engineering life, I was trained to remove ambiguity by solving problems precisely. For those bothered by constant confusion and unending ambiguity, project-based organizations are a very uncomfortable place to work in.

Following is a quotation from a Mintzberg book that was published more than twenty years ago. The quotation explains the reality in most external project-based organizations:

Many creative people like an innovative project-based organization structure because of their democracy and limited bureaucracy (as opposed to a more machine-like top-down organization structure with many controls and monitoring). However, many people need neatly organized predictable environments (even though they may claim otherwise). Many of them see project-based organizations as a nice place to visit but not to spend a career. Even dedicated members of project-based organizations periodically get frustrated with the fluidity, confusion, and ambiguity. In these situations, all managers some of the time and many managers all the time, yearn for more definition and structure. The managers of these organizations report anxiety related to the eventual phasing out of projects; confusion as to who their boss is, whom to impress to get promoted; a lack of clarity in job definitions, authority relationships, lines of communication; and intense competition for resources, recognition, and rewards. Along with ambiguities and interdependencies, these companies can emerge as a rather politicized and ruthless organization—supportive of the fit, as long as they remain fit, but destructive of the weak.[3]

As Mintzberg understood very well, many engineers say they find new technology challenges and fast-paced projects exciting, but in reality they crave the stability and predictability available in hierarchical and bureaucratic organizations. As a result, there is significant turnover in project-based organizations; some voluntary and some not. Staff members do not always understand that some of the turnover arises out of the structure itself. Managers, even if they grasp the circumstances, are reluctant to accept the high turnover rate, for fear that their company will look bad compared with other organizations. If they stay with the company long enough, they will eventually develop the perspective that high attrition is an expected feature of the organization's functioning and will stop worrying about it.

Machine Organizations

Machine organizations are designed for efficiency and can scale up as the business grows. These organizations are the most successful businesses and are becoming more common in almost all industries. We love them for their everyday low prices, reliability, and consistent quality. As a consumer or a buyer, I benefit when my supplier offers better goods every year at the same or lower price (think of cell phones and falling tariffs). I choose to fly IndiGo Airlines every time I travel between Mumbai and

Hyderabad for their low fares and on-time performance. I use Internet retailer Amazon to deliver my purchases at a good price, on time nearly every time. Similarly, we use Dell computers to deliver great products at a reasonable price. Most of the smaller computer assemblers cannot compete with the quality and price offered by large machine organizations.

Almost all big companies use a machine organization structure in some or all of their operations. In such structures, work is clearly divided, assigned to specialists who perform a very narrow set of activities well.

Many organizations recruit MBA graduates to become a part of their selling machine (called marketing) or their manufacturing machine (called operations). Unfortunately, most hires do not realize they will be a part of a machine organization, performing a narrow set of activities repeatedly. Every year, they will be asked to do more in less time or with fewer resources. If they can't deliver more, they will be replaced by another set of graduates the following year at the same or lower salary levels. The organization's drive to survive in a competitive marketplace requires higher performance and increased efficiency. Only a few MBA graduates who master their work will be promoted to supervise and design work rules, which will, in turn, enable new hires to deliver goods or services more efficiently the next year.

When a mid-sized company grows, it mostly transitions to a machine organization with well-developed rules. This transition can be challenging for employees accustomed to the old ways of doing things.

One of our early employees used to work for Shurgard Storage Centers, which rented temporary storage space to the public. He was a management graduate of the University of Washington, Seattle. As a part of store operations, he answered phone calls, marketed storage space to individuals and walk-in customers, provided customers with storage units and collected payments. His job was very varied.

In 2006, Shurgard Storage was sold to PS Storage Solutions. What was originally a real estate play became a 'let-us-improve-our-operational-efficiency' move for PS Storage.

The new company brought a centralized machine approach to the acquired company. The leadership team centralized all marketing and sales of storage space to a call centre in California. Retail operations were limited to providing physical access to storage spaces. By centralizing sales operations, the storage spaces could be marketed to consumers consistently and uniformly by a well-trained telephone sales team. The sales performance of individual telephone sales team members could be monitored centrally. New discounts and promotions could be offered depending on the availability of space in individual facilities. As a result, the company simplified store operations, allowing it to hire individuals with less training at salaries 30–50 per cent lower earlier.

Over time, automation took over. Telephone-based marketing moved to an only-web-based reservations system. Expensive call centre workers were replaced by semi-automated websites, resulting in fewer mistakes.

Mobile phone apps allowed consumers access to storage spaces, reducing costs even further. While these efficiencies helped the company reduce costs, they made work at the company less interesting for our management graduate from the University of Washington, Seattle. That was why he joined our firm. Shurgard's was not an isolated case. There are many other companies whose story is the same.

Here are ten common characteristics of machine organizations:

1. **Machine organizations simplify operations.** As a result, they lower costs by using less-skilled and low-paid workers. These organizations' use of technology to automate work has been replicated across all industries for centuries with varying levels of sophistication.

2. **Managers set up elaborate processes to ensure that employees follow the same procedures every time they service a customer (simple steps, repetitive work).** Some of these procedures are due to regulatory concerns. I recently spoke to an airline attendant. In the past, airline rules required each flight attendant to carry a 2 kg, 4-inch-thick operating manual on every flight. The manual provided detailed instructions for dealing with nearly every situation that may arise before take-off, during flight and after landing. For the industry and its regulators, millions of flights over the years have led to encounters with almost every problem that could arise. Because airline safety is a

matter of life and death, managers want to minimize failures. (My flight attendant, however, was beaming with joy because the large and heavy manual was now loaded on to her new 200-gram mobile phone. She no longer needed to carry heavy binders to stay on top of company procedures.)

3. **Machine organizations require a strong support organization to develop, revise and monitor well-developed company procedures.** For example, in the case of emergency landing of an aircraft, there is no time for a meeting or a conference call. There is no time to come up with a plan or to assign responsibilities. The operating procedures manual clearly specifies everyone's role and the sequence of steps airline personnel should follow. As a result, these machine organizations make flights safer than car travel.

4. **Even customers of machine organizations must follow a strict set of rules.** As a consumer, I like the discounted low prices resulting from the extreme efficiency machine organizations provide. But I also desire the flexibility offered by full-service providers. Unfortunately, I can't have both. Customers of machine organizations experience limited—if any— flexibility on pricing or on the quality of goods and services they are delivered.

Sometimes this is disappointing. For nearly twenty years now, I have relished the south Indian fast food at Ramakrishna restaurant near Vile Parle East railway station in Mumbai. Ramakrishna is a high-volume, low-price operation designed to cater to commuters who are rushing to office by train. Ramakrishna offers the same efficient and fast service to everyone. Its prices and quality are unmatched for an expensive metro city like Mumbai. What Ramakrishna does not offer is menu customization. It serves certain dishes in a set way. Its goal is to serve customers quickly so that the table is freed up for the next set of customers. Many times I have made the mistake of ordering customized dishes and then regretting it when the cook got my order wrong. Sometimes I've come in search of a quiet place for a business meeting and found the rush of activity in the restaurant overwhelming.

Ramakrishna is a machine organization. If I want to dine in a leisurely environment, I have learned not to go there. McDonald's, with thousands of restaurants worldwide, is another well-known example of a machine organization. Their joints are designed to maintain an extremely high rate of efficiency, which allows them to deliver food quickly and at incredibly low prices. They are fundamentally a 'food machine'.

5. **Over time, machine organizations become calcified owing to their past bad experiences.** These organizations are run by administrators who hire people that operate by the book. As a result, the organizations develop procedures for every kind of unusual situation that could occur at the company. They rely on detailed, often time-consuming procedures for everything. Basically, there are

procedures to develop procedures, which can be good in some instances but time-consuming in others.

6. **They are less nimble and agile than growth companies.** In growth companies, there are no policies, only guidelines. As companies become machine organizations, guidelines must become detailed, and specific policies and procedures must be developed and followed without fail. There is no discretion. In some cases, even their best customers suffer as a result of this rigid approach.

Fraud prevention procedures are one example. From the start, our company has paid employees their salary on the last working day of the month across all locations. Because we were a new and small company, many employees were sceptical as to whether they would be paid on time. We did not want to miss payroll because of delays or mismanagement (or worse, because of lack of cash). To ensure that our funds were safe, we opened our company account at a large multinational bank, which has locations across multiple countries. The bank is so large that it 'never sleeps'. I assumed that its success partly came from its elaborate policies to prevent fraudulent withdrawals.

On Thursday, 29 March 2007, I happened to be in our Mumbai office. It was end of the fiscal year and payroll week. We were busy setting up our Hyderabad engineering centre, so the rest of the management team was in Hyderabad that week.

As part of the payroll procedure, every month an authorized signatory would send a signed letter and a signed cheque authorizing our bank to withdraw money from the company account and deposit salaries into the bank accounts of our employees. Because I was locally available and an authorized signatory, I signed the letter and the cheque for the total salary amount to be deposited promptly into the employee accounts. Once we delivered the signed letter and cheque, the bank official would sign the letter to acknowledge the branch had received our instructions.

To me, as a business customer, this was a routine procedure. I assumed the salaries would be deposited the following day. However, late the next day, at around 6 p.m., I received a call from the bank. They told me I was not authorized to sign the salary deposit instructions. As depositing payroll in employee accounts without fail (with no excuses, no explanations) was one of my obligations as head of the company, I was shocked. Just one month earlier, I had signed exactly the same instructions and sent them to the bank, and the money had been deposited correctly.

I pleaded with the bank official concerned not to delay the salary payment. He had a signed cheque from me. Somehow, the bank's records were not showing that I was authorized to sign the salary deposit instructions. I reminded him that the same instructions were sent the previous month and signed by me, so I *must* be authorized. Somehow, the bank had cleared the salary payments in February without any problem, but was now refusing to do the same the very next month.

Unfortunately, the procedures manual at the bank did not allow me to sign salary instructions. As a result the salaries were deposited on Monday, 2 April 2007 instead of on Friday, 30 March 2007. As a machine organization, the bank had strict controls. The procedures did not allow the bank official to deposit our employee salaries. I was disappointed. In a follow-up meeting, I requested that the bank official visit us and explain the glitch.

Since that incident, we have moved to another bank. Machine organizations, when they work, are a model of efficiency. Their level of service and fees are unmatched. We often have no choice, however, but to abide by their rules as customers or employees. There is little flexibility. Their model does not support deviations from standard procedures. Sometimes these deviations are necessary, and the better machine organizations build policies and procedures to allow for human judgement. In this case, the bank was too rigid to meet our company's needs, and I was compelled to find a more suitable bank.

7. **For employees of machine organizations, the virtues of efficiency and sticking to requirements play out differently.** Just as customers of machine organizations have limited choices and freedoms, employees too must strictly follow rules and procedures to ensure a consistent customer experience. Rigid guidelines

do not always lead to a satisfying work experience. It's often the case that the better the experience of customers with a company, the less attractive the company is to its employees.

Working in machine organizations is not fun. Most of the thinking is done by a centralized staff working to increase efficiency (with the ultimate end goal: reduce costs per sale). Unfortunately, many people join machine organizations at an entry level, seeking fun. Just ask a Disney park employee or a Café Coffee Day barista.

In reality, customers are the only ones who have fun. The employees have to show up on time without fail, stand, be alert, and be ready to serve customers all day. In a machine organization, management views employees as a cost, not as an investment, and seldom appreciates their unique contributions.

8. **Most of the top managers handle only 'crises' or exceptions to operating procedures.** Otherwise, daily operations are routine and well documented. These daily operations require little judgement or coordination from top managers.

9. **Machine organizations either shape the external environment or operate in environments that match their products or services.** In the context of semi-conductors, Intel created an environment where it provided a personal computers (PC) ecosystem. Intel set the standard for chipsets, networks and memory modules, and the market adapted itself around it. Essentially, Intel's head, Andy Grove, 'willed Intel

into a powerhouse'. The approach in this type of organization differs greatly from that in project-based organizations, which are built to adapt to changes in the external environment.

10. **Nothing is permanent.** If the external conditions change drastically, beyond the machine organization's capability to absorb the changes or to shape new technologies to adapt to them, this firm's prominence is at risk, as we observed from the attrition on the Fortune 500 list. Because of the highly mechanized or bureaucratic nature of machine organizations, change is difficult. Many of these companies do not survive change.

Despite all the negatives associated with machine organizations, more companies are moving a greater percentage of their operations towards a machine-organization approach when it comes to routine work. For non-routine work, they follow project-based or innovative structures.

Most operating units in machine organizations face a dilemma when forced to change. No matter what, they have to meet current production needs (sales, units produced, etc.) to survive. They cannot stop the assembly line, break to reconfigure, then start producing again. Professor John Kotter, writing for the *Harvard Business Review* in November 2012, suggests that companies (invariably machine organizations) should follow a dual operating system approach to bring about change. Kotter defines a dual operating system as one combining a traditional management hierarchy (which is good at addressing daily production tasks) with a strategy network (which is flatter and can quickly innovate and respond to industry changes). The strategy network comprises volunteer employees with a zeal to attack growing markets. 'Because a dual operating system evolves,' Kotter wrote, 'it doesn't jolt the organization the way sudden dramatic change does. It doesn't require the organization to build something gigantic and then flick a switch to get it going.'[4]

Even in our project-based organization, we relax our team members' schedule a little bit so that their attention is freed up to lead 'change' initiatives. Instead of forcing change from the outside, a volunteer network of employees can implement in-context change solutions while maintaining a sense of urgency. Like most mid-sized companies, ours faces a shortage of good people. As a result, we must seek employee volunteers and engage them in the change effort while providing top management support.

Division-Based (Diversified) Organizations

Division-based organizations are large conglomerates with branches operating across geographies.

In 1988, after completing my master's degree in engineering from Iowa State University, I joined the Laundry Division of White Consolidated Industries (WCI) in Webster City, Iowa. WCI was formed during the consolidation of the appliance industry. It had many divisions, including the washing machine and dryer unit (called the laundry division), the kitchen range division, the dishwasher division, the air conditioner division, the vacuum cleaner division and many others.

Some of the brands owned by WCI were Frigidaire (which makes refrigerators and is responsible for the American slang word 'fridge'), Kelvinator (a big refrigerator brand in India—in fact, my family's first refrigerator was a Kelvinator. They were so proud of it), and Tappan (a well-known kitchen cooking range brand in its day). WCI also purchased appliance units from Westinghouse Electric Corporation.

The home appliance industry is a mature industry with limited growth, if any (1–2 per cent per year). Most homes already have appliances, and do not have any reason to replace them unless one of them breaks down.

Two years before my joining the company, AB Electrolux of Sweden purchased WCI to expand its presence in the north American market. AB Electrolux was a diversified organization, headquartered in Stockholm, Sweden. In a company with more than 50,000 employees worldwide, I was one of the youngest and probably the junior-most engineer.

As Mintzberg explains, diversified organizations form because they seek to grow their revenue. Unable to increase sales organically, the parent company (usually a very large conglomerate) acquires companies outside of its geography or acquires related businesses within the country.

That was the case with AB Electrolux. In the late 1980s, and into the 1990s, there was little uniformity in appliance specifications across different countries. In the US, clothes washing machines were top-loaders; in Europe they were mostly smaller and were front-loaders. The differences arose from local customs, energy costs and water conditions. For example, due to high energy and water costs, European washing machines were initially smaller and more energy-efficient than the north American models. The global headquarters later decided to develop and introduce more energy- and water-efficient European designs to the north American market to meet local needs and regulations. The strategic direction was provided by the headquarters in Sweden to their operating divisions worldwide.

By acquiring WCI, AB Electrolux had purchased access to the US, the single largest appliance market at that time. By following the divisional structure, it could expand its presence to many countries worldwide.

In accordance with Mintzberg's description, this was our situation as a diversified company:

- Key managers at the global headquarters (HQ) decided strategy for the company, which was then implemented by the divisions worldwide.
- Headquarters managed divisions through operating metrics that, at times, included financial returns and market share, etc.
- Headquarters provided independence to the operating managers in the divisions. There were tensions between HQ and the local operating managers who sought more independence than provided by HQ. As a result, managers played games to get around HQ's directions.

- Our division manager had to compete with other Frigidaire divisions for financial and technical investments as well as for adequate attention from HQ.

One incident during my time with AB Electrolux in the late 1980s vividly illustrated these traits for me. We had signed a volume purchase agreement with IBM to provide AB Electrolux with hardware, software and related maintenance services. In return for the volume purchase commitment, the company received a significant discount on the high-priced IBM equipment. At the division level, we were striving to computerize our engineering team by introducing PCs. For our infrastructure at the division level, we needed to set up a local area network (LAN). There were three competing networking standards at the time (IBM token ring, AppleTalk, and Ethernet, the last of which was supported by every other vendor).

My local supervisor was an Apple fan and preferred to buy Macintoshes for their ease of use. At the time, Macintosh users were proud of their choice and the superiority of the computers. HQ and the global IT staff, however, were against introducing Macintoshes in the company because of their limited compatibility with IBM mainframes and minicomputers. My former supervisor could get approval at the local division from the financial controller by breaking down the computer purchase order (PO) to an amount below $2000. A PO exceeding that amount for computers needed additional scrutiny, because assets would be capitalized.

As a low-level engineer helping the division advance by implementing new computing hardware and software,

I had to persuade my supervisor to toe the line on global strategy to ensure that our division complied with it. HQ wanted to ensure that we purchased only IBM hardware so that the independent divisions could share their expertise with other divisions, exchange best practices and increase overall efficiency at the company. Before the dawn of the Internet, however, we could not even send an email to one another, so information sharing without an in-person meeting was difficult.

Because HQ had given financial performance metrics to the independent divisions, divisional managers could freely choose to invest (so long as they met the goals set for return on assets and profit) where they wanted. Essentially, HQ managed control over the independent divisions through metrics or by replacing non-performing or non-aligned divisional managers.

As a result, I had to work with an HQ-strategic supplier (IBM), understand its products and implement them so that we could move ahead. The divisional managers were afraid to go against HQ's direction for fear of alienating it. The president of the division did not want to come across as leading a rogue business unit even when delivering solid financial results. Being a rogue division is even harder when the division is in investment mode (i.e., not profitable).

Many Fortune 500 diversified companies are riven by similar tensions between the strategies driven by HQ and the independence sought by divisional managers. Taking the late Professor C.K. Prahalad's advice to corporations to 'focus on their core competence', some of these diversified organizations morph into machine organizations. Even Mintzberg dropped references to the divisional structure as a separate entity in his latest work.

I felt nostalgic during a recent visit to Webster City, Iowa, where I was once part of all the excitement around new investments. Globalization had taken a toll on the manufacturing plant. The factory where I'd worked had been shut down, and manufacturing had been moved to a lower-cost location in Mexico. It was totally contrary to what I would have expected when I was working there. For so long we'd been afraid of Japan taking over the manufacturing industry. It ended up being Mexico.

Chapter Summary

Key Points

- Company processes and managerial roles vastly differ, depending on the size and age of the company.
- Entrepreneurial organizations:
  o Are managed by a single person.
  o Operate in niche areas.
  o Are relatively small.
  o Respond quickly to market conditions.
  o Employ people who are results-oriented.
- Project-based (innovative) organizations come in two varieties:
  o Those that work on internal projects (administrative).
  o Those that work on external projects (operations).
- Internal project-based organizations:
  o Work on innovative projects to sell in the market.

- o Are often young technology companies.
- o Have relatively short/rapid project cycles.
- External project-based organizations:
  - o Develop innovative solutions for outside customers.
  - o May have specific technical skills and market knowledge or may help staff in other businesses.
  - o Assemble small teams of specialists (professional bureaucracy) to meet specific customer needs.
  - o Must stay on top of industry developments or risk losing customers.
- Machine organizations:
  - o Successfully deliver standard goods and services at low prices.
  - o Are designed for efficiency and scalability.
  - o Divide work among specialists who perform a narrow set of activities very well.
  - o Work to simplify operations, cut costs and automate processes.
  - o Have procedures and workflow that are not flexible.
- Division-based (diversified) organizations:
  - o Are large, multifaceted organizations.
  - o Are slow to respond to industry change.
  - o Decide strategy for the company at global headquarters.
  - o Grant divisional operating managers *some* independence.
  - o Allow divisions to compete for company resources.

3

Why Do We Need Managers?

'I swore to myself that if I ever got to walk
around the room as manager, people would
laugh when they saw me coming, and would
applaud as I walked away.'

—Michael Scott
In the TV programme *The Office*

No one likes being managed. If you ask employees, most of them will say they don't need managers. For a long time I agreed with this view. Ask company founders if they need managers and many of them will say they hope to never hire middle managers. No one grows up aspiring to be a manager. Yet almost all companies continue to have managers. Why? The answer is simple: we need them.

Around the time I completed my MBA, I received a letter from the IIT Kharagpur Alumni Foundation. Vinod Gupta, one of our more successful alumni, was starting a school of management at IIT Kharagpur (now called the Vinod Gupta School of Management). Gupta ran a very successful company, which he took public on the US stock market. (Thirty years ago, it was uncommon for a first-generation founder from India to take a company public on the highly competitive US stock market.) Gupta had contributed US $2 million and a lot of personal effort to start the IIT management programme.

As an engineer, my initial reaction was, 'India doesn't need more managers. We need more and better engineers.' My response was wrong. As a CEO who perhaps struggled with the challenges of hiring and developing good managers, Gupta knew something that I did not. Now, as I reflect on his contribution twenty years later, I agree that we need better managers.

When I speak to senior business leaders in the globalized world, I repeatedly hear that the lack of middle managers is a key problem in India. Management studies show that India, China and Brazil—which collectively account for nearly 40 per cent of the world's population—face a huge shortage of trained managers.[1] As of 2014, India's management practices ranked below China's and Brazil's for manufacturing. Decades of choking regulations, underinvestment in industry and limited management training have resulted in a significant shortage of good managers in the country.

The shortage of good managers is aggravated by the fact that companies worldwide appoint the wrong people as managers 82 per cent of the time.[2] In Indian businesses, the deference shown to people who have spent years at the company makes it difficult to promote the most capable employees to managers.

This is particularly true in engineering organizations, where longer tenure is often seen to reflect superior technical expertise and knowledge of customers. Appointing a person with less experience almost guarantees that the more experienced person will quit. Experience and technical expertise, however, do not equate to good management. Injudiciously appointed managers struggle to communicate effectively with, and lead, their direct reports. Poor people management results in miserable subordinates and suboptimal team performance. Managers become frustrated as their teams do not produce at the same level as other, well-managed teams. After a few years, some of these ineffective managers return to technical-specialist roles. The company then starts the process of appointing new managers all over again.

Superior management practices start with middle managers. A good manager reduces employee attrition and improves customer satisfaction, productivity and work quality. Some managers create unique and highly motivating microcultures within a larger organization. These managers are talented leaders who energize their team members by modelling desirable behaviours. In short, good managers increase their companies' profitability and growth.

An economy with fast-growing companies will create jobs and encourage investment. If India grows its base of good middle managers, the country's improved management practices will result in increased wages and a higher standard of living. Such is the contribution and impact of a good manager!

Management Fills a Human Need for Hierarchy

Our society has always had managers. Kings and their ministers needed to manage large numbers of people.[3] At a local level, affairs were managed by landlords (zamindars), landowners, traders and priests. Many of these officials appointed managers who administered their affairs.

One reason why managers have existed for so long could be because management structures meet human psychological needs.

Research conducted by Professor Justin P. Friesen of the University of Waterloo, Canada, confirms human's need for structure. Friesen's research concluded that:

- Organizations use hierarchical structures (top-down) because they satisfy our 'core motivational needs' for order. Hierarchy creates structure, which provides comfort in chaotic situations.[4] Religious organizations, governments and companies have relied on hierarchies for as long as they have been around.

- Humans need to view their world as well structured and organized. In situations that are beyond our control, we find it comforting that authority figures (e.g., managers) exist. In case we don't know what will happen (uncertainty) or cannot change outcomes in our favour, we find authority figures a reassuring presence.

For example, during recent discussions on a change in policy regarding the H1B visa programme in the US, the environment of our industry was, uncertain and chaotic. Even though I did not have any unique insights, our company wanted me to address the employees. In the session, I did not state anything new. Team members, however, felt much better and reassured after the session.

- As managers enjoy power and the associated privileges, it is natural to expect that people at the top prefer hierarchy. Surprisingly, people at the bottom too prefer to work in hierarchical organization.

Industry changes around the world result in frequent company reorganization, which creates a lot of anxiety. However, the hierarchy in organizations helps reduce anxiety among staffers. Job security remains one of the top concerns for employees. Because many of these reorganizations are outside our control, people prefer to be part of a company that offers them managerial support and is organized.[5]

Hierarchical organizations are not perfect. Unfairness is rife, resulting in undeserved benefits for certain people. However, hierarchical structures may be more efficient for some organizational tasks or goals.

I have seen these dynamics first-hand in my voluntary work with several NGOs. Most of these NGOs are run by people who are passionate about the cause. Even so, running an NGO requires hierarchy and structure.

One of these NGOs is the IIT Kharagpur Alumni Foundation. All executive committee members of the foundation are volunteers who came together to support a common cause. Even as a purely volunteer organization, we had to develop a governing hierarchy to coordinate our activities and to get things done efficiently. The NGO was structured such that all decisions required quorum and majority approval. A few times, meetings could not be held because the quorum was not available. Scheduling these meetings was difficult because the board members lived in various time zones and travelled frequently. Getting majority approval on operational matters was a challenge. As a result, issues took time to progress.

Two years ago, I attended one of the organization's board meetings. On the agenda was a request to fund travel expenses for a business plan competition at Rice University, Texas. The requested budget was only a few thousand dollars and was well within the organization's means. All board members on the phone conference had equal say, making it difficult to come to a decision.

Due to the limited hierarchy, the president had to answer all the questions. There were questions about whether the case study competition was prestigious enough, whether the organization should set a precedent, if student travel should be automatically approved, whether there could be any lasting benefit to IIT

Kharagpur, etc. What should have been an easy task proved difficult because of the lack of hierarchy.

After more than a decade of dissatisfying governance, the IIT Kharagpur Alumni Foundation proposed the following three-tiered hierarchy to speed up decision-making and execution:

1. **An advisory board** consisting of non-voting members passionate about advancing IIT Kharagpur. These members would not have any decision-making or management roles but would be informed of the foundation activities.
2. **An operating board** consisting of absentee members and donors who could significantly influence the organization's decisions.
3. **An executive committee** consisting of three or four members to run the non-profit on a daily basis. The executive team would comprise the president, secretary, and treasurer. This group would decide and manage the activities of the foundation.

Once the new structure was put in place, operational decisions were easily made by the executive committee without delay. It appears unnatural that such a hierarchy was necessary in a volunteer organization where people with good intent were working towards a common goal. But even under ideal circumstances, getting things done requires structure.

While managers are sometimes resented by their employees, they are necessary for a well-functioning workplace. Management hierarchy provides structure and freeing subordinates from worrying about company-wide operations. The subordinates can instead focus on their immediate tasks at hand, allowing them, and the company as a whole, to be more productive.

Chapter Summary

Key Points

- There is a significant shortage of good managers worldwide and especially in India.
- Managers are often promoted based on their years of experience, not their capability.
  - o Experience and technical expertise don't equate to good management.
  - o Injudiciously appointed managers struggle to communicate effectively with their teams.
- Good managers reduce employee attrition and improve productivity, work quality and customer satisfaction.
  - o Improving the quality of middle managers will result in increased wages and a higher standard of living for employees.
- Managers have always been necessary because:
  - o They satisfy our need for structure.
  - o There is a human need to view the world as well organized.
  - o People at all levels of a company prefer hierarchy.

4

What Does a Manager Do?

'The man who knows "how" will always have a job. The man who knows "why" will always be his boss.'

—HARRINGTON EMERSON

Every year we see recent MBA graduates and newly promoted managers fumble because they lack clarity on their roles as managers. What does a manager do? What is the difference between a leader and a manager? What do engineers want from a manager? How does a manager delegate effectively? To succeed as managers, we need to understand the answers to these questions.

Based on my experience as both a subordinate and a manager, I have learned that I must consider these questions in terms of my contribution to the organization and the managerial roles described in this chapter. The job of a manager depends on many factors, including his or her placement in the organization's hierarchy, the type of organization, the life stage of the organization, the cultural context and the competitive landscape. A first-level manager of front-line workers plays a different role from what a manager of other managers does. Likewise, a manager who oversees software engineers does not operate in the same way as a manager who supervises assembly line workers. Entrepreneurial organizations require different managerial roles than mature organizations.

Not all managers manage people. Many managers manage other resources, such as schedules, budgets, risks and communication. Traditionally, managers gauge their success by the number of people they supervise. Peter Drucker, father of modern management, advises us to focus on our contribution, on how we add value to our organization:

The effective person focuses on contribution. He looks up from his work and outward towards goals. He asks, 'What can I contribute that will significantly affect the performance and the results of the institution I serve?' His stress is on responsibility.

The head of one of the large[st] management consulting firms always starts an assignment with a new client by spending a few days visiting the senior executives of the client organization one by one. After he has chatted with them about the assignment and the client organization, its history and its people, he asks (though rarely, of course, in these words), 'And what do you do that justifies your being on the payroll?' The great majority, he reports, answer, 'I run the accounting department,' or 'I am in charge of the sales force.' Indeed, not uncommonly the answer is, 'I have 850 people working under me.' Only a few say, 'It's my job to give our managers the information they need to make the right decisions,' or 'I am responsible for finding out what products the customer will want tomorrow,' or 'I have to think through and prepare the decisions the president will have to face tomorrow.'[1]

As Drucker's anecdote illustrates, it is essential to focus on our contribution to the organization and to the broader community if we want to make a difference. Most of us fail to recognize how we fit into the larger context.

Joan Magretta, a well-regarded business scholar, offers an insight in *What Management Is: How It Works and Why It's Everyone's Business*. She points out that the genius of management is in eliminating complexity, trivializing specialization (so that everyone can do the work previously done by a specialist, also called deskilling of labour), and getting work done simply.

An example of deskilling in the software industry involves automating the deployment of software on production servers. With software getting updated on an almost daily basis (Facebook users get a new version of the application several times per week), software engineers must load or deploy software multiple times on production computers. In the past, this deployment was tedious, time-consuming, and error-prone because there were numerous software code files as well as their versions. As a result, highly skilled engineers were needed to deploy the software to the servers. Now, with some programming and customization, new software tools deploy software without any manual intervention by an engineer.

Critics of this approach argue that capitalist managers are driven to deskill the labour force to lower production costs. There is some truth to the argument that automation has replaced low-skilled and middle-skilled jobs. However, there is another side to the story. Automation of software deployment has freed skilled engineers to take up more interesting problems. Overall employment has not gone down. Automation has liberated those who have developed their technical prowess to use their skills to work on more complex and enjoyable activities. Highly talented technical employees may find increasing enjoyment in activities such as improving algorithms and honing a software program's design and architecture.

Similarly, during the days of manual typewriters, when simple memos and documents had to be typed, errors were difficult to correct and consumed a lot of time. Today, I do not know of many people who use typewriters or employ specialized typists (who have no job skills other than typing). Many typists, such as those employed by transcription services, have learned to apply their keyboarding skills to the PC and the Internet in a variety of administrative tasks. They add value to the company by processing documents in addition to providing useful information from the Internet.

Deskilling of labour and automation are just two examples of companies' desire to simplify production processes. But even when organizations are driven to simplify, complexity always creeps up. A manager must continuously reduce complexity by implementing new technologies in order to develop and run a high-performance organization.

Managerial Roles

Most growth companies recognize employees for their positive behaviours, strong performance and loyalty. Then one day, the company promotes these employees to supervisors. Now, superior technical skills and positive behaviours do not necessarily mean the employees will be good managers. Nonetheless, as the employees have been promoted, they are given teams to manage.

While many of us aspire to be managers, we must realize that we will then be responsible for the output (production) of an entire team. We must manage the flow of work. Many new managers are happy to accept the title and the rewards, but they struggle to produce the output expected from them and their teams.

Many new supervisors are also unable to read the expectations of the organization or of their newly appointed teams. They could use some clarity about their new roles.

The situation is even worse for MBA students. Many of them complete their MBAs with the expectation that they will become managers right after graduation. Speakers at business schools typically come from the executive ranks. Most of these senior leaders visit campuses to promote their companies so that they can recruit the best graduates. During their visits, the speakers are motivated to present the opportunities at their companies in a very positive light.

Many companies use case studies during their presentations, featuring graduates who have risen to senior positions. Case studies can be misleading. While they showcase graduates who have progressed quickly, most may not rise to that same level and at the same pace.

As a starry-eyed job applicant, it is easy to picture yourself in the same successful role as those in the presentation. To rationalize our perception, we immediately look for and find similarities between these people and ourselves, even if they are as insignificant as a shared gender, a last name or a prior qualification. As a job candidate listening to such speakers, I dreamed I would hold the CEO title within a few years of graduating.

Lack of clarity about the role managers play in an organization leads to such unrealistic expectations among MBA students.

In my career over the last twenty-five years, I have realized that there is no single answer to what a good manager does. The job of a manager depends on many factors, including his or her placement in the organization's hierarchy, the type of organization, the growth stage of the organization, the cultural context and the competitive landscape.

It is possible, however, to provide generalized descriptions of management roles. Mintzberg, in *Mintzberg on Management: Inside our Strange World of Organizations*, classifies the work of a manager into the following three types of roles, which may entail the duties described below:

- Interpersonal roles (managing people)
  1. Production leader
  2. Figurehead or ceremonial role
  3. Liaison or coordinator
- Informational roles (managing information)
  1. Monitoring information
  2. Sharing information
  3. Being spokesperson
- Decisional roles (decision-making)
  1. Entrepreneur
  2. Crisis manager
  3. Allotter of resources
  4. Negotiator

Mintzberg notes that the effectiveness of managers significantly improves when they gain insight into their work.[2] I find that most managers have good intentions and are motivated to do a great job. Senior managers, however, regularly tell me they are frustrated that their first-level managers are not performing well. They complain these managers are not stepping up to handle one of the ten roles they have been assigned every week, leaving matters to the senior managers to tackle.

On the other hand, first-level managers are often astonished to learn they are not meeting their managers' expectations. First-level managers tend to focus on ensuring that their daily work is completed with little drama. They must deal with unexpected absences, technical blockages and customer demands.

Focused intensely as they are on this, first-level managers often forget the pressures senior managers face. As a senior manager at MAQ Software, my challenge is to ensure that our managers work in alignment with the tasks at hand and that our priorities are clear. With the availability of dashboards and performance metrics across organizations, managers now have greater clarity on what is expected of them. Nonetheless, they still need to expand their thinking beyond their simple concern for excelling in their immediate work.

Even after earning my MBA, and despite many years of experience, when I first came across Mintzberg's management roles a few years ago, it was an eye-opener. None of the job descriptions I had ever seen mentioned these roles for a manager. The roles might have been implied. My senior managers had modelled them in the past. But because I am a poor observer, I needed to be told explicitly.

I did not realize that I had made myself ineffective by ignoring some of these roles. For example, I am an introvert. I do not enjoy being in the limelight, so I find the figurehead or ceremonial role difficult. But as a manager I do not have a choice. Teams need to hear from me and want to see me cutting the ribbon. Teams have a certain image of the leader. I needed to act the part.

As Mintzberg explains, these roles are integrated and a manager must play all of them depending on the context he finds himself in. A manager cannot select the roles he likes and avoid the ones he dislikes. For example, we have had managers who were extremely talented in technical matters, but were introverted. They avoided conflict. They did not like asserting themselves or having announcing any bad news to their teams. They were not successful—which was not surprising. Mintzberg says none of the ten roles can be removed from his framework.

In my experience, when a manager plays which of these ten roles and for how long depends on the industry and the company. Not all roles require an equal emphasis or are to be given equal time. For senior positions, ceremonial roles become important, and have a larger impact than do other roles. In a technology company, a manager spends a lot of time inventing new products and services. People responsibilities have a smaller scope for such a manager. In contrast, a manager in a sales and distribution company spends more time on interpersonal roles and customer support activities.

When I was a first-level manager with a small team, I had to perform *all* these roles, sometimes at the same time. I had no choice. As our teams have grown, I still play these roles but I have some discretion as to how much time I spend on each.

If my experience is any indication, I think many managers will benefit from a clearer understanding of Mintzberg's roles. The following sections examine each role in greater detail.

Interpersonal Roles

Interpersonal Role #1: Production Leader

Every team in an organization must deliver a product or a service. A team may produce software, uncover sales leads, generate revenue, or prepare PCs for new hires. Managers have formal authority over their teams and are responsible for the teams' output.

A production leader's responsibilities include training, project on-boarding, hiring, managing the performance of subordinates, motivating the team, and reconciling individual employee needs with the company's goals.

In my experience, training workers has become an increasingly significant managerial role. The rapid technological advances of today require companies to update their processes and systems much more frequently than before.

For example, nearly thirty years ago, when I was working for Frigidaire Company, we produced one million washing machines every year. The manufacturing equipment and capital expenditures were designed to last ten years. Once we completed a production set-up, there were little, if any, changes to a washing machine model for the next decade. A worker who learned how the washing machine was manufactured did not have to learn new skills during that period. Now, it is unthinkable that the same washing machine model could be assembled by the same person in the same way for ten years. Technological advances, along with changing consumer preferences, will almost certainly lead to changes in design. As a result, a new process will be put in place, requiring the worker to learn a new job. Invariably, the manager must learn the new job first to be able to then train the worker.

A similar story can be told of the automobile industry. In the past, car manufacturers would release new models every year, but would only redesign their cars every seven years. Due to advances in technology, most car companies have now started to change their designs every five years.

A few years ago, Tesla appeared on the scene. Tesla operates like a technology company, using Lean software development and manufacturing practices to produce new car firmware every ninety days. The company relies heavily on robots to produce cars. The managers, however, must train workers regularly on new techniques.

Interpersonal Role #2: Figurehead or Ceremonial Role

In this role, managers fulfil internal and external ceremonial duties. For our managers, this work may involve handing out recognition and award certificates at employee anniversaries, attending a subordinate's wedding, speaking at a quarterly or annual team celebration, hosting a dinner for visiting clients, or using email or social media to recognize a team milestone.

Most of these routine activities do not require any decisions to be made. However, many first-time managers are not comfortable with all this public attention. They do not realize that these activities cannot be ignored; they are part of their managerial role, and very important for the company.

I have learned to devote more time to figurehead activities. I reserve ten to fifteen minutes every day for digital activities that meet my ceremonial role. On social media sites such as Facebook and Yammer I can easily 'like' or comment on posts put up by people in the company. Since we have a distributed workforce, these tools offer a simple and efficient way to connect with people in different locations. Nonetheless, my activity on social media does not eliminate the need to show up for ceremonial activities in person when the situation demands it.

Interpersonal Role #3: Liaison or Coordinator

As knowledge-based organizations have moved to matrix structures, the role of the liaison or coordinator has become more critical. In this role, the manager gathers information that is important both to peers and to groups external to the company. Managers spend considerable time with their peers (managers in other departments, as opposed to bosses or subordinates), suppliers, clients and trade associations. A lot of this contact requires strong verbal and written communication skills. Managers also meet with other managers in similar companies as part of alumni networks and professional groups, both online and offline. Many of these activities are informal and one-to-one, but they are very much part of the process of building the managers' network.

Informational Roles

Because managers have key contacts within the company and industry, they have more information than their subordinates or anyone else in their division.

Business email has made information flow much faster. Managers must keep up with industry trends, company advances and immediate project details to develop a broad perspective and improve their judgement. Many managers provide their real email addresses and Twitter handles to worldwide audiences in their presentations to gather and share information in real time. Prominent managers who share their email addresses include Jeff Bezos of Amazon and Steve Ballmer of Microsoft. (My email address is available on our company website.)

Informational Role #1: Monitoring Information

According to Mintzberg, managers are always scanning their environment for information, gathering data from subordinates and interacting with their industry contacts. The manager may receive unsolicited intelligence from sales people or from a network of personal contacts developed over time. Some information comes from email broadcasts and social media. Other information is received orally as gossip, or as speculation from people within the company. By virtue of their position, managers easily develop contacts, receiving more information than anyone else in their division. The activities of effective managers in this role include:

- Setting up Google alerts and following the Facebook and Twitter feeds of their employers, key competitors, trade associations, industry blogs and key technology suppliers (such as Microsoft Cloud and Amazon Web Services).
- Attending and contributing to local college alumni meetings to network with industry peers and collect information. For example, I have attended every Pan-IIT Alumni Conference held in the US at a significant investment of time and expense.
- Connecting with industry peers (even if it is for a cup of coffee for twenty minutes) when visiting a different city.

Ineffective managers in this role:

- Fail to review quarterly and annual reports of publicly traded companies in the industry. These reports are full of company and industry information. Managers who do not review these reports miss an easy opportunity to gain insight.
- Neglect to visit the websites of competitors.
- Miss optional informational meetings. Companies may customize information discussed in these meetings to provide relevant information efficiently. Because many managers are focused on immediate production work, they do not bother to attend these meetings.

Informational Role #2: Sharing Information

The manager must continuously share information with subordinates and colleagues in the company. Many subordinates do not receive the information necessary to help them understand how their contribution fits into the big picture. Such information can, arguably, help them perform better. To bridge information gaps, the manager must synthesize, simplify and share information that is relevant and actionable for subordinates. This information doesn't only come from the top levels of the company. To my surprise, I often have to pass on information from one of my subordinates to another. I am flabbergasted that my own team members do not talk to each other. To prevent these communication challenges, we have ten-minute 'scrums' (daily meeting, in engineering terms) so that everyone is clear about the work being completed.

Informational Role #3: Being Spokesperson

As a spokesperson, a manager must share information outside of his team. That may mean providing status reports and informing the relevant people on a different team of any dependencies. An IT manager may need to update a supplier on new hardware and software standards in the company. A development manager may ask the IT department to add additional hard disk space or memory to laptops.

The spokesperson's role also extends outside of the company. At senior levels, a CEO must spend a lot of time influencing customers, suppliers, trade organizations (e.g., NASSCOM or ITSAP), government bodies, NGOs and other influential groups.

Recently, I attended an annual IIT alumni meeting in Silicon Valley, California. While there, I engaged in all three informational roles. Many senior officials and directors from IITs attended the alumni conference. As a spokesperson for my company, I shared my optimism about it and talked about the opportunities in the software industry. I also asked IIT officials about campus recruitment trends and contemporary student aspirations. In my information-sharing role, I passed on the information I gathered from this meet to our managers handling campus recruitment efforts to help them improve their planning.

As noted earlier, sometimes a manager may play more than one role simultaneously. While my primary role at the alumni event was as a spokesperson, I also took advantage of the opportunity to gather information. The get-together was also an opportunity to catch up with some of my old friends, some of whom work in the industry. One friend mentioned a new service that would help large companies increase the effectiveness of their sales force. His clients use salesforce.com and he develops advanced statistical models to predict the probability of closing a sales deal based on a prospect's sales force history. This is an emerging growth area for the entire industry.

While we do not directly offer this service to our clients using salesforce.com software, I passed on the information to our engineering team so that they could seek opportunities using Microsoft and Amazon machine learning tools.

Another classmate works as an adviser to IT service providers to help them secure US government contracts. In my information-monitoring role, I sought information from him about the feasibility of securing these contracts and the effort required to win them. My classmate provided me with a realistic assessment of the commitment needed to start working with the US government. In our short conversation, I had verified and updated my knowledge about how large government contracts work.

Decision-making Roles

Managers play a major role in decision-making. Unit managers use data from various sources and take into account current information about their team members to make critical decisions. There are four roles a manager plays as a decision maker.

Decision-making Role #1: Entrepreneur

Managers seek to improve their teams constantly so that they can adapt to changing environments. Managers play an entrepreneurial role when they initiate a good idea as a corporate development project. A manager may delegate the initiative to an employee, who may at times require approval of the final proposal.[3]

As an entrepreneur, the manager must select the correct approach and adapt it as markets shift. What may be a custom product or service at one point in time may become a mass-produced offering requiring cost reduction at a later time. On the other hand, some mass-produced items and services need to be personalized to offer exclusivity and differentiation.

In their entrepreneurial role, managers must be aware of the options available to do this. They may be able to personalize what they sell through services driven by software.

Recently, I had to choose between a traditional taxi service I have used for years and Uber to get to the airport. I called the taxi service, which ended up arriving late. I vowed to call Uber next time. I missed the personalization Uber offered. Without repeated calls to the taxi service, I could not estimate where my taxi was or when to expect it to arrive. With Uber, the service provider and the driver know my location, my car-size preference, my preferred payment method and my regular destinations.

It is no wonder then that the taxi industry is falling behind or that many other traditional companies have been forced into rapid change. Managers who are unable to transform their firms quickly risk losing business.

To succeed in their entrepreneurial role, managers also need to understand how to mix the three systems of production (production of unique products, process-based production, and mass production) as new companies and new industries emerge.

For example, a large-scale software project, which is unique or one-of-a-kind, falls under the production of unique product production. Think of building a very complex operating system like Windows. Hundreds of engineers would be assigned to such a project. With the process engineering approach, however, we can produce a new version of the software every day. Delivering new software combines unique product production and process-based production. In the entrepreneurial role, the manager must forecast trends and decide which production approach to pursue.

Decision-making Role #2: Crisis Manager

In the entrepreneur's role, the manager initiates change voluntarily. But sometimes the manager must act as a crisis manager when responding to changes beyond his or her control. Some examples of crisis include an unexpected bank strike causing delays in loan approval and affecting a company's cash position, inability of a key supplier to deliver on time, or sudden loss of a customer. Two leading management thinkers, Peter Drucker and Leonard R. Sayles, who studied the job of a manager, say that managerial work requires managing crises or handling unexpected events.[4] For a well-run company, the manager can create a set of standard operating procedures that can predict outcomes. Mintzberg says that some crises arise because ineffective managers ignore threatening situations until they reach a crisis point. But even good managers can't anticipate the consequences of all the decisions that they make.

A significant portion of a manager's time goes into handling crises every day. For example, information security is an area where companies are vulnerable to internal and external threats. Improving security requires changing processes and spending money on training and technology. As a manager, it is difficult to prioritize and improve security procedures proactively. The budget is always limited. We cannot slow down the production line to implement new processes. But once a security incident happens, the crisis forces the budget decision as well as the required downtime to implement secure processes and new technology.

Decision-making Role #3: Allotter of Resources

Managers decide how to distribute resources to team members. Managers look for optimal utilization of the resources they have at their disposal. Some of the apportioning they have to do pertains to:

- **Their own time:** One of the most important resources managers have is their time. It is by access to the manager—who is the unit's nerve centre and decision maker—that unit members get exposure and learning opportunities. Because high performers choose to spend time with other high performers, human nature dictates that a manager will often opt to work alongside the best performers in the team, whether this seems fair or not.
- **Work allotment:** A company manager decides the size of the team for an initiative or innovation. With Agile engineering practices and the flattening of organizations, the unit structure is similar throughout

the company. Still, managers of larger groups can decide on the broad informal structure of their teams.

A manager also decides how work will be allotted to individuals and who will do what. For software projects, not all work is equally challenging. Coding and testing certain portions are more interesting and desirable to some individuals. Despite our movement towards self-organizing teams, the team manager still decides informally who does what, and has the final say in allotting work. The manager is under pressure to ensure that project deadlines and commitments to customers are met.

Local optimization by managers is often a problem faced by many organizations. This happens when a unit manager is incentivized to do what is best for his unit without any regard to the overall benefit of the company. Because many decisions are interrelated, they must at some point pass through a single person's brain. If power or decision-making is fragmented, it will result in disjointed strategies. Lean principles strongly discourage local optimization by unit managers. As Mintzberg says, the overall optimization is done by the chief executives.

- **Potential initiatives:** In our experience, we must select from many worthy and equally great proposed initiatives that will consume a significant amount of effort and financial investment made by the company. Choosing the 'winner' initiative depends on many factors.

For example, we were recently grappling with the question of whether or not to triple our engineering facility in Hyderabad from the current 33,000 square feet of special export zone (SEZ) space to 99,000 square feet. SEZ unit approvals require a minimum leasing commitment of five years. The investment would quadruple the space for our engineering team. Of course, there would be a proportionate increase in maintenance expenses.

Some of the factors that helped us make the decision were: (1) *The political climate.* Following the division of Andhra Pradesh into two states, the future of Hyderabad was shrouded in uncertainty as the new capital was outside Hyderabad. Also, with a new government at the Centre led by a new prime minister and a new finance minister, SEZ rules and policies were likely to be revised. (2) *The impact on overhead.* One key question is whether the sales team can generate enough business to absorb the additional facilities in a foreseeable future (one to three years). (3) *The impact on the company.* In considering the expansion, we asked ourselves: are we ensuring that our current team will not be overextended? Do we have the support of the broader management team? Can we generate enough management depth and support staff to handle the expanded infrastructure? We decided not to expand.

To ensure that proper decisions are made, chief executives rely on the recommendations of the executive team. The executive team *and* the project manager must buy into the final decision so that everyone presenting the investment is involved in ensuring the success of the proposal.

- **Tools and equipment:** The manager decides the most desirable office location to which to send the latest computer hardware and shared resources (administrative helpers).

Decision-making Role #4: Negotiator

Managers spend considerable time in negotiations. Negotiations are a 'way of life' for a sophisticated manager. A first-level manager may negotiate or persuade a team member to align his vacation schedule with the project deliverables. At other levels, a negotiation may require deciding on a salary package for new MBA hires from a leading MBA programme. At other times, managers may negotiate with key suppliers on the rental rates for a new SEZ facility.

In customer situations, a manager may need to persuade a client to agree to a revised teamwork plan that is more expensive but will improve the desired outcome. Mintzberg mentions that the manager is the only player who has 'real-time' information about the resources that are required in negotiations.

Bestselling author Daniel Pink notes that all of us are constantly selling or persuading others to adopt our point of view.[5] But managers must sell or persuade more often than others to get the desired outcome to meet their goals.

Good Managers Are Leaders

'First rule of leadership: Everything is your fault.'

—A Bug's Life

'Leader' and 'manager' are terms frequently used to describe the roles responsible for an organization's performance. Is there a difference between a leader and a manager? Ultimately, managers must motivate their workers to deliver great value to customers. Leaders must set broad company goals, create a vision for their team and inspire them. All credit—and most of the blame—starts and ends with these two roles. Their work is closely related; both leaders and managers are necessary in any successful company. Often the same person plays both roles.

In the 1960s and 70s, the manager was portrayed as the 'villain' of the organization. More recently, TV serials like *The Office* and comic strips like *Dilbert* have mocked managers, especially managers in office environments. The negative stereotype of the manager resulted from the harsh economic realities that have surrounded us. With globalization, competition increased. Though managers did not control all aspects of the business, they still had to deliver superior results. People hated the manager, even though he was often just the messenger of bad news related to job cuts, pay reductions, increased workloads, etc.

Given this negative stereotyping of managers, many talented people opted out of moving up the ranks.

To reverse this situation and to make the management role more appealing, companies tried to inspire managers to think beyond their stressful daily operations. To motivate managers to broaden their horizons and think bigger, companies tried to improve their self-image. Using a new word—'leader'—to describe the manager's role made it easier. Many of us have had managers remind us: 'We are leaders, not managers.' Managers were also asked at the same time to broaden their thinking by looking at the competitive landscape or the 'big picture'. With the shortage of skilled workers, managers now had to focus on inspiring and leading people, and not on 'micromanaging' them. As leaders, managers were asked to delegate all work and not get involved in execution.

In *First, Break All the Rules*, authors Marcus Buckingham and Curt Coffman describe the difference between a manager and a leader.[6] The difference, they write, lies in their focus. A manager is internally focused. A leader is externally focused. Essentially, the authors are asking managers to think of the external landscape, which includes competitors and customers. In the past, the same managers may have only been expected to think of internal operations, such as the company's cost structure or streamlining of a product's assembly.

John Kotter discusses the functions of management and leadership in his 1990 book, *A Force for Change: How Leadership Differs from Management*. Kotter explains that managers provide order and consistency to organizations. Leaders produce positive change in companies, driving them towards a brighter future.[7] Kotter says that management and leadership activities are both required for a company to prosper, as outlined in the following table:

Table 4.1: Management and Leadership

Management Produces Consistency	Leadership Produces Change
Plan and Budget • Establish priorities • Set timelines • Allot resources	Establish Direction • Create a vision • Clarify the big picture • Set strategies
Organize Staff • Provide organizational structure • Hire and fire people • Establish rules and operating procedures	Align People • Communicate goals • Seek commitment • Build teams and alliances
Control and Solve Problems • Develop incentives • Provide creative solutions • Take corrective action	Motivate and Inspire • Inspire and energize • Empower followers • Satisfy unmet needs

While Kotter emphasizes the need for increased leadership, I have found that good managers act as change agents. Leaders and managers do not need to be separate people. *All good managers must be leaders. But not all leaders are good managers.* Some managers are great at inspiring people but poor at managing operations. Some people are great at leading operations, but cannot and should not manage people. Every company of every size needs a combination of both sets of skills. Every responsible job role requires both management and leadership skills. Some of us are better at one or the other.

In my review of organizational charts of many companies of every size, I have not come across two parallel career tracks, one for managers and one for leaders. Senior managers in particular must embody both management and leadership traits. Most large companies have a chief *executive* officer (CEO) at the top. The CEO is responsible for managing and leading the company. Just below the CEO are the vice-presidents or the management team. They are responsible for organizing the company and delivering great performance across all measures. These measures include profitability, market share, stock price, customer satisfaction and employee engagement. The vice-presidents must uphold these responsibilities while preserving the long-term viability of the company. Depending on the company's needs, the vice-presidents also act as leaders and managers.

One of the most recent and public examples of how leaders and managers must coexist at the executive level comes from Steve Jobs, the late founder of Apple. Nobody would disagree that Jobs was a visionary leader. Conventional wisdom implies that, as the CEO of Apple, Jobs should have simply communicated his vision of the iPhone to his employees. His employees would then be responsible for its actual design and production. Through delegation, Apple would get its employees to fulfil their CEO's vision and deliver lovely products to consumers.

However, even with a visionary leader at the company's helm, the reality at Apple was different. A former Google mobile executive, Vic Gundotra, recounts an anecdote describing Steve Jobs' involvement in the operational details of the iPhone. Gundotra's Google+ post appeared on 24 August 2011, while Jobs was hospitalized battling pancreatic cancer. Jobs passed away on 5 October 2011.

The incident Gundothra describes happened just a week before new iPhone features were announced at the much-anticipated trade show. At that time, Jobs contacted Gundotra. Here is Gundotra's account of their conversation:

One Sunday morning, January 6th, 2008, I was attending religious services when my cell phone vibrated. As discreetly as possible, I checked the phone and noticed that my phone said, 'Caller ID unknown.' I choose [sic] to ignore.

After services, as I was walking to my car with my family, I checked my cell phone messages. The message left was from Steve Jobs. 'Vic, can you call me at home? I have something urgent to discuss,' it said.

Before I even reached my car, I called Steve Jobs back. I was responsible for all mobile applications at Google, and in that role, had regular dealings with Steve. It was one of the perks of the job.

'Hey Steve—this is Vic,' I said. 'I'm sorry I didn't answer your call earlier. I was in religious services, and the caller ID said unknown, so I didn't pick up.'

Steve laughed. He said, 'Vic, unless the Caller ID said "GOD", you should never pick up during services.'

I laughed nervously. After all, while it was customary for Steve to call during the week upset about something, it was unusual for him to call me on Sunday and ask me to call his home. I wondered what was so important?

'So, Vic, we have an urgent issue, one that I need addressed right away. I've already assigned someone from my team to help you, and I hope you can fix this tomorrow,' said Steve.

'I've been looking at the Google logo on the iPhone and I'm not happy with the icon. The second O in Google doesn't have the right yellow gradient. It's just wrong and I'm going to have Greg fix it tomorrow. Is that okay with you?'

Of course, this was okay with me. A few minutes later on that Sunday, I received an email from Steve with the subject 'Icon Ambulance.' The email directed me to work with Greg Christie to fix the icon.

Since I was 11 years old and fell in love with an Apple II, I have dozens of stories to tell about Apple products. They have been a part of my life for decades. Even when I worked for 15 years for Bill Gates at Microsoft, I had a huge admiration for Steve and what Apple had produced.

But in the end, when I think about leadership, passion and attention to detail, I think back to the call I received from Steve Jobs on a Sunday morning in January. It was a lesson I'll never forget. CEOs should care about details. Even shades of yellow. On a Sunday.

To one of the greatest leaders I've ever met, my prayers and hopes are with you Steve.

—Vic[8]

Even though Apple employed some of the best designers and managers in the industry, one of the tech industry's most visionary leaders found it necessary to get involved in the very specific details of his company's products.

Critics of Steve Jobs' management style rightly assert that he was a micromanager, which many consider a bad thing. I believe his micromanagement must be viewed in the larger context. Steve Jobs produced 'insanely great' products that are loved by many and command price premiums in the otherwise commoditized cell phone industry. It is hard to argue with his results.

In his 1993 book, *The Working Leader: The Triumph of High Performance over Conventional Management Principles*, Leonard R. Sayles discusses the futility of

Generally Accepted Management Principles (GAMP). He notes that some managers incorrectly perceive that their job is to 'maintain the status quo' in the department 'keeping output high and their boss' anxiety low'.[9] In the past, management also assumed that:

- Goals should be clear and fixed permanently.
- Technology that is delivered on these goals does not change.
- Central support groups will deliver new recruits, offer training, procure goods and services and take care of accounting.
- Managers should delegate everything.
- Metrics should be established after which one should get out of the way.
- People and technology issues are separate.

Some companies, particularly those in monopolistic industries, still adhere to the dated conventional management principles that Sayles rallied against. A company with strong managers but with no leaders will be very bureaucratic. The organization will never change. Work will be performed using the same procedures and the same tools to produce the same goods that were produced twenty, thirty or even fifty years ago. If customers do not require new versions of the products and competitive dynamics do not change, there is no need for any change either. Theoretically, effective managers are all that is needed in such an organization.

On the other hand, if a company has no management and only leaders, there will be change just for the sake of change. Some of these changes may be counterproductive.

In reality, neither a purely management-based nor a purely leadership-based company would last very long. A complacent organization with no motivation to change will die when a new technology or competitor appears. A company that changes without solid managerial inputs will suffer from poor performance. That company too will die.

The job title of 'leader' does not exist. Company organizational charts do carry the title of 'manager', of course. We come across the job titles of 'production manager', 'software engineering manager', 'project manager', and so on. They reflect the well-defined nature of the job and what employers expect the person in that role to produce. Even at senior levels, job titles refer to executives. In other words, the titles indicate that the roles include responsibility for execution. Common executive titles are 'executive director' and 'executive vice-president'. That distinction and focus on execution and delivery means that, as managers, we must deliver today. And, as leaders, we must introduce change.

What is the proper mix of managerial (execution) and leadership (change) roles for an executive? Which of the two is more difficult? Which is more desirable? Which is more rewarding?

In my experience, most organizations rely on their executives to introduce change. Such changes may revolve around people's capabilities or around process improvements through new technology, new sales and new marketing techniques (e.g., advertising using Google AdWords instead of printed newspapers). Because companies have to adapt to stay competitive, it makes sense for them to ask their executives to lead production and change initiatives.

Peter Drucker proposes another way of viewing the leader-versus-manager dichotomy. Drucker mentions that the manager has three broad roles: that of the thinking man, the production leader and the front man or the public face. Drucker cautions that it is difficult for one person to handle all three roles simultaneously. Companies have recognized this. Over time, new management structures have evolved along the lines of the CEO and COO/CTO framework, even at the departmental level. Depending on the company and industry, two people may share these responsibilities, which may gain or lose importance over time.

For example, in technology companies the 'thinking man' usually has the title of chief technology officer and the 'execution man' may be the vice-president of engineering. The 'front man' may be the CEO, who is really the marketing man.

In my assessment, while Steve Jobs was heading Apple he focused on the design of 'insanely great' Apple products. Jobs was also the public face (front man) of Apple. Tim Cook was the execution man who, as the COO, oversaw the efficient manufacture and distribution of Apple products throughout the world.

To Delegate or Not to Delegate?

Delegation is a *process* managers use to involve team members in getting work done. Good delegation increases team output, develops the team members' skills and boosts team morale. Managers who learn how to delegate effectively also reduce their own work hours, leaving them with more time for important personal activities.

Some managers learn to delegate well. Other managers take the misguided approach of *delegation by abdication* of their responsibilities. In the latter case, managers often fail to set up proper metrics and systems to establish accountability among their subordinates. Without accountability, subordinates may not be able to work effectively without close supervision.

Given the creative nature of the specialized and increasingly technical work many of us do, getting work done involves collaborating with globally distributed co-workers, departments and even suppliers. Delegation is not always easy in this environment, but with training and practice, we can learn to delegate effectively.

Challenges Faced by New Engineering Managers

The story about Steve Jobs' concern over the shade of yellow in the iPhone Google logo may suggest, on the surface, that good leaders do not delegate. On the other hand, virtually all management literature advises us to delegate everything. For most managers, the reality is somewhere in between. Even when managers delegate, they should remain engaged.

In *The Working Leader*, Sayles explains that it is futile for active managers to define boundaries separating their work and their subordinates' work.[10] As he explains, active managers use 'interactive delegation' to deliver superior results. 'A manager is responsible for keeping track of when and how to intervene, despite ambiguities,' he notes.

While Sayles's book was not tailored to meet technology organizations' needs, his work is applicable to the software development industry. In our business, managers must remain engaged even when they are delegating—a daunting challenge for many new managers.

Many companies, including ours, use Agile software development practices. An Agile team of six engineers may be brought together to work on a project that will last three to six months. As the new team is forming, the team manager will ask one of the engineers to lead the team (this person often being called the point of contact, or POC). Usually, managers select a POC based on his or her superior technical ability and positive performance indicators. The rest of the team is usually fine with being supervised by the POC because they respect that person's expertise. POCs are responsible for their own work output as well as for the output of their five team members.

New POCs start out by assigning work to themselves and to their team members. The POCs, however, face a challenge. They received promotions precisely because of their superior technical skills. Their team members are not so skilled as they are, and may make mistakes or miss deadlines. If a member does make a costly mistake, the POC will be accountable for the misstep. The POC will likely step in and rescue the team by putting in long hours. In effect, the work was reverse-delegated to the POC, who also has to de-escalate the missed delivery deadline or defective work issues with his manager, and potentially with the sales and customer service teams.

Because of such scenarios, many POCs become afraid to delegate. They worry their team members will make mistakes, so they end up taking on many more assignments than they should.

It is understandable why new POCs do not want to delegate. When I assign work to another team member, I am still responsible for the completion, quality and timely delivery of that work. And because I am accountable for the deliverable, I often find it easier to do the work myself.

This 'if-you-want-something-done-right-you-have-to-do-it-yourself' mindset is damaging, for several reasons. First, it results in my doing more and more work and may even make me a bottleneck to the task at hand. Second, refusing to delegate limits the growth prospects of my team members and the departments under me. One of my managerial responsibilities is to motivate my team and improve its capability. I cannot fulfil this duty if I do not delegate.

Common Barriers to Delegation

I describe below some of the common situations that prevent managers from delegating work:

1. As managers, we lack clarity on the expected outcome. As a result, we are not clear in defining the expected outcomes. If a subordinate asks for clarifications, our answers are likely to be unclear and unhelpful. It is as if we expect people to read our minds.

2. We feel vulnerable and personally insecure. If other people learn the task, will they replace me?

3. Most of our information comes to us orally. A lot of the information and considerations required to do the work are in the manager's head. Sometimes, it may take more time to describe and write what is expected than to do the work ourselves.

4. We do not spend enough time developing procedures and documenting them for others to follow.

5. We do not spend enough time training and developing people.

6. We have had bad experiences in which a subordinate did not do a good job with a delegated task. As a result, we develop the view that subordinates are incompetent. Sometimes we believe they are already overloaded with work. In some cases, we believe they are unwilling to take on more responsibility.

7. We like work done our way. When it comes to creative work this approach makes matters difficult. Sometimes we underestimate the team's capabilities.

8. We underestimate the amount of time it takes to do a task, leading to missed deadlines. As a result, we get frustrated and angry.

As a manager, I have experienced many of these issues myself. We can address many of these barriers by setting up the proper environment for success before we delegate work.

Thinking Through the Delegation Dilemma

Before I delegate work, I must have clear answers to the following questions:

1. What am I delegating? Is it a task (like collection of weekly time sheets or logging a bug)? Is it a project (such as developing the architecture of a software application or putting together a sales presentation)? Is it a function (like accounting, sales or marketing)?
2. Who will do what and by when?
3. How will the work be completed? In today's knowledge-based organizations, it is difficult to separate the 'how' of a work from the actual work itself.
4. Who is responsible for completion of the task?
5. Who is ultimately accountable for the work?
6. Who has the authority to commit company resources to the assignment?

Mixing Up Authority, Responsibility and Accountability

I find it useful to review the ideas of authority, responsibility and accountability. The terms are somewhat overlapping and are frequently used interchangeably by managers and subordinates.

The *Business Dictionary* provides the following definitions for responsibility, accountability and authority:

- **Responsibility**: A duty or obligation to satisfactorily perform or complete a task. Failure is penalized. Multiple team members—including the manager and subordinates—usually share responsibility for completing the task or project.[11]
- **Accountability**: An obligation of an individual or group to account for its activities, accept responsibility and share results. While multiple people may be responsible for a project, usually one person is held accountable for the outcome.[12]
- **Authority**: A formal power to commit resources (e.g., budgets, engineers, etc.) and give orders, which are expected to be obeyed. The authority comes with credit for our positive actions and liability for failure to act. Usually, the senior managers retain this authority.[13]

When we work with our clients to develop custom software, there are multiple software engineers *responsible* for the development work. The project manager, however, is *accountable* to the customer for ensuring the software quality (i.e., delivering properly working software on time). The accounts manager or the engagement manager has the *authority* to sign the legal contract and commit to the schedule and company resources.

As you can imagine, one of the difficulties of management is that managers are accountable but do not usually have authority. 'Without proper authority, how can I be held accountable?' is a common concern.

There are several facets to this question. First, most people are not even aware they are accountable. Just asking the accountability question helps clarify that aspect. Second, depending on the company and the project downside or risk, authority is granted or shared with multiple people.

We find an easy example of shared authority in the field of computer security systems. By default, experts advise giving subordinates only as much authority as is necessary to do their work. Over time, this authority is expanded as subordinates prove their competence to do the work correctly. For low-peril projects, we can start out with a higher level of trust for the new team member. In those cases, authority is given earlier.

At the highest level of government, our elected prime minister has the authority to run the country. Even with his legitimate authority, however, the prime minister is accountable to other elected leaders and has the responsibility of meeting the expectations of the people.

Reversing Reverse Delegation

Reverse delegation takes the work of subordinates and places it on managers. The classic *Harvard Business Review* article, 'Management Time: Who's Got the Monkey?' provides some guidance on reversing reverse delegation.[14]

The article invites readers to imagine work tasks as monkeys. When workers approach their managers with problems, the monkeys are perched on the subordinates' backs. If managers take ownership of the problem from their subordinates, the monkeys jump on to the managers' backs. To keep the monkeys on the subordinates, managers must refuse to solve problems for their workers. Managers accomplish this goal by establishing five clear rules:

Rule 1: Is the task necessary?

Decide whether the monkey, or the work, needs to be done. If a monkey is unnecessary, immediately inform the subordinate to eliminate the task. If a task needs to be handled, the subordinate must follow-through with it. A neglected task without any follow through requires additional discussion by the manager.

Rule 2: Limit the tasks to be discussed

The manager can limit how many work items will be discussed by the subordinate. A properly defined task can be discussed in less than fifteen minutes. Otherwise, meetings take an inordinately long time.

Rule 3: Discuss pending tasks

Set up an appointment to discuss the pending tasks. This simple technique forces the subordinate to follow up on the tasks and discuss what blocks his progress. The manager should not be the one following up on neglected tasks.

Rule 4: Hold meetings in person

To save time, meetings should be held in person. In case of remote teams, we insist on videoconferencing. By avoiding email discussion, we ensure that the subordinates are not waiting for the manager to respond before moving forward (monkey on manager's back again). Reports and status emails can supplement but cannot replace the in-person meeting.

Rule 5: Set follow-up times

For every task or monkey, the next follow-up time should be set. The subordinate should know his or her five options. Does he have to (a) wait until told, (b) ask what to do, (c) recommend and then act, (d) act and inform immediately, or (e) act independently and report? As the subordinate develops her skills and demonstrates proficiency, she can graduate to acting independently. The article suggests, however, that subordinates should be aware of their boundaries.

New software tools such as Trello, Slack and Microsoft Teams help us ensure ownership of and clarity on work items. These simple dashboards and workflow tools clearly identify who has the monkey and for how long.

Insights from the Situational Leadership Model

As a manager, I need to assign tasks or projects that are appropriate to a subordinate's development level. Depending on the skills and abilities of my team members, I must select the scope carefully. As a new manager, a mistake I made frequently was to assume that all my team members were equally skilled and equally committed.

The Situational Leadership Model provides a useful tool to gauge a person's ability to perform a task. The model has been widely taught to millions of managers and is useful because of its simplicity. The model allows managers to adjust their management style (directing, coaching, supporting, or delegating) to match the development level (competence and commitment) of their subordinates. The model explains that most people go through four stages of development:

1. **Enthusiastic beginner:** Low competence and high commitment—cannot do the job, but is willing to do the job. When I was a new MBA graduate, I was eager to make an impact in my first job. But beyond theoretical equations and case studies, I did not know how to complete a project in the new company setting. I wanted to be told what to do, how to do it, and I was open to close supervision, aka micromanagement.

   Most of our new hires from colleges probably fall into this category. Managers overseeing stage 1 employees need to adopt a *directive* style. In this first stage of employee development, the manager should structure the work, teach how the work is done and closely supervise his wards. In a software development organization, new developers are eager to write code and ensure that the code is in production. This is the first time their code is being utilized by actual users. At this stage, the manager works with developers to teach them software version control tools, download the latest software code into their computers and understand how the earlier changes were made.

As part of their learning, many of our developers study how previous software projects at the company were organized. They are provided with the coding standards and best practices they must follow. They are given non-critical and low-risk tasks. In the first three to six months, new engineers are mostly changing existing code and fixing errors. Once the work is completed, the supervisor must check the completed work to ensure that it was done correctly. Frequent review, feedback and direction build confidence.

2. **Disillusioned learner:** This employee has some competence but is low on commitment. He is mostly able to do the job but is not willing to do it. Even after we have worked for a few months on projects, we are still inexperienced and relatively unskilled. Engineers, for instance, know how to code, and they understand the underlying technology. But they are not experts. In the next six to eighteen months, they add to their skills by writing new code and checking it in the source code repository. The occasional bug or error easily frustrates and overwhelms them. As a result, they give up easily.

We need to closely supervise and monitor employees at the 'disillusioned learner' stage to ensure that their work is completed correctly. At this stage, we need to explain what needs to be done and how it must be done, then check if the work was done correctly. We need to adopt a *coaching* style, in which we provide specific feedback, answer questions and review suggestions. Up to this point, the worker's input is limited to the existing software architecture and libraries.

To build the worker's commitment, we need to include him in decision-making (e.g., whether to implement the suggested approach, whether to implement a particular architecture, new software libraries, new micro-services, etc.) and praise his inputs in order to build his confidence and self-esteem.

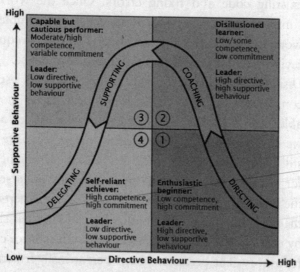

Figure 4.1: Situational Leadership Model

3. **Capable but cautious performer:** This employee has moderate-to-high competence but variable commitment. She can do the job, and may do the job. By this stage, the team member has worked on at least six sprints and delivered software. The person is skilled and knows how to write code, understand customer requirements and deploy software. Her manager is confident she can do her work well. Other team members and customers are starting to look up to her for her decisions on the software architecture, the proper software library, or the underlying software server platform. Some of these bigger decisions involve unfamiliar approaches and may be risky.

   In these situations, the person has occasional self-doubts and may not be willing to take risks. To boost her confidence, we need to listen to the person's concerns and suggestions. But this employee, because of her skills, does not need monitoring or micromanaging. Once managers recognize that the employee has advanced skill levels, they need to back off from close supervision (which is easier for some managers than it is for others). We need to adopt the *supporting* style. At this point, the manager mostly needs to provide the employee her assignment and general direction. Once the assignment is given, the worker needs management support and approval to increase her commitment to the project.

4. **Self-reliant achiever:** High competence and high commitment characterize this worker. The person both can and will do the job. This employee can

understand customer needs and team capability. He consistently and independently translates customer requirements into superior software solutions. Every company has these highly desirable team members. They are a joy to work with. With them, we need to adopt the *delegating* style. Because of their commitment and superior skills, management teams are often guilty of not paying them enough attention or of not spending enough time with them. Most managers give self-reliant achievers coveted assignments and independence in decision-making. Managers step in only to help 'unblock' their path, should something impede their progress. Managers need to highlight these workers' accomplishments and help them reach new heights.

Not all of our assignments are equally challenging. When we start working on new projects, we must consider the complexity, speed and volume of work necessary to complete the project. Some projects are technically very complex. We assign our technically advanced people who are already at stage 3 to take on these projects. Some projects are about volume and not technical complexity. We then set up the processes and monitoring mechanisms to deliver the desired outcomes. Stage 1 and stage 2 team members do well on these assignments and still feel challenged. In other words, we tailor project assignments based on project demands and the individual worker's stage of development. Just because a person was at stage 3 in a project of low technical complexity, we do not assume he will be at stage 3 in a technically complex project.

Deciding Which Assignments to Delegate

In their zeal to delegate, some new managers try to delegate everything. Some managerial activities are time-consuming and negative in nature (e.g., firing, providing difficult feedback, etc.). Eager to maintain relationships, many conflict-avoiding managers jump at any opportunity to delegate these activities. To my mind, delegating unpleasant tasks is never a best practice.

So, what can you delegate? And what are the tasks that you must do personally?

Start by listing the activities that, as a manager, you should not assign away. In *Delegating Work*, the *Harvard Business Review* cautions that managers cannot delegate the following activities:[15]

- Aligning the team with the company goals.
- Hiring and firing team members.
- Directing, inspiring and motivating the team.
- Evaluating team members' performance.
- Delegation of work delegated by someone else; when I receive a rare escalation from a key client manager who wants me to review our project quality, I own it, I follow up and I respond.
- Handling complex negotiations with clients, regulators and suppliers.
- Tasks that match our specific or unique abilities.

Other tasks can be completed by many of one's team members. As mentioned earlier, managers can also do these tasks. We, as managers, may be good at them and may even enjoy doing them. But many others can perform them equally well. As a manager, I must narrow my contributions to just the activities I am uniquely good at, i.e., work the other team members *cannot* do yet.

Creating the Right Environment

Managers set up our environments for successful delivery of our customer commitments. Creating an environment of success for our employees depends on the employees' stage of development. If a team mostly comprises enthusiastic beginners (stage 1 employees) and disillusioned learners (stage 2 workers), managers must spend more time on training and development. In such situations, the manager's span of control (or team size) is smaller. Teams comprising stage 1 and stage 2 software engineers may have around five people each.

Many Agile teams consist of very capable performers (stage 3) and self-reliant achievers (stage 4). In these teams, a manager's span of control extends to roughly thirty employees who report through a flat hierarchy. These team members do not require supervision; managers are only required to lightly support their teams' efforts. Improved collaboration tools and a focus on efficiency allow for these larger spans of control.

Google asked its engineers to define good management. According to the *Harvard Business Review*, Google's extensive surveys and data crunching showed that a great manager:[16]

1. Is a good coach who helps identify and develop subordinates' individual genius or superpowers.
2. Empowers the team and does not micromanage.
3. Expresses interest in and concern for team members' success and personal well-being.
4. Is productive and results-oriented.
5. Is a good communicator who is a good listener and also shares information.
6. Helps workers with their career development.
7. Has a clear vision and strategy for the team.
8. Has the key technical skills for advising the team.

The Google study confirms that highly skilled engineers want their managers to be good coaches. A good coach offers advice and specific feedback in a positive way. Being very skilled (stage 3 or stage 4), the engineers do not want or need to be micromanaged. Google engineers also wanted technically capable managers with a clear vision and strategy for their teams.

As mentioned above, a manager adjusts the environment based on the readiness of the team and its composition. In our engineering projects, we follow certain techniques (albeit inconsistently) to bring stage 1 and stage 2 employees into stage 3 and stage 4. Some of the techniques include:

1. Ensuring that the team members have received proper technical training to complete at least basic tasks.

2. Selecting the right person with the needed skills as opposed to the next person available (which may be of convenience to us).
3. Providing a process or procedures manual (These manuals seem to get outdated the day they are written. In my experience, we do not spend enough time to update our documents regularly).
4. Preparing and using checklists to remind people to do their work correctly.

Once the proper environment is set up, the manager needs to adjust his supervision from being directive to providing support.

Chapter Summary

Key Points

- Managers contribute to their organizations by simplifying tasks and reducing specialization.
- Effective managers must perform three roles: interpersonal roles, informational roles and decisional roles.
- All good managers must be leaders; not all leaders are good managers.
- Good delegation:
  - o Increases team output.
  - o Leads to team members' growth.
  - o Boosts morale.

- Good delegation skills are required in the modern work environment to effectively deal with globally distributed co-workers, departments and suppliers.
- Refusing to delegate limits the growth prospects of team members and departments.
- To efficiently delegate, managers must:
  - o Communicate clear expectations.
  - o Develop clear procedures for others to follow.
  - o Train team members properly.
  - o Trust team members.
- Managers must be aware that they are *accountable* for the outcome of projects, even if they are not *responsible* for developing the project and lack the *authority* to set the terms of the project's contract.
- Managers must refuse to solve task-related problems for their workers by:
  - o Deciding whether the task is necessary; and if so get the subordinate to follow through.
  - o Designing tasks that can be explained in fifteen minutes or less.
  - o Setting up appointments to discuss pending tasks.
  - o Holding meetings in person or by videoconference (avoiding email discussion).
  - o Setting follow-up times for subordinates.
- Managers must determine their subordinates' development levels and assign tasks accordingly.
- Effective managers create the proper environment for their subordinates' success, then switch from a supervisory role to a support role.

5

Please Understand My Style

'I myself am made entirely of flaws, stitched together with good intentions.'

—Augusten Burroughs
Author, *Running with Scissors*

Throughout my career, I have been a part of many teams. In every team, each member had unique personality traits. Based on my research on management, I knew that to be productive I needed to work effectively with various kinds of people. But knowing something and doing it are two separate things. It took me years to understand my own personality well enough to be able to work with other personality types. While talking to new managers, I notice that many have the same lack of self-awareness that I did.

When I applied for MBA programmes, universities asked evaluators to comment on my 'self-awareness' in their recommendation letters. At the time, I felt confident that I knew myself. After all, many people relied on me for input, direction and decisions at work. But the reality was I didn't understand myself at all. Beyond taking the time-bound personality examinations, I did not have many tools for self-reflection. Because I did not understand myself, it was not possible for me to understand other people.

During my engineering education at IIT Kharagpur, I was required to take only one psychology class during my second year. The only topic I remember from that class was gestalt perception theory. As a young person, my focus was on completing the coursework. The professor's abstract concepts had little relevance to my future employment in mechanical engineering (or so I thought). During my master's work at Iowa State University, I was expected to focus on engineering design and analysis. Humans and their behaviour or social styles were not a part of my formal education.

As I worked as a mechanical design analysis engineer at Frigidaire Company, our engineering team took the DISC (dominance, influence, steadiness and compliance) assessment. The DISC measures personality types and behavioural styles. When I saw the results, I was fascinated. It was like discovering that an astrologer had accurately read my horoscope. The test correctly reported my behaviours—how I responded to conflict and what motivated me. It clearly revealed what caused me stress and how I solved problems at work and in life. That test and my experience of applying the results to my career were critical to my development as a manager.

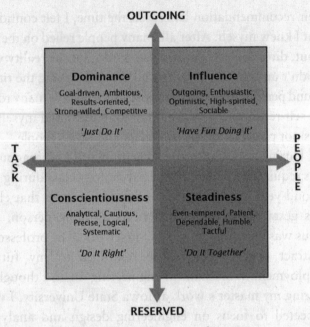

Figure 5.1: DISC personality types

The DISC test rated me very high on Dominance (D) and relatively high on Conscientiousness (C). My test results in some areas were flattering and in others so revealing that they made me a little uncomfortable, especially when they related to how I interacted with others.

Giving me a high D score, the test reported that I can be blunt and straight to the point. I see the big picture, emphasize on 'the bottom line', accept challenges and am results-oriented. I am always overconfident (sometimes to the amusement of others), even when I am wrong.

With a relatively high C score, I place emphasis on complying with processes and procedures, as well as on the quality and accuracy of my work. I get into the details and objective reasoning.

However, I tend to gloss over my interactions with people, including their concerns, feelings and emotions.

My influence (I) score was low, as the survey concluded that I place little or no emphasis on influencing or building personal relationships with others. No one would accuse me of bubbling over with enthusiasm or collaborating with many people. My co-workers see me as detached, analytical, critical and sceptical.

My lowest score, for steadiness (S), reflects my intense, undiplomatic and impulsive responses and behaviours. I like the fast pace and do not value security over certainty. Many of my co-workers have a high S score, which is a boon to our team. They provide stability and consistency over time—counterbalancing my traits.

The results were interesting and certainly increased my self-awareness. Working in the slow-paced appliance industry in Iowa was not a good fit for me, given my fast-paced, aggressive style. The pace of business was even slower than what it is today. If a meeting was needed, we usually scheduled it for the next week or the next month. Today, a meeting of similar importance is held the next day, if not on the same day. I was in a relatively relaxed environment. Everyone was nice and genuinely friendly (there is a term called 'Iowa nice' for that). With my limited self-awareness, I could not understand how my co-workers could be so relaxed and easy-going.

To increase my self-awareness and thus my effectiveness as a manager, I found it useful to rely on personality tests. DISC is only one of the tests that can help managers take an objective look at their own personality, allowing them to better position themselves in their workplace. Another well-respected test is the Myers-Briggs Type Indicator (MBTI).

The same year I joined the MBA programme at the University of Michigan, the school embarked on a new initiative to help students increase their self-awareness. From what I recall, it involved the MBTI tool. As a new student, I took the MBTI test for the first time.

Isabel Briggs Myers and her mother, Katharine Briggs, developed the MBTI instrument. It is based on Carl Jung's theory of personality types. The MBTI tools have been adopted and refined over the years. Many free[1] assessments are available on the Internet. Millions of people have used these assessments to understand their behaviours and strengths.

It is important not to assume that any personality trait is better or more desirable than another. As an engineer, I have a very limited understanding of humans and their psychology. But most of my survey results were written in a flattering way (at least as I saw it). Based on my answers, DISC described me as *pioneering*, *assertive*, *competitive*, *confident*, *positive*, and a *winner*. I preferred to focus on these results.

I was delighted to accept my positive personality attributes from the DISC and MBTI tests. I could not, however, comprehend how others could view my strengths as anything but a positive. I didn't want to believe that my co-workers would see me as *demanding*, *nervy, egotistical* and *aggressive*. Nor did I choose to acknowledge that, under extreme pressure, stress, or fatigue, I am seen as *abrasive, autocratic, arbitrary* and *opinionated*. For some time, I was in denial. I paid more attention to the compliments and felt vindicated. Just like many other reports, I saved the survey results in a folder to review later.

In retrospect, being a little sceptical about the results may have been wise. A general problem with the MBTI and DISC tools is that their effectiveness is dependent on how the test taker feels about the results. The results may be accurate, but what they mean for the candidate is based on the *test taker's* perception of himself. These tests are only effective if the test taker is willing to engage in honest, objective self-analysis.

Because my context and work groups changed over the years, I never went back to my team members and asked what they thought of my results. I maintained my biased views and continued to operate the way I always had. I was a task-oriented manager. I did not know how to analyse or understand team members beyond their work deliverables. I did not have a structured way to learn about my co-workers' natural work styles.

It wasn't until many years later that I finally realized I needed to do some serious work on my self-awareness or I would never become the leader I hoped to be.

Nearly ten years ago, as our company and industry were growing rapidly, we reached a critical stage of having more than 250 employees worldwide. Our people issues were becoming more pronounced. Many of our star performers delivered great software but were unhappy. There was increasing team and management conflict.

As a result, we decided to make a concerted effort to improve team development and management skills. The first step of the effort was to increase my awareness of my own work style. While researching on this, I came across *People Styles at Work* by Robert and Dorothy Bolton.

In their book, the Boltons describe the Social Style model, which was first developed in the 1960s by industrial psychologist David W. Merrill.[2] Merrill's model focused on the behavioural differences between people. Instead of asking individuals to answer questions about their own preferences and behaviours, Merrill asked *others* to identify certain behaviours of the individual under study using a statistical factor analysis technique.

Merrill found four distinct clusters of personality traits across two dimensions: assertiveness and responsiveness (refer to Figure 5.2 below).

The first dimension is *assertiveness*, which refers to how firmly a person communicates. People with low assertiveness 'ask', while those with high assertiveness 'tell'. We all know highly assertive people who use a strong, loud voice to tell others what to do, regardless of their hierarchy in a company or social structure.

The second dimension is *responsiveness*, which refers to whether a person prioritizes tasks or people. On one side, there are project managers who only care about results. People, and their feelings and opinions, do not matter to individuals who are considered low in responsiveness. All of us know very successful project managers who are good at getting things done, but no one likes to work with them.

Highly responsive managers, on the other hand, care a lot about people and their feelings. Highly responsive people may have a low task or results orientation. I have known many employees for whom people are the only concern and for whom task completion is an afterthought.

As a CEO, I have to be aware of these traits in my team. If I am not, projects can quickly derail—either because of bruised feelings or missed deadlines.

Based on the two dimensions—assertiveness (ask vs tell) and responsiveness (task vs people)— Merrill broadly divided people into the following four quadrants:

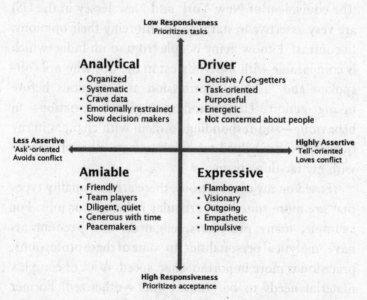

Figure 5.2: Four Social Styles–Each quadrant represents 25 per cent of the population

It's worth noting that Merrill mentioned 'versatility' as a third dimension, which is independent of the first two. His observation is that many successful people can adapt their primary work style to match the needs of their role (formal or expected), situation (social or organizational) and individual needs.

In *People Styles at Work*, the Boltons further developed the Social Style model. To ensure successful relationships, the Boltons advise us to 'flex' or adjust our behaviours to work effectively with others who may have different styles.

Stereotyping is not fair, but I will go out on a limb here. In my experience, people from Haryana and Punjab (the equivalent of New York and New Jersey in the US) are very assertive in stating and enforcing their opinions. In contrast, I know many people from south India (which is comparable with the Midwest in the US) who are soft-spoken and 'ask' for permission and opinions before taking action. Understanding regional variations in behaviour—and responding to them with changes in my own style—has helped me communicate more effectively with my far-flung team.

Based on my observations, there are personality types that are more suited to particular industries or jobs. For example, many professors, engineers and accountants have Analytical personalities. In some of these professions, precision is more important than speed. A lot of complex material needs to be studied and synthesized. Former prime minister Manmohan Singh displays a highly Analytical style.

In service industries such as health care, Amiable personalities thrive. Concern for other people is of utmost importance. Customers and patients need to feel that they have been heard and understood. Customer service, human resources and account management offer a natural fit for Amiable personalities.

Across almost all industries, managerial and CEO roles are dominated by Expressives. They create the vision for their companies and mobilize people around it. They are assertive and relate to many different personalities. Most of us enjoy working for Expressive managers. The most beloved public figures share this personality style. Some prominent examples are former Indian prime minister Atal Bihari Vajpayee, former US president Bill Clinton, and GE CEO Jeffrey Immelt.

Finally, Drivers are often at work as entrepreneurs, starting new companies. Even when Drivers are wrong, they are supremely confident. In the early stages of a company, you need to ignore all naysayers. Industries and companies that need to move through a period of significant change are often led by Drivers.

To increase the effectiveness of our managers, we train them to understand Boltons' four work styles. The following sections look at these key personality types and how to work with them.

Drivers

These highly assertive individuals are action-oriented. They make decisions and start executing them. Even if they are not sure about matters, they behave as if they know what they want, where they are going and how to get there efficiently. They always come across as certain and confident. They are micro managers and want everything done *now*, their way, to the last detail. Drivers focus on getting things done as opposed to making people happy. These individuals talk fast. If you see a group of people walking into a restaurant for lunch, you will find Drivers in the front. They are the first to enter the restaurant and they decide where the group will sit.

Drivers do not enjoy working with people. Over time, they realize that people slow them down. People drain their energy. These individuals rarely have the time for, or feel the need to, explain their motives or actions to other people. As a result, others find them uncommunicative, sometimes harsh and pushy. Based on their seniority, Drivers are supported by people-oriented peacemakers who explain the Drivers' objectives to affected people.

Though Drivers do have emotions and do care, they demonstrate their feelings through their actions rather than sharing them verbally. Depending on the situation, Drivers can be pleasant and charming too.

Time Horizons: Drivers are focused on the present and decide quickly how to handle the current situation. They are not concerned with the past or the future. To communicate with Drivers, one should get to the point quickly and not waste their time. Drivers get restless with long-winded explanations.

Decision-making: Drivers make their own decisions and do not like being told what is to be done. To work with

Drivers, it is always better to present facts and data (not opinions or feelings). It is best to give them options so that they can choose. They have strong opinions about matters that concern them. When their objectives are not met, they become heavy-handed or 'autocratic' and use strong action to force desired outcomes.

Team Interactions: Despite their shortcomings, every organization uses Drivers to bring about change and keep things moving. Drivers are often 'first generation entrepreneurs' and project managers. They are usually appointed (not elected) as senior managers when a major change is needed.

A prominent example of an appointed Driver is Jack Welch when he took over as CEO of GE. With globalization and increased competition, GE needed to change. Welch's first act was to fire 18,000 long-term employees and shut down many plants and divisions. Welch's actions devastated lives and many communities. At the time, he was called 'Neutron Jack' due to the explosive impact of his rapid decision-making. Jack Welch and Drivers like him are wartime CEOs.

Our current prime minister Narendra Modi is a Driver. He is highly assertive and confident about his vision and ideas. He is personally engaged in key initiatives and ensures they are on track. As an elected leader within his party, he has provided a compelling vision to his party members. The nation needed an assertive leader with a strong voice; it elected him with an overwhelming majority.

Not everyone, however, responds well to his tendencies as a Driver. Opposition parties find him 'dominating' and 'pushy', even dictatorial. After many years as the chief minister of Gujarat, he realized that he did not need to spend time answering questions after his speeches. Modi's speeches are a one-way communication with the audience.

Unfortunately, for the opposition parties, our prime minister is not going to change his primarily dominant style any time soon. Because of this, his opponents will continue to accuse him of centralizing power, of micromanagement and of heavy-handedness in his decisions and treatment of bureaucrats and ministers. Most recently in the US, President Donald Trump represents the 'Driver style', with his assertive and aggressive no-nonsense talk.

Many fast-changing industries and companies have been started or transformed by people with a Driver style. Some of the most prominent and successful Drivers include Infosys founder and CEO, N.R. Narayana Murthy, Microsoft founder and CEO, Bill Gates, and Apple founder and CEO, Steve Jobs. Each of them had a very different view of their industries. If they waited for approval from others, they would not have acted. Many of these CEOs appoint themselves because others typically will not select them due to their sometimes abrasive or harsh demeanour.

Expressives

People with an Expressive style successfully integrate assertiveness with a high level of emotional responsiveness. They are warm, friendly, energetic, approachable and ambitious. They share their feelings and thoughts with others easily. They dream big, they are competitive and they frequently enlist others to support their projects and causes. They are visionaries with fertile imaginations full of creative ideas. They experience and exhibit their emotions easily. Some days they are very happy and full of energy; other days they are down and unhappy.

Expressives are often surrounded by people; they like to be in the middle of the action. They love to be in the limelight and crave appreciation and approval from others. They are usually the life of a party. People with an Expressive style are energized by their interactions with others. They are great at mobilizing people by selling their vision through great speeches, personal interactions and sometimes dramatic or theatrical actions. They describe everyone as a close friend. People with other personality styles will describe a similar relationship as merely an 'acquaintance'.

Time Horizons: Expressives spend their time and energy on their future dreams. Because they tend to be undisciplined, they are late to meetings and their meetings run long. They spend time dreaming about the future, sometimes forgetting to address specific details in the present.

Decision-making: Expressives use their intuition, feelings and opinions of other important people to make decisions, as opposed to using logic and facts. Because they are willing to take risks, they decide and act quickly, on emotional impulse. As a result, they take risky decisions and may make mistakes. They move on to their next set of activities quickly. However, they are willing to change.

Team Interactions: To manage and work with Expressives, one needs to recognize their need for social recognition and prestige. Because they lack follow-through and the attention to detail needed to complete their projects, it is usually wise to pair them with someone who is thorough, detail-oriented and familiar with the current groundwork.

Because of their assertiveness and their ability to mobilize people, Expressives progress quickly through the ranks of most companies to lead teams and departments and become CEOs. They are the peacetime CEOs; they can mobilize people and take them along. After Jack Welch left the CEO position that he held at GE for nearly twenty years, Jeffrey Immelt took over and led with an Expressive style. He likely invigorated the stakeholders—including employees and customers—with his people-oriented ways.

Former prime minister of India, Atal Bihari Vajpayee, represents an Expressive style as well. His speeches were full of energy and included his personal poetry, humour and exuberance. He drew energy from people and large crowds. He connected well with members of his party and other leaders of the world. Demonstrating his ability to act quickly and take risks, one of his first acts as prime minister was to detonate a nuclear bomb to draw attention to India. Everyone in the country was instantly proud and mobilized by his assertiveness and the demonstration of their country's power. (In response, within five days, neighbouring Pakistan responded by detonating its own nuclear bomb. Unfortunately, the nuclear bombs triggered economic sanctions by the US and other Western countries against India and Pakistan. Both countries suffered economically for many years.)

As an Expressive, Atal Bihari Vajpayee moved on to his next dream of establishing a train service to Pakistan (the Samjhauta Express). This effort had limited success over the years.

I estimate that more than 70 per cent of established organizations are led by people with an Expressive style. Senior managers in these companies are either elected or become 'consensus' candidates to meet the approval of a broad set of constituents. The constituents include customers, employees, suppliers and other stakeholders. These stakeholders look for varying degrees of assurance from the candidate. Employees look for continuity, assurance and an assertive leader with a big dream and vision. Customers want to be 'sold' or assured they are in good hands and will continue to receive great value and service from their relationship with the company. Shareholders want great returns on their investments. Community groups want communication, engagement and participation from the senior leaders. Expressive leaders love to engage and draw energy from these relationships. They connect well with every group.

Some prominent and successful examples of Expressive leaders include Rajat Gupta, former McKinsey managing director (he was elected for three four-year terms by McKinsey partners), Jeffrey Immelt, GE CEO, and Steve Ballmer, former Microsoft CEO.

Analytical

People with an Analytical style are calm, strive for facts and live life according to logic, principles and careful assessment. As thinkers, they are 'ask'-oriented and 'task'-oriented as opposed to 'tell'-oriented and 'relationship'-oriented. They are deliberate and thorough and comply with rules and policies. In social settings, they are unassuming, low-key, reserved and quiet. Others may see them as aloof. They are usually private and do not like to share a lot of personal information (in contrast to Expressives, who often share more than one would want to know). Former Indian prime minister Manmohan Singh displays an Analytical style.

Time Horizons: Analyticals have a long time horizon. To work with them, one should not rush them into deadlines or quick decision-making. I remember going to a restaurant with a group of co-workers who represented all the styles. While everyone else had placed their order, the 'Analytical' was still studying the menu and was the last to decide.

Decision-making: Analyticals ask a lot of questions and need to complete their analysis before deciding. They may appear slow to decide because they may not have all the information. Once they have the facts, they are conservative in their decisions and tend to avoid risk. Instead of relying on personal opinions, they want to rely on data or facts. Once they decide, they stick with their choice for a long time.

Team Interactions: To team members and subordinates, Analyticals may come across as indecisive. Analyticals avoid conflict. They avoid people, topics and situations where they are likely to face disagreement. In many meetings, they defer taking decisions until more information is collected and additional surveys can be completed. Once they complete their analysis, however, their recommendations are thorough and appropriate. As a result, they provide a much-needed counterbalance to Drivers, who decide first and justify later. Expressives (who are likely to be in managerial roles) need support from Analyticals to gather facts, logic and reasoning that go beyond people and relationships.

Amiables

Amiables are people-oriented. They are friendly, easy-going, warm, cheerful and full of energy. They develop personal relationships and seek harmony—skills that are an asset when working with others. They do a lot of work in a dedicated manner without complaining or drawing attention to themselves. As a result, a lot of their work is not appreciated or even noticed. They bring calm and peace to contentious meetings.

Time Horizons: Similar to Analyticals, Amiables take a long time to decide and to take action. Because other people are their foremost concern, they spend a lot of time helping or being concerned with others, sometimes forgetting their own priorities and deadlines.

Decision-making: Amiables are concerned with the thoughts, needs and feelings of others. Like Analyticals, they are slow and cautious in their decision-making. They avoid risks and touch base with people before they announce their decisions.

Team Interactions: Amiables are 'people'-oriented (as opposed to task-oriented). They are generous with their time with team members. If a team member needs to talk or discuss something, they drop everything and spend time with that individual to ensure the team member's needs are met. Instead of declaring, 'Let's use cloud architecture,' they may say, 'Do you think that we should use cloud architecture?' Alternatively, they may say, 'Many people are using cloud architecture. Should we also use cloud-based architecture?'

Amiables are quick to start a discussion rather than push a decision. In fast-paced situations, team members may expect a decision, not a discussion. But Amiables will not complain that they were not heard or that their feelings were hurt.

An Amiable manager tactfully provides difficult feedback to team members without sounding harsh. By mostly concealing their true opinions, Amiables maintain their relationship with others.

One of my favourite Hindi movies is *Sholay*. Nearly every personality type is represented by the movie's lead characters. Veeru, played by Dharmendra, is outgoing, jocular, assertive and a people's person—all traits of an Expressive personality. Basanti, played by Hema

Malini, has an Amiable personality. In the well-known scene showing the tonga ride, she is concerned about ensuring the comfort of the passengers. Throughout the ride, she does most of the storytelling. Gabbar Singh, played by Amjad Khan, is one of the Drivers who plays by his own set of rules. If his people do not deliver the goods, he eliminates them. Jai, played by Amitabh Bachchan, is a man of few words but also a careful planner. He has the many traits and behaviours exhibited by Analyticals.

In our society and workplaces, all four personality styles are equally present (25 per cent each, according to the Boltons). Each style is a gift, so long as it is complemented by the other styles. Different styles make life more interesting. We were three brothers in my home. We represented three different personality types (Analytical, Expressive and Driver). Over time, we gravitated towards roles suited to our natural styles.

In my experience, the Boltons' Social Style model is easy for managers to understand. Using the Boltons' model, I have collaborated with managers at MAQ Software to better understand the natural talents of our staff. I categorized myself and our team members into one of the four quadrants based on our natural preferences. With this simple model, a few of my co-workers provided me with inputs based on their interactions with me. We now notice our own behaviours and recognize our own individual Social Styles. With our added awareness of our Social Styles, we have reduced our interpersonal conflicts. Now, team members know how to work with other styles to achieve the best results for the team. Project roles are assigned according to team members' natural strengths, resulting in happier and more productive teams.

How do we use the Social Style Model?

> '*A team is a small number of people with complementary skills who are committed to a common purpose, performance goals and approach for which they hold themselves mutually accountable.*'
>
> —KATZENBACH & SMITH
> *The Wisdom of Teams*

Once we became familiar with the Social Style model, we decided to help our team leaders implement it within their teams. During the rollout, we had to ensure that we were not 'labelling' people and hurting their feelings or self-image. Once the team members understood the Social Style model, they assessed their own behaviours for assertiveness and responsiveness. After the individual team members recognized their primary style (Driver, Expressive, Analytical or Amiable), they shared the details of how they would flex their interactions with other members of their team.

My sample for my interactions (as a Driver) with the team members is provided in Figure 5.3.

Figure 5.3: Flexing my interactions with the team

To further increase our effectiveness, I shared my action plan with my team members, checking to see if my assumptions were correct. Usually, three to six months after new recruits join our company, we ask them to identify their Social Styles and share their action plan with their teams.

We continue to search for innovative means to understand each other's personality styles. A tool we've recently found useful is StrengthsFinder 2.0. This is an online assessment that helps our experienced engineers determine their innate talents. Once these talents are discovered, the engineers become more self-aware and approach their work keeping their strengths in mind.

Over time, I have gravitated towards assignments that use my strengths. To promote openness and build trust, I have shared my StrengthsFinder 2.0 report with our management team. We are just beginning our journey with StrengthsFinder 2.0, but I am confident that continuing our exploration of the personalities and strengths of our team will pay off.

Chapter Summary

Key Points

- To understand others, managers must understand themselves.
- Once they understand themselves, managers must also get to know the different personality types on their teams and manage them accordingly.
- The DISC test rates personalities based on Dominance, Influence, Steadiness and Compliance.
  - o Outgoing people rate high on Dominance and Influence.
  - o 'People's person rate high on Influence and Steadiness.
  - o Reserved people rate high on Steadiness and Compliance.
  - o Task-oriented people rate high on Compliance and Dominance.

- The Social Style model uses the assertiveness and responsiveness attributes to divide people into four styles:
  - o Drivers (assertive, action-oriented).
  - o Expressives (assertive, emotionally responsive).
  - o Analyticals (fact-driven, logical).
  - o Amiables (people-oriented).
- Companies use the Social Style model to:
  - o Familiarize team members with their own style.
  - o Help team members develop strategies to interact with other styles.

6

Training

'Good management consists of showing average people how to do the work of superior people.'

—JOHN D. ROCKEFELLER
First US billionaire and richest person in US history

In May 2015, *Fortune* magazine asked Fortune 500 CEOs about the challenges facing their companies. 72 per cent of the respondents identified the rapid pace of technological innovation as one of their biggest challenges.[1]

The Fortune 500 list represents the largest, and some of the most successful, companies in the world. In the mid-twentieth century, the average age of a Fortune 500 company was about seventy-five years. Only six companies have managed to stay in the top twenty of the Fortune 500 list over the last forty years.[2] The companies that retained their positions adapted to changing business climates and embraced new technologies successfully.

The same *Fortune* survey mentions that 34 per cent of Fortune 500 CEOs cannot find skilled or qualified workers. By definition, they were heading successful companies that ought to be desirable places to work at. This means that at least one-third of Fortune 500 companies cannot operate at their maximum capacity and certainly cannot grow to their full potential. Given the shortage of available talent, employers must spend a significant amount of time training existing employees to fill the positions for which they can't hire.

In February 2014, I attended the India Leadership Forum organized by NASSCOM. Conference attendees included the CEOs of Tata Consultancy Services (TCS), Mindtree, Cognizant Technology Solutions, Wipro and HCL Technologies. Collectively, these five companies represented more than 800,000 employees worldwide. These organizations help support the digital transformation of thousands of companies all over the world, affecting millions of workers. The NASSCOM conference theme revolved around SMAC—loosely representing technological advances in social media, mobile, analytics and cloud technologies. CEOs expressed significant anxiety about the unprecedented pace of technological advances. This pace of progress requires companies to retrain their existing workforces faster than ever.

Many of these firms' employees learn to deliver services with specific processes and tools. Eventually, new hardware and software tools are introduced, which all employees must then learn.

Companies must adopt these technological innovations to deliver better, faster and cheaper products and services. Senior managers, operating managers and employees all must learn and implement new technologies faster than their competitors and upstarts can.

The need to train for emerging technologies has been a perennial issue—existing long before the digital era. Peter Drucker mentioned technological obsolescence in the context of companies operating fifty to sixty years ago. And nearly eighty years ago, Austrian economist Joseph Schumpeter explained 'creative destruction'.[3] The term describes how new companies form to take advantage of novel processes and structures. Creative destruction kills companies that do not adapt to market shifts and technological advancements. Kodak, for instance, lost its market dominance when digital cameras took hold. Advances in cell phone technology led Micromax, Apple, Samsung and Nokia to dethrone one-time market leader Motorola.

I faced a similar challenge while working as a mechanical design engineer at Frigidaire Company nearly twenty-five years ago. I was helping a team of engineers and draftsmen who were producing two-dimensional (2D) drawings using IBM CADAM software. By today's standards, our working conditions were almost primitive. The mechanical engineers did not have a computer at every desk. We did not use email. We had about ten IBM drafting stations run by an IBM

Mainframe (System 370). Our company relied on IBM to supply us with most of the hardware, software and the necessary support.

In the following years, the arrival of UNIX-based workstations made it feasible for companies to buy more powerful software, which included three-dimensional (3D) design capability. AB Electrolux chose IBM Catia, sold by Dassault Systems of France. Headquarters wanted every division to transition from CADAM 2D-based systems to Catia 3D systems. The new system required retraining our team of about ten draftsmen. Most of the team had used 2D CADAM software for more than eight years—a span that seems unimaginable when you consider how quickly we learn new software today. Prior to that, the draftsmen used paper-based drawings.

Many team members voiced concerns about the new technology. Would the new technology eliminate the need for 2D drawings? Would drafting jobs be eliminated due to mechanical engineers now being able to design using 3D models? Would the draftsmen be able to use the new, unfamiliar system? Would they need to learn the new software while managing their existing workload on the old system? How would data migrate from the old system to the new system? Would they have the choice to return to the old system if they were unhappy with the new system? After all, the old system worked yesterday. Were they better off going to a new employer who wouldn't expect them to learn a new system?

Eventually, the team adapted and found that the 3D system was much more efficient. No one's job was eliminated. In fact, by freeing us from our rudimentary approaches, the new software enabled us to take on more challenging projects that were more personally rewarding.

Because we focus on providing expertise regarding new software tools and architecture at MAQ Software, we regularly face training challenges. About five years ago, we invested in and developed significant expertise in the Microsoft SharePoint 2007 software system. Many of our engineers had used the software for several years and were skilled at developing custom applications using the system. Soon after, Microsoft released SharePoint Server 2010, which was better designed and offered new capabilities. We could work faster and deliver richer applications for our clients.

From a management perspective, we needed to adopt the new system quickly to ensure our clients received superior applications. Our challenge was to persuade our engineers to learn and gain proficiency in the new system quickly. Many of our existing engineers were reluctant. For our engineers, the easier option was to leave for an employer who needed a person skilled in SharePoint 2007.

What ultimately persuaded most of them to stay was the highly efficient training system we developed. It made learning any new system much easier than it otherwise might have been. In this system, we first work with our existing team to form small study groups of eight to ten engineers. Our study groups meet twice a week for an hour. Each member of a study group presents one topic related to the training assignment to the rest of the group.

Employees complete Microsoft Self Study Training Guide assignments on their own and then take internal quizzes and examinations that we administer. Within six to twelve weeks the team developed enough expertise to use the system successfully.

Eventually, our training leads to independent vendor-based certifications. The certifications add to the team members' professional qualifications and their pride in their technical expertise. Many of the team members are promoted, receive additional leadership responsibilities, or are asked to perform more complex project work as a result of their increased proficiency. Independent vendor-based certifications are a significant annual expense for the company, but we view them as an investment for the future success of our team members.

Admittedly, when we ensure that our engineers are experts in new technologies, they may become more marketable and attractive to other employers. Many first-time managers fear we are training our employees so that they may easily find other opportunities.

That is a risk we are willing to take. As managers, we have two options. The first is to hire and train great employees with a strong interest in learning and growing themselves over time. Because of their training, these engineers do great work. We risk losing some of them if we cannot generate opportunities for them quickly enough. We view this as a positive challenge for our management team. If we create an amazing culture and compensate our employees appropriately, our most capable team members will have no reason to look elsewhere.

The second option is to hire great employees but *not* invest in their training. These engineers would perform average work. As a result, many of them would not have any current or marketable skills. Such unskilled employees would never leave us. But because of their stagnation, we would risk becoming a company of people with outdated skills.

Which route would you take if you were a CEO? To me, the decision is obvious.

Within our individual companies and industries, we must have an abundance-oriented mindset. That includes making generous investments in training people to the best of our ability. By enabling our team to learn or upgrade one new technology or software system every quarter, we prevent the company from becoming obsolete and ensure that our team will have somewhere to work in the future.

Many of our people are excited about the opportunity to research and explore new technologies. Others remain comfortable with older technologies. Some of them end up leaving the company for job opportunities based on the old technologies, but because these employees are not likely to contribute to our growth in the future, their departures are healthy for the company.

In Tom Peters' bestselling book *Thriving on Chaos*, he describes ten attributes of successful training programmes. Here is how MAQ Software has applied them:

1. **Extensive entry-level training that focuses on exactly the skills in which you wish to be distinctive.** The software industry in India has been training new

engineers extensively for decades. Our training programme stands out because it focuses on teaching technical skills around the latest software technologies that are used by our customers.

2. **All employees are treated as potential long-term employees.** For years, we have offered comprehensive and rigorous training to all employees. Although training everyone can be expensive, we want to ensure that each employee (including temporary employees and interns) completes the training. Given the high attrition rate in the software industry, it is tempting to just teach the basics. We lean, however, towards comprehensive training.

3. **Regular training is required.** As practising engineers, many of us are comfortable with our ways of working. At MAQ Software, however, we require all our employees to regularly learn new technologies in order to remain up to date and employed. By regularly, we mean frequently. Team members typically go through a new training cycle every quarter.

4. **A lot of time and money is invested.** Much to the frustration of our finance team, we continue to reimburse employees for relevant industry certifications. Though it is difficult to quantify the direct benefit of investment in training, any company's success can be attributed to a well-trained staff.

5. **On-the-job training matters.** Our team learns by doing. As soon as possible, we assign engineers to projects where they can apply what they have learned. Over time, the project work adds to their learning.

6. **There are no limits to the skills that can be taught to everyone profitably.** We work with team members to help them improve their English, their presentation skills and skills in technologies (such as machine learning) that may not be immediately relevant to their projects, but help us to serve our customers better.

7. **Training is used to commit to a new strategic direction.** Because the software industry requires new skills every few years, we commit to training in the new areas where our company is focused. In the past years, we were committed to cloud and mobile technologies first. Now, all of our new work revolves around artificial intelligence (AI). We have expanded our training to ensure that everyone is focused around an AI-first strategy.

8. **Training is emphasized at a time of crisis.** Every few years, our projects end. After working at a fast pace, all of a sudden we have a large team without any projects to work on. A large number of people without any active projects creates anxiety and sometimes a feeling of crisis in the company. To combat this, we refocus our energy on learning new technologies until the next project begins.

9. **All training is driven by operating managers.** As the CEO, I actively participate in training discussions. Every year, no matter how busy I am, I spend several days giving training to our team members. All our managers drive the training. So far we have avoided a separate training department that is disconnected from the reality of our project work.

10. **Training is used to teach the organization's vision and values.** Because our senior-most managers lead and coordinate the training effort, they also model the company values and share the company vision. In our experience, it is very effective to have different managers share their own examples and anecdotes demonstrating the company values. Trainees remember these stories.[4]

So far as I can tell, all successful companies have a great training programme that includes these attributes. You will notice that many of these attributes appear in the sections that follow.

How Do We Train New Engineers?

Every year, more than 1,00,000 computer science and IT engineers graduate in India. From this group, we hire about 150 engineers every year for short- and long-term assignments. In India, we hire from engineering colleges in Mumbai and Hyderabad, and from the NITs and the IIITs. In the US, we primarily hire from the University of Washington, Seattle.

With teams that are increasingly globally distributed, we need to show our clients that we can perform up to their expectations. Many of our engineering projects utilize multiple problem-solving approaches. In many cases, there are numerous potential solutions and countless opportunities for innovation and ingenuity. Our clients expect the same level of technical expertise and productivity from our engineers in India as they do from engineers trained and educated anywhere else in the world. To deliver software that meets our clients' demands, we need to ensure that our engineers are properly trained and technically proficient. In many other professions— including medicine, aviation and the military—proper training and certification are required before a person is assigned to work. We take a similar approach.

Most of the new engineers we've hired over the past fifteen years have been very talented and motivated. They are eager to start developing and testing new software applications. Many computer science graduates, however, are not technically prepared to start working on projects immediately.

This readiness gap is due to the uneven faculty staffing levels at many engineering colleges, low student attendance and sometimes obsolete curricula. Many engineering colleges rely on rote learning and memorization. Some students rely on paid tutors or classmates to complete their assignments. We usually don't discover these shortcomings until after we have hired someone and found he lacks the basic knowledge we expect of recent graduates.

The situation is improving with the availability of online classes such as Codeacademy, Coursera and EdX. New graduates, however, often do not take advantage of these training resources before looking for a job. We must accept this challenge and work actively to find solutions to train them appropriately.

Upon joining us, many new engineers expect to sit in a classroom where they will listen to lectures by an expert trainer on basic engineering topics. Addressing the gaps in skills, however, requires a very different approach.

We have created an active training programme that allows new graduates to contribute to projects as quickly as possible. Our new graduates are joining the industry for the first time, so we need to increase the strength of their belief in their own abilities to complete tasks and reach their goals. Additionally, the training programme needs to be cost-effective and scalable to accommodate many inductees.

Increasing Self-Efficacy

'Meet your people where they are. They may not be as good as they can be, but they are as good as they believe they can be.'

—Susan C. Foster
Former CFO, NASA's Marshall Space Flight Center

Fostering an active learning mindset in our new hires is a challenge. In college, students are often steered towards the right answer. As mentioned earlier, many completed their assignments with the assistance of tutors or friends. While this may have given them good grades, it did not help them develop the problem-solving skills needed to succeed in the workplace. Many students believe they cannot solve problems on their own because they have not actually done so. Psychologists describe this as low self-efficacy. Self-efficacy is defined as the strength of your belief in your ability to complete tasks and reach your goals.

Developing and testing new software requires high self-efficacy. Usually, we are not doing repetitive work. Our projects are comparable to designing, building and flying an aeroplane for the first time. Many of our engineering problems may be solved through multiple approaches. Our engineers must be flexible and confident enough to pursue many different types of solutions.

By focusing on increasing our new hires' self-efficacy, our training programme improves their ability to persist at and succeed at a task. These engineers are extremely talented. Our training is aimed at working with these new hires so that they can maximize their talents.

In our experience, self-efficacy directly relates to how long an engineer will stick to solving a particular bug or software deployment problem. We find that engineers with high self-efficacy stay with a challenge and solve the problem. In a similar situation, engineers with low self-efficacy give up on the challenging assignment or 'write it off' as impossible.

To succeed as a manager, it is important to help employees build their self-efficacy. According to the Stanford University psychologist Albert Bandura, 'self-efficacy affects learning and performance in the workplace.'[5] Self-efficacy also influences how individuals approach tasks and challenges.

High self-efficacy enables employees to:

- **Set more challenging goals.** They develop strong commitment, interest and a deeper connection to these personal goals.
- **Work hard to learn how to perform new tasks,** because they are confident they will be successful.
- **Persist when engaging in challenging assignments.** Employees with high self-efficacy are confident they will complete their tasks. They view difficult tasks as challenges to master.
- **Experience less stress and anxiety when they engage in a task.** As a result, their performance on the job improves.
- **Sustain their efforts in the face of a setback or failure.** They can recover faster from wrong turns and disappointments.
- **Attribute setbacks to their own insufficient effort or knowledge.** In a workplace, additional effort can be applied with revised timelines, and additional knowledge can be gained through research and training.

Conversely, employees with low self-efficacy:

- Set less challenging goals for themselves.
- Consider difficult tasks as threats to avoid.

- Believe that more difficult tasks are beyond their capabilities.
- Experience burnout and stress when assigned challenging tasks.
- Give up easily upon failure and negative outcomes.
- Lose confidence in their abilities quickly.

New engineers with low self-efficacy are not comfortable with challenging assignments. We work with them during their training to improve their belief in their own abilities. Improving their self-efficacy is a top managerial priority. We believe that by creating a team with high self-efficacy, we contribute to a great company culture.

We increase self-efficacy in the workplace through a seven-step approach:

1. **Hire better engineers.** We strive to improve our hiring practices to ensure that new hires are better qualified than our previous hires. To build teams with high self-efficacy, we recruit from higher-ranked universities and insist on ever-better academic records. Strong and consistent academic performance usually reflects a high commitment to tasks beyond the university curricula.

   In a competitive market, it is not easy for any company to keep its hiring bar high. Over the years, we have debated lowering our hiring standards. In the rare instances when we compromised and brought on people with lower academic performance, we have suffered. We have vowed not to repeat the same mistake. Although having a degree from a great school does not guarantee managerial success, achieving high academic performance does correlate with doing a good job at our company. Our mistakes have served as great reminders of what not to do and offered learning opportunities for our managers.

2. **Offer the right role models.** We assign key managers to serve as mentors and trainers to new hires. We strongly encourage these managers to take advantage of the certifications and extended training programmes we offer. This gives them additional professional development and learning opportunities. When new trainees see that others in the company who participated in our training have experienced professional growth, they feel confident and persist in learning, increasing their own self-efficacy.

3. **Follow Agile and Lean software development practices.** With this approach, team members are assigned tasks based on their interests, abilities and project needs. As engineers gain proficiency, they are moved to more challenging and interesting job assignments. Over time, engineers gain the mastery, perspective and confidence to autonomously handle complex problems. With self-management, we also increase management's span of control and reduce overhead.

4. **Show confidence in our teams' ability to master tasks quickly and provide great solutions.** By using continuous and incremental software delivery approaches, we quickly increase self-efficacy with

every build that is deployed. With daily delivery of software and work products to clients for review, we increase team self-efficacy every day.

5. **Set reasonable daily goals.** Our engineers receive small work items that do not last more than six-and-a-half hours, based on feedback from our team. Barring unknown challenges, most team members can reasonably complete the tasks in one eight-hour day. By limiting work items to bite-sized chunks, we can break down complex problems with long cycles into everyday successes.

   On the other hand, if a team takes on a complex challenge and fails, the team members' self-efficacy may decrease. These failures may result in a downward spiral of increasingly lower self-efficacy, which creates a drop in performance.

6. **Help improve self-management skills, such as time management.** Time management skills include punctuality, self-organization, discipline and setting realistic personal goals. Most organizations cover these soft skills through orientation training, ongoing discussions and role modelling. Over the years, we have worked hard to share these practices through role modelling, individual development plans and technical certification goals.

7. **Provide constructive feedback and appreciation to team members.** These activities also increase self-efficacy. Research shows that 65 per cent of workers received no recognition in the workplace in the last year.[6] I am sure all companies—including

ours—can do more to recognize our employees' everyday performance.

Recently, we have started using social media tools such as Facebook and Yammer at work, to publicly thank employees for specific performance. As a practising manager, I need to do more in this regard. Ideally, I would like to recognize someone for doing something right every day.

We want our engineers to start thinking independently, as opposed to expecting to be routinely spoon-fed. They need to get away from a passive mindset. We want to move to a self-managing team model, at least on technical aspects. In our experience, the best way to accomplish this is to foster self-efficacy in all our employees. This, in turn, will lead to a stronger sense of self-belief. As Bandura once said, 'Self-belief does not necessarily ensure success, but self-disbelief assuredly spawns failure.'[7]

The Origins of Our Training Programme

Since the inception of our company in the year 2000, we have used peer-based active learning to train our engineers. Our training programme is very different from the classroom-style of education used in the broader software industry.

We stumbled on our active training programme by accident and by sheer necessity. In December 2000, we had only five developers. Each developer, on average, had less than one year of experience. We could not find or afford a senior trainer. One of our key challenges was to quickly develop the team's technical expertise in order to help us deliver database applications.

As you would expect from any start-up, we were looking for any help or resources we could get. At that time, Arpita Agarwal, a senior data warehouse developer, was visiting Mumbai. Our local team leader was desperate to find some means to improve the technical expertise of the team. He requested that Arpita teach our junior developers the data warehouse techniques used by the industry. Arpita started teaching advanced data warehouse material to the junior developers with great enthusiasm.

After a few sessions, Arpita realized that her hard work was going to waste. The students felt the lecture-oriented material was too theoretical. The developers could not learn or relate to many of the topics she was teaching. Arpita decided to change her approach. She asked each developer to read one chapter from the Microsoft Official Courseware (MOC) on SQL Server 2000. The developer then had to present the topic to the group. Arpita changed her role from teacher to facilitator, answering the developers' questions when they struggled with a topic.

We didn't realize it at the time, but Arpita had discovered a very effective training technique. We have been using peer-based active learning for nearly fifteen years now. To my knowledge, MAQ Software is one of the largest users of peer-based education in the industry. Our first formal extended peer-based ninety-day training programme (informally called 'Bootcamp') started in July

2003 with twenty engineers. The goal was to officially induct each new engineer into the company.

The research of Eric Mazur, a renowned physics professor from Harvard University, confirms our belief in the effectiveness of peer instruction. For over twenty years, Professor Mazur has been studying the benefits of peer-based learning. His findings indicate that interactive learning can triple knowledge gains and improve students' retention of new information. 'Nothing,' according to the Mazur Group website, 'clarifies ideas better than explaining them to others.'[8]

Our Current Peer-Based Training Programme

By the end of our rigorous training (which can last up to three weeks) attendees are expected to have a base-level understanding of the software tools and relevant technologies that were taught. Trainees must demonstrate this by obtaining independent vendor certifications.

Currently, we divide new hires into groups of about fifteen to twenty each. Even if there are unplanned absences, groups of this size will still have at least twelve to fifteen members present each day. Experienced engineers act as facilitators who provide technical support and general guidance when trainees need help.

We always pair two students to work as a team. Based on a well-defined curriculum or set of topics (say, ten chapters from a book), we assign chapters to specific teams. These teams learn and present their chapters to the rest of the group.

Each attendee's presentation lasts sixty to ninety minutes. After the presentations, the group works on assigned programming exercises and workshops.

When designing our active peer learning programmes, we incorporate educational materials from many sources. We use Codeacademy, Coursera and EdX material. We also use Microsoft Certification Training Kits for relevant products. Such materials serve a dual purpose. In the short term, they provide the content we need to teach new hires about Microsoft tools. Additionally—and perhaps more importantly—they show new engineers a number of available resources. When these engineers encounter a problem in their work, they will know where to start looking for help.

Peer-Based Training: Flipping the Classroom

As the conventional wisdom goes, we learn the most when we teach a subject. In other words, the teacher quite often learns more than the students. Peer-based active training programmes promote student-initiated learning by 'inverting' or 'flipping' the classroom. The flipped classroom intentionally shifts instruction to a learner-centric model. The students become the teacher. The instructor acts as a facilitator, monitors progress and provides help when needed.

In a flipped learning environment, students must review educational materials before coming to class. Materials take the form of textbooks, videos, online and in-person discussions and Internet research. Our peer-based learning is workshop-oriented. Attendees learn by actively solving programming problems in the classroom.

One of the pioneers of peer-based learning and flipped classrooms is Salman Khan. Khan, whose parents hail from Bangladesh, holds an undergraduate degree in mathematics from the prestigious Massachusetts Institute of Technology (MIT). He also holds graduate degrees in electrical engineering and computer science (also from MIT) and an MBA from Harvard Business School.

In 2006, Khan founded Khan Academy, a non-profit educational organization. Through the organization's website, video lessons on a wide variety of subjects are available for free. All a student requires is an Internet connection.[9]

Khan Academy encourages flipped classrooms. Students do their traditional homework in the classroom rather than at home, with the help of other students and the teacher. Students review their Khan Academy lessons before coming to class.

Around the world, Khan Academy videos have been incorporated into flipped classrooms. The Bill and Melinda Gates Foundation, Google, and the Carlos Slim Foundation have donated millions of dollars to further Khan Academy's contributions to worldwide learning.

Online instruction videos, such as those provided by Khan Academy, can serve as quality learning material. When millions of people view a lecture, mistakes are addressed through crowdsourcing—that is, they are identified and clarified by viewers. Sometimes students may even provide better explanations or faster ways to solve a problem.

Khan Academy videos also standardize classroom lectures, which limits dependency on the quality and knowledge of teachers. If today's teachers are anything like mine, some are probably routinely late, improperly trained, or are simply lacking in knowledge. Uniform video lessons help eliminate the problems resulting from the shortcomings of traditional teachers.

Khan Academy lessons have been translated into several languages, including Hindi. While the website initially focused on maths, numerous other topics have been added. It even has videos on preparation for IIT's Joint Entrance Examination (JEE). I have personally used Khan Academy to learn about many topics related to economics and the sciences.

The New '3Rs'

American high schools used to emphasize the 3Rs: reading, writing and arithmetic. The old 3Rs were considered the foundation of a skills-oriented education. Not having attended middle school in the United States, I was introduced to the concept of 3Rs at a ceremony at Lakeside School, Seattle, in the spring of 2007. At the ceremony, Bill Gates was launching a significant initiative aimed at reforming high school education in the United States.

The Gates Foundation's 3Rs of high-school reform stand for 'Rigour, Relevance and Relationships'. Gates explained that, under the new 3Rs, students need challenging courses, classes that relate to their lives and adult role models who will help them succeed.[10]

To maximize learning, our training follows the new 3Rs:

1. Rigour

We hire some of the top computer science graduates who have cleared one of the toughest recruitment processes in India (so far as software services companies are concerned). Our training needs to be fast-paced to ensure that these attendees are not bored. Our pace is designed to keep up with the fastest students. Slower students can work over the evening and weekends to catch up on class material.

A side benefit of our rigorous training is that about 10 per cent of our recruits drop out. These trainees may accept a less challenging position within or outside the company. Our projects are challenging and demand a lot of effort. If new hires are not capable of performing the work, it's better for everyone if they leave early.

Our training programme is not easy. When I think about the classes where I learned the most, I recognize that they were taught by the most demanding professors. These professors stretched us beyond our comfort zones. In classes where I merely listened to lectures and appeared for easy examinations, I did not learn or retain much. While attending the rigorous classes, I did not appreciate the assignments or the tough grading. Years later, however, I can appreciate how well they prepared me for challenges in life. I thank those teachers to this day.

2. Relevance

We make sure that training topics are current and relevant to our software project work. Relevance ensures that attendees will retain the material because they will use it as soon as they join the project teams. In the past, we found that disconnects between training materials and project work left both supervisors and trainees dissatisfied. As a result, we regularly revise the training programme and materials to ensure that we use the latest technologies, products, books and Internet resources.

3. Relationships

We do not hire external trainers to teach basic software tools and technologies. Instead, we use our existing software engineers and project managers as facilitators. If trainees run into roadblocks during class, they turn to these experienced facilitators for guidance.

In addition to developing a lifelong relationship with the students, facilitators can use the training to refresh their own technical skills. Facilitators also evaluate trainees and use these evaluations to lobby for the best performing trainees to join their project teams.

Because of their status, facilitators are able to describe how the training content applies to current company projects. Facilitators also share the company history and their experiences in working on and delivering some of the stretch assignments.

By contrast, an external trainer would have to rely on hypothetical examples and refer to fictional companies such as Fabrikam (used in Microsoft demos). It's often the case that external trainers use examples that are irrelevant to our project work.

How Do We Evaluate the Attendees' Performance?

To reduce the load on facilitators, we ask attendees to rate the assignments completed by their peers every day. Based on the scores, a ranked list is published and shared with senior management. Many students and facilitators are initially shocked to see the rank-ordered list (say, from one to twenty) shared widely. Over time, however, a camaraderie develops among the trainees. They work together to ensure that the overall quality of the assignments improves.

Many facilitators are not comfortable with the competitiveness and conflict the 'ranked order' lists stir up. We do not consider these consequences bad. We have found that attendees still help one another. Competitiveness and conflict exist in any workplace, so it does no good to shield trainees from them.

Instead of avoiding conflict, we think of real project situations. When working on real projects, we share our code and documents with the entire project team *and* the client in the online Source Code Control system (e.g., GITHub or Visual Studio Online). The quantity and quality of the code written by each individual engineer is visible to all. Before check-in, a peer reviews the code. The reviewer's comments are visible to the entire team. If the code is buggy or performing poorly, it is better to share the feedback with the engineer early. We try to fix and improve the quality of the code before it goes to the client review builds.

For the integrity of the overall software development process, it is better to become comfortable with providing and receiving honest and accurate feedback from fellow team members. After all, we are on the same team and are working towards common goals. Public feedback is no different from what we see in open source projects where code shortcomings are openly discussed and rated for quality by peers.

Indirectly, we also use the power of peer pressure to improve our work quality and to deliver great software to our clients. On a daily basis, many engineers may not care what their managers think of them, but most of us do not want to look bad in front of our peers. While managers have a lot of influence, not all early-career subordinates realize it. Many of them give far more weightage to their peers' opinions than to their manager's.

How Do We Know Our Active Training Approach Works?

We engage in a multi-step process to evaluate the efficacy of our active training approach.

First, we ask project supervisors about the readiness level of the new engineers and their ability to contribute to active projects. Whenever we execute correctly and follow the 3Rs, the feedback from supervisors is very positive. Because many of the supervisors completed a similar training programme a few years earlier, they know the strengths of the approach.

Second, we speak to the engineers who completed our active learning programme years earlier. We ask if they found the active learning training effective. We also ask whether we should change our approach to a traditional classroom-based approach. Most of the past attendees indicate that the programme was quite rigorous. After they completed the programme, they started believing they could solve many work challenges on their own. Many previous attendees do not want us to change the active learning approach. They say that this was the best way for them to learn.

Finally, we review the software that we deliver to our clients on regular basis. By increasing the self-efficacy of our team members, we ensure our engineers continue to adopt new technologies faster than their counterparts at our industry peers. Our clients feel satisfied with the quality and pace of our deliverables.

As we reflect on our experience over the past fifteen years, it is obvious that we did not start with a well-researched strategy document that indicated we should use a 'peer learning' approach. Since starting, however, more than 1500 engineers from all types of engineering colleges have completed our training programme. I am certain that, over time, more organizations will adopt active learning techniques.

Management Training

Training efforts at MAQ Software are not limited to new engineers. We take management training very seriously as well. When new managers are hired, I lead training discussions in a facilitator-type role. I share with them the context of the company, our industry and our clients. Management training also provides me the opportunity to evaluate our new managers and vice versa.

Jack Welch used a similar approach. Throughout his twenty-year tenure as CEO of GE, he spent two to three months every year training the company's senior managers. In turn, all the senior vice-presidents and presidents of the many GE companies taught their managers. Many observers see this training method as one the key factors that helped Welch grow the company's annual revenue from US $20 billion to over US $100 billion.[11]

Chapter Summary

Key Points

- Technological advances require managers to train their teams quickly.
  - o Adapting to changing business climates and new technology is crucial for business longevity.
  - o Successful companies have great training programmes.
- Many new engineering graduates lack project skills and have low 'self-efficacy'.

- Peer-based training:
  - o Improves retention and comprehension of new information.
  - o Compels students to master the material to be able to instruct other students.
  - o Requires students to review the material before coming to class.
- To increase self-efficacy, managers:
  - o Must improve the hiring process to ensure new hires have a belief in their abilities.
  - o Act as role models for new hires.
  - o Follow Agile and Lean development practices so that team members are assigned tasks based on their interests, abilities and project needs.
  - o Have confidence in their teams' abilities.
  - o Set reasonable daily goals.
  - o Improve self-management skills (such as time management).
  - o Provide constructive feedback to team members.
- Employee training should follow the new 3Rs: Rigour, Relevance and Relationships:
  - o **Rigour:** Training should be fast-paced to ensure top recruits are not bored.
  - o **Relevance:** Training materials must be current and relevant to project work.
  - o **Relationships:** Utilizing existing employees instead of external trainers helps develop team bonding, strengthens the facilitator's knowledge

and makes it easier to evaluate trainees for project team placement.

o   Sharing of peer-ranked assignments with students develops competitiveness and teaches the peer review process.

o   Reliance on active learning increases self-efficacy and fosters better quality and timely delivery of projects.

• Management training is as important as non-manager training and can yield enormous benefits for the company.

7

On Motivation

'Employees involved in high performance settings are more likely to be motivated than those working in average or mediocre organizations.'

—Leonard Sayles
Columbia University professor and
management scholar

New managers often ask me, 'How do I motivate my team?' This question is rooted in the manager's need to improve the performance of engineers on her team.

Highly productive, high-performance engineers are desirable in all firms. Collectively, these individuals make for high-performance teams. Customers are likely to choose companies with high-performance teams. These teams offer a competitive advantage to customers because they get more done with less effort, thus increasing productivity.

The benefits of increasing productivity extend far beyond a company's bottom line. When middle managers develop highly productive teams, they help improve the standard of living for their entire country. In 1957, Fred W. Harper, a Cornell University economist, established that wages increase as productivity increases.[1] At a macro level, economists have found that average worker productivity determines a country's standard of living. At a micro level, assuming an efficient marketplace, highly productive, high-performance engineers command good salaries, which raises their standard of living.

Managers are often asked to deliver superior performance from an existing team delivering existing services or products to existing customers. Because new managers do not have much freedom to change the services, customers or team members, team efficiency is vital.

New managers sometimes worry about the consequences of pushing their teams to increase productivity. They ask themselves questions such as: *Will we have smaller teams as we now expect fewer people to do the same amount of work? Because consulting revenue depends on billing for man-hours, will smaller teams reduce company revenues?*

Fortunately, demand for software is growing rapidly, so it is unlikely that these managers will put themselves or anyone else out of work. Even with productivity advancements, there are not enough engineers to produce all of the software that needs to be written. This has been true for my entire career. Demand for software is huge. All industries are being reshaped by advances in software technology. As leading venture capitalist Marc Andreessen famously stated, 'Software is eating the world.'[2]

Assuming that demand for software is continually increasing, more software will need to be produced to help people achieve more in all areas of their lives. The overall market expands when software is produced cheaply and efficiently. But even with demand for software work increasing exponentially, managers can't afford to have unproductive teams.

Motivation enters the equation as managers try to establish highly productive, high-performance teams. Teams consist of *people*. Managers who do not address their subordinates' psychological needs will quickly face unmotivated and disengaged teams.

In 2015, Gallup surveyed more than 80,000 employees worldwide. Only 32 per cent were actively engaged in, enthusiastic about and committed to their workplace. Over 50 per cent were not engaged and 17.2 per cent were actively disengaged.[3]

While physically present, disengaged employees have mentally resigned from their jobs. In our experience, unmotivated employees exhibit some or all of the following behaviours:

- Frequently take unplanned days off
- Make many mistakes
- Miss deadlines
- Refuse new assignments
- Miss team meetings
- Gossip
- Complain

Managers facing unmotivated employees may be tempted to seek easy ways out. They might try to throw money at the problem, hoping that a higher salary will keep the employee happy. They might fire employees who exhibit disengaged behaviours. Great managers, however, consistently find ways to turn disengaged employees into motivated and productive team members.

I have studied business books and management articles for years, searching for actionable motivational models to apply at MAQ Software. The following is a survey of what I've found.

Motivational Models

In the 1960s, Douglas McGregor developed a model for motivation in newly industrialized economies: Theory X and Theory Y. Theory X assumes that people dislike work; they want to avoid it and do not want to take responsibility for it. Theory Y assumes that people are self-motivated and thrive on responsibility.[4] Industrial demand was so high that businesses needed to do all they could to produce more. McGregor brought managers' attention to Theory Y just as prosperity was setting in and worker shortages were being experienced in the developed world.

Before McGregor, in the early 1900s, Frederick Taylor conducted time-motion studies. He suggested that there was one best way to do a manual task in a factory. Following Taylor's time-motion studies, companies adopted rigid procedures to have workers perform the same tasks, the same way, every day and every week.[5] Obviously, workers were bored once they learned how to do something. In their zeal to improve productivity, however, companies increased the speed of their assembly machines.

In 2009, author Daniel Pink published his book *Drive: The Surprising Truth about What Motivates Us*, which went on to become one of the bestselling books about motivation. Pink identified *three* motivational factors: autonomy, mastery and purpose. His model primarily applied to US workers between thirty-five and fifty-five years of age. Many of these workers had been part of the workforce for fifteen to twenty years. At this point they knew their jobs very well. An accountant with twenty years' experience, for example, perhaps knows more about bookkeeping and charts of accounts than his supervisor.

Pink noted that many experienced workers have mastered their crafts long ago. These workers often seek the autonomy to be able to do their work their own way. Their way, they believe, is better than what was written in the procedures manual decades ago. They want to be recognized as masters of their work.

Finally, many of the older members of this group are empty-nesters who are looking towards bigger goals in life and may be seeking their life's purpose, probably outside of their work. They may be less concerned about meeting their cash flow to pay rent than the younger workers.

While I found these theories interesting, they didn't seem to apply to our company. While surveying various motivation theories, I realized that many authors took a narrow view that only addressed specific situations, specific industries, specific economic conditions or specific demographics. After sifting through many models, I found the following three frameworks most useful for our company's needs:

1. Herzberg's two-factor motivation theory.
2. The Gallup list of employee-engagement questions.
3. A comprehensive performance model described by David A. Whetten and Kim S. Cameron.

Herzberg's Two-Factor Motivation Theory

Psychologist Frederick Herzberg studied US worker satisfaction during the 1950s and 1960s. At that time,

World War II had ended. Many young soldiers had returned home from the war. The US economy was booming as a result of new demand for consumer goods from young families. The Baby Boom (1950–64) had helped jump-start the American economy. During this period, demand for quality goods generally exceeded supply in the marketplace. There were not enough workers to produce the goods and services these new households needed.

Herzberg published a two-factor model of satisfaction for workers. He initially studied engineers and accountants to understand their attitudes towards their work.[6] His findings showed that while most supervisors have limited control over company administration policies, work conditions, or work location, they can do many simple things to improve their team members' sense of achievement.

The first factor of Herzberg's motivation theory relates to 'hygiene factors'. When it comes to our physical health, good hygiene prevents illness but does not make us healthier. Similarly, in the workplace, addressing Herzberg's hygiene factors may prevent job dissatisfaction or unhappiness, but will not motivate employees.

The second factor of Hertzberg's motivation theory relates to 'satisfaction factors'. Meeting these needs results in intrinsic motivation, increasing job satisfaction and creating happiness among employees.

A comparison of hygiene factors versus satisfaction factors is given in Table 7.1 on the next page:

Table 7.1: Herzberg's study on hygiene versus motivators[7]

Hygiene factors causing unhappiness	Satisfaction factors causing intrinsic motivation (Happiness)
• Company policy and administration • Supervision • Relationship with supervisor • Work conditions • Salary • Relationship with peers • Personal life • Relationship with subordinates • Status • Security	• Achievement • Recognition for achievement • Work itself • Responsibility • Advancement • Growth

If managers address the hygiene factors, employees feel their basic needs are covered. Creating intrinsic motivation, however, requires managers to focus on satisfaction factors.

To motivate people, Herzberg suggests making jobs more interesting for individuals. Instead of horizontal loading, or increasing the quantity of work (e.g., running 300 test cases per day instead of 100), he suggests *vertical loading*.

In our context, vertical loading could include:

• Offering autonomy, so that employees control how they do their work, but are also accountable for the results.

- Increasing their span of control (the employee is accountable for a complete module or a functional team).
- Inclusion of employees in key meetings and discussion threads.
- Providing employees additional training opportunities and assignments involving new technology areas (AI, cloud, mobile, etc.).

The Gallup List of Employee Engagement Questions

More recently, leading market research firm Gallup studied more than 80,000 employees. Gallup's list of employee engagement questions is the gold standard. Many companies use this list to gauge the motivation levels of their employees. During its multi-year pursuit, Gallup found there are four stages of growth for team members in a company.[8]

- Stage 1: What do I get from this role?
- Stage 2: What do I give?
- Stage 3: Do I belong here?
- Stage 4: How can we all grow?

Employees in stage 1 are concerned with what Herzberg classified as dissatisfiers or 'hygiene factors'. Employees in stages 2 to 4 are becoming progressively more skilled, self-aware and independent. These employees are concerned with Herzberg's intrinsic motivation factors.

The manager will decide the employee's stage based on their history together and an assessment of the employee's current performance. The manager will then use the most relevant questions from Gallup's list to meaningfully engage with the employee and make the most of one-on-one interactions with the employee.

Stage 1: What Do I Get from This Role?

The first stage is quite basic for any employee. In this stage, employees are *concerned about their pay, job role, their workspace, their computers, and, of course, their commute.*

To gauge employee motivation during stage 1, Gallup suggests that managers ask employees to reflect on the following questions:

1. Do I know what is expected of me at work?
2. Do I have the materials and equipment I need to do my work?

In the Agile work environment, the entire project is set up as a sprint. A sprint contains stories, which are explained by storyboards. The stories are then divided into 'tasks'. Modern software tools allow any team member to review the epic (big picture), storyboards and tasks (or work items).

Similar to Lean production techniques, these tasks (work items along with the estimated effort or duration they will take) are visible to the entire team on a kanban board. Not all organizations have adopted the Lean and Agile techniques equally. However, the movement is accelerating.

In their morning meeting, team members can pick individual work items and complete them for the day. As a result, expectations of any employee are available daily to all team members. The status of any task is visible to all team members at any time. In the olden days, we used to rely on a monthly or weekly report from our departments.

With continuous software delivery techniques, the pace is even faster. Now, almost all of us receive daily reports. We are aware of the progress of all work items at any time.

In the earlier days, sending daily reports would be considered as micromanaging and was viewed as a threatening act. If a manager needed to terminate someone, she would ask for a daily work report. Asking for a daily report was tantamount to a person being shown the door. Today, things have changed. Regular and almost real-time reports are necessary to meet tight deadlines.

The second question—*Do I have the materials and equipment I need to do my work right?*—relates to the hardware and software required to do the work. Over the past two decades, companies have been aggressively adopting email, Microsoft Office, faster Internet access and newer software and hardware. Modern software tools allow everyone to achieve more every day. At our company, our intent is to adopt new operating systems, new software versions and newer workflows to increase our efficiency. Most of the new software is designed to help us do more in less time. These tools are improving every year, increasing employee satisfaction by freeing them from cumbersome tasks.

Stage 2: What Do I Give?

In the second stage, according to the Gallup researchers, employees are focused on *their individual contributions*. At this stage, employees ask: *Am I excelling in my role? Am I becoming an expert? Are others helping me improve? What do others think of my performance?*

To gauge employee motivation during stage 2, Gallup suggests that managers ask employees to reflect on the following questions:

1. At work, do I have the opportunity to do what I do best every day?
2. In the last seven days, have I received recognition or praise for doing good work?
3. Does my supervisor, or someone at work, seem to care about me as a person?
4. Is there someone at work who encourages my development?

Managers can help create an environment that enables subordinates to feel satisfied about what they've given at the workplace. In the Agile work environment, workers select work items from the kanban board every morning. Many of us can pick tasks that we enjoy and are good at.

Most of the tasks are broken down into smaller work items that can be completed in six-and-a-half hours (usually, about one-and-a-half are devoted to meetings, email and shadow work). Selecting tasks that we can complete gives us autonomy.

As Pink mentions in *Drive*, autonomy is a key human desire.[9] Most programmers have the autonomy to show creativity by creating superior algorithms and producing optimized code that follows coding standards and industry best practices. Customers like standards and following best practices because someone else will have to maintain the software eventually.

In a typical organization, a first-level supervisor has previously performed, over several years, all of the jobs that his or her subordinates do. Once someone masters the basic work, he or she may be promoted to supervisor.

In manufacturing plants, due to heavy capital investments in tools, dies, robots and production systems, the job of a typical worker does not change every day. Any modification of product design or manufacturing process is expensive. Change may require modifying the dies and machines, or reworking the assembly line. A first-level supervisor knows and has probably mastered the work the subordinates are doing.

With an increased amount of work shifting to knowledge-intensive industries, the situation for supervisors has changed. By the time a team member becomes a supervisor, some of the tools he or she has mastered may be obsolete because of changes in technology. What the supervisor has learned about the company, its customers and its industry, however, remains relevant. This allows the supervisor to provide judgement in ambiguous situations.

The supervisor is also an individual contributor. In modern Agile engineering environments, a project team comprises six to nine engineers. The team includes a formal supervisor or informal leader (POC). Within the team, many engineers work independently to complete a work item (writing new software code or modifying existing software). Almost all team members have the required permissions to check their modifications of the software into the common repository.

To maintain the pace of work, supervisors don't review the work of all other members before it is submitted to production. Supervisors can't realistically keep pace. Over time, sub-teams develop from this eight- or nine-person subgroup. In this scenario, only one or two members handle the work related to a specific area, so it is clear what they must give.

People in these subgroups become experts in their own areas in the project. They continue to master skills that are recognized by the management team and the customers.

In the Agile context, the entire team is part of the project discussions. For the last sixteen years at MAQ Software, we have included the entire team on all project-work-related discussions. In some cases, the extra communication created an email overload. In many cases though, the extra visibility helped new team members recognize the correct way to get things done.

It also allowed supervisors to assess the work of the new members. Recently, the Slack tool has brought visibility to the entire conversation and reduced email clutter.

With Slack, because the work is available to everyone for review, everyone recognizes the capability and contributions of team members. Still, most of us can do more to recognize our team members for their contributions and their impact on the overall system. At our company, we offer monthly spot awards and champion-of-the-quarter awards to recognize outstanding contributions.

In high-context societies such as India, where people are more familiar with and involved in the lives of their co-workers, I have seen co-workers go to extraordinary lengths to provide support to one another.

Stage 3: Do I Belong Here?

In the third stage of the employee's tenure with a company, she is concerned about her *impact on the workplace*. In our context, many engineers are driven by use of the latest technology and techniques. There is a significant focus on improving the quality of our solutions by incorporating the latest technology. There is a lot of focus on attention to detail, which shows up as superior software.

Over time, a high performer will have mastered the required technical skills and become a 'go to' person in at least one, if not many, areas. Such individuals are recognized by everyone and promoted. Their ideas, language and excitement resonates with everyone in the team. It becomes clear to these workers and their colleagues that they belong in the company.

Many workers ask themselves, however, if their company is a good fit for them. To gauge employee motivation during stage 3, Gallup suggests that managers ask employees to reflect on the following questions, which will also make it clear whether they belong:

1. At work, do my opinions seem to count?
2. Does the mission/purpose of my company make me feel my job is important?
3. Are my co-workers committed to doing quality work?
4. Do I have a best friend at work?

It is important for managers to help create a sense of belonging in the team by encouraging friendships in the group. We found that employees with similar interests hang out together. Many engineers are interested in the latest technical advances in the fields of cloud computing, machine learning and AI. They read and engage in discussions about the same technical advances. They download and install early-release versions of new software on Friday night. They work through the installation difficulties over the weekend. They cannot wait to show their implementation to the broader, sometimes informal, group on Monday.

Many others do not relate to these Monday conversations. Over time, some adopt excitement over emerging technologies. Others, however, do not share these interests and don't quite feel a sense of belonging.

They may even leave the company. Asking themselves Gallup's four stage 3 questions results in their finding an environment that is a better fit for them.

Stage 4: How Can We All Grow?

In the advanced stage, employees are working on *making things better around them*, to grow and to innovate.

To gauge employee motivation during stage 4, Gallup suggests that managers ask employees to reflect on the following questions:

1. In the last six months, has someone at work talked to me about my progress?
2. This last year, have I had opportunities at work to learn and grow?

Our regularly scheduled one-on-one meetings and biannual performance reviews include a formal section on Individual Development Plans. We help set specific technical and managerial learning goals for our team members. As a software-oriented company, we found that engineers who were interested in implementing the latest technologies tended to stay with the company. Many interested engineers will research and implement the latest technical advances for their customers to save them time and money.

Pink, in *Drive*, describes the third and fourth Gallup stages as the human need for mastery and purpose. Regardless of how motivation is described at these stages, it is essentially about contributing in a way that makes a difference for the company and for the broader community.

Performance = Motivation x Ability

I am constantly looking for ways to improve our company's performance. One way is to search for different methods of motivation. Scholars have proposed and tested more than fifty motivational theories over the last century. The consensus has been that our work motivation depends on our individual mindset and our interaction with organizational traits.[10]

As a manager, I needed an actionable approach to motivation. The model I consistently return to is in a textbook widely used in MBA programmes: *Developing Management Skills* by professors David A. Whetten and Kim S. Cameron.[11] Whetten and Cameron explain that a person's performance is determined by motivation and ability. The authors then break down motivation and ability into five factors:

$$\textbf{Performance} = \text{Motivation x Ability}$$
$$\text{where}$$
$$\textbf{Motivation} = \text{Desire x Commitment}$$
$$\textbf{Ability} = \text{Aptitude x Training x Resources}$$

Motivation Factor #1: Desire

There are two types of desires that lead to motivation: intrinsic and extrinsic.

In intrinsic motivation, we have an internal desire for new challenges and acquiring knowledge. We enjoy the task itself without any external pressure or desire for reward.

In extrinsic motivation, we desire external rewards such as higher pay, promotions and status. The problem with extrinsic rewards is that they do not last. As soon as we receive higher pay, our self-image changes and the higher pay becomes our new normal. Within a short time, we need another pay raise to stay motivated.

Motivation Factor #2: Commitment

The second factor in motivation is an employee's commitment or grit—the ability to persist despite difficulty and setbacks. In *Grit: Passion, Perseverance, and the Science of Success*, Professor Angela Duckworth notes that grit is the most important success factor. 'Our potential is one thing,' Duckworth writes, 'What we do with it is quite another.'[12] When new engineering graduates join us, many are intrinsically motivated to excel in the software field. They have an innate desire to learn software tools quickly. Many work hard and demonstrate a very high level of commitment to their projects.

Grit goes hand in hand with a growth mindset. People with a growth mindset believe they can develop their skills with effort. Our mindset determines who we are, how we live and what we become. According to Stanford psychology professor and researcher Carol Dweck, 'The view you adopt for yourself profoundly affects the way you lead your life.'[13]

For our customers, we have delivered more than 10,000 man-years over the last seventeen years. To deliver so much software, we had to align ourselves with our customers' thinking and their way of serving their own clients. When we analysed our successful team members, we found their mindsets were aligned with our customers'. They understood what our customers needed and organized the company to deliver along those lines. Likewise, these team members aligned with the company mindset.

To ensure the success of team members, businesses need to hire people whose mindsets align with the mindset of their clients and of their own company.

Based on our experience, we have articulated eight growth mindsets that explain our approach to personal success: (1) Manage Oneself, (2) Manage Learning, (3) Manage Delivery, (4) Use the Latest Technology, (5) Manage Teamwork, (6) Manage Customer Success, (7) Be Grateful and (8) Take Ownership. Next, we share positive and negative behavioural indicators to help our team members. We review the eight mindsets and the related behavioural indicators in recruitment and performance evaluations. (See Appendix B for additional information on these eight growth mindsets.)

One of our key managers is John Doe (name changed). He completed his degree from an eastern India engineering college. He graduated with poor grades (second division). Despite his four-year degree, he has limited knowledge of English. More than 80 per cent of the engineering graduates in India are deemed unemployable. John is one of them.

Most employers, including us, rarely hire such graduates. Based on a friend's recommendation, we hired John for a temporary assignment as a software tester. His job was to find defects (bugs) by manually installing and testing software. He needed to repeat this work day after day, week after week.

What John lacked in his earlier education, he made up for through dedicated effort. Most of our other engineers did not last on this job. But John continued working harder than anybody else to master the software. He was always energetic. He was rarely late or absent. He rarely called in sick. He was internally motivated. John has the grit that Duckworth describes.

As John became more proficient in his work, he started teaching other engineers how to do their work. Soon, however, to bring in additional efficiencies, we automated manual work by writing software programs. John did not give up when the nature of his work changed. He started leading efforts to specify how to automate software testing. Over time, he worked on improving his English.

Every year, John's managers recognized his contributions and rewarded him for his role as a key player in the workplace and in meetings. Now John is leading crucial initiatives in some of the most advanced areas, including machine learning and AI. If my experience is any indicator, senior positions in most companies are occupied by people like John, who demonstrate grit and drive even when society tells them they don't have perfect credentials.

In my interactions with young graduates, I find that many are not aware of the commitment and grit displayed by the top performers in every field. Hard work does not guarantee success. But failure is guaranteed if we do not work hard.

Next, we discuss the ability factors that contribute to superior performance.

Ability Factor #1: Aptitude

Aptitude describes a person's physical and mental skills and abilities. Managers must assess each subordinate's aptitude and determine what training and resources are necessary for the employee to perform.

The aptitude of a recent computer science graduate will usually fit within this profile:

- He understands the basics of programming languages, with around three months of internship experience using those languages.
- He has the raw intelligence to comprehend the algorithms behind most of our company's software projects.
- He has limited client interaction skills.

Ability Factor #2: Training

Managers must train employees to remove any skill gaps and enable employees to succeed. Even motivated employees are unlikely to perform well if they do not know how to deliver. Many new engineering graduates lack proper technical education. As a result, they do not perform well initially.

Most managers want to hire well-trained candidates, but they must recognize that training is part of the job. Ready-to-work, fully trained candidates are a rare find. Because developing technical expertise continuously is critical to our company's survival, we work hard to train our team members. This hard work has resulted in the success of employees such as John Doe.

With the ever-increasing pace of technical change, training has become even more necessary. Fortunately, new technologies are easier to learn than technologies of the past. New and better software tools help one correct mistakes faster.

Ability Factor #3: Resources

The third ability factor relates to resources. In some of our early projects, highly capable and trained people could not perform well. To my surprise, those same people were wildly successful on other projects.

When we considered the performance difference, we found a definite gap in the resources that were available for the projects. In our early projects, we did not have the required information, the necessary computer hardware and software, or access to the appropriate people. When we realized this, we made resources a priority. I now follow up daily with our project teams to ensure their work is not blocked because of any lack of resources.

Understanding Which Factor to Address

Managers faced with an underperforming employee may not know which of the above factors needs to be addressed. Whetten and Cameron offer four questions that managers may ask themselves to diagnose whether an employee's performance problems result from lack of motivation or ability factors:

1. How hard is the individual trying to succeed at the job?
2. How much improvement is the individual making?
3. How difficult are the tasks being assigned to the individual?
4. How capable is the individual?[14]

Once managers have answers to these four questions, they can act on the information they have. Ability questions can be addressed through technical training and guidance, which is relatively easy. As discussed earlier, motivation issues are more difficult to address.

Does Money Matter?

In my experience, most first-time managers may influence, but do not decide, their subordinates' pay. A company decides pay levels based on many factors, including company performance, the criticality of the employee, the employee's performance and potential, and the current market environment.

Early in my career, I became acquainted with a colleague who was unhappy with his pay. This was when I was working for Frigidaire Company as a mechanical design engineer. Randy Anderson (not his real name) worked in the IT department and supported our engineering computer workstations. He attended Iowa State University nearby, and worked evenings at our company. With Randy's support, we advanced our computing infrastructure. In my informal discussions with him, he mentioned that he was dissatisfied with his pay.

I badly needed Randy's help to get my work done and I was afraid he would leave if his pay did not increase. I lobbied his case to the assistant controller, an elderly gentleman with years of experience in accounting and management. He patiently heard my concerns, then cautioned me about motivating people using money alone. When I became a manager myself, I began to understand what he had been trying to tell me. So far as I know, Randy did not receive a pay increase immediately, but he continued to help our department. Despite the pay he was unhappy with, the project was interesting to him and he was learning useful technical skills.

New managers confronted with an employee who wants higher pay often react the way I did. They assume that a pay raise alone will make the dissatisfied employee happy. In reality, trying to resolve employee dissatisfaction by increasing pay rarely works. Employees may appreciate the higher pay for a few months, but they will quickly fall back into unhappiness if they are not intrinsically motivated to do a good job.

Moreover, managers are accountable for the sustainability of salary structures. Salaries need to work during both strong and weak economic times. When the economy takes a downturn (which it inevitably will), high salaries are often unsustainable.

I have modified the following table from Cameron and David, *Developing Management Skills* to reflect the needs of our engineers in India at various stages of their careers:

Table 7.2: What do workers want?

	New graduates (< 2 years of experience)	Graduates with 2 to 10 years of experience	Graduates with over 10 years of experience
1	Good wages	Job security	Interesting work
2	Job security	Interesting work	Appreciation
3	Promotion and growth	Appreciation	Job security
4	Interesting work	Involvement in decisions	Involvement in decisions
5	Appreciation	Good wages	Promotion and growth
6	Involvement in decisions	Promotion and growth	Good wages

Source: Adapted from Developing Management Skills[15]

For new graduates like Randy, wages take priority over other aspects of work because workers like him are looking for financial freedom and independence. Next, young engineers are energized by interesting work that offers technical growth and promotion opportunities.

Mid-level engineers value job security over salary. Engineers with two to ten years of experience usually have families and/or own homes and need to cover fixed expenses.

In senior management roles, people value interesting work and recognition for their achievements. Most senior managers are well paid, so negotiating salary becomes a lower priority.

When we hire from engineering campuses in India, new graduates usually focus on salary. There is limited information available to them regarding the projects and growth opportunities at their employers'. Even if financial information is available, most graduates can't apply that information to estimate their job security at a later stage.

So, how can a company meet new graduates' high salary expectations? We follow the model used by several US companies such as Container Store and Costco. These companies pay junior employees 25–40 per cent more than their competitors do. The higher wages are offset by improved employee productivity. To ensure high productivity, the companies invest more than their competitors in employee training. Managers at these companies also simplify processes so that it is easier for employees to get work done.

Chapter Summary

Key Points

- Higher productivity leads to higher wages, leading to a better quality of life.
- Businesses increase productivity by hiring managers who deliver a high level of performance.
- Performance = Motivation x Ability.
  - Motivation = Desire x Commitment.
    - Desire = Intrinsic + Extrinsic.
      - Intrinsic Desire: An internal desire for new challenges and acquiring knowledge.
      - Extrinsic Desire: Desire for external rewards such as higher pay, promotions and status.
    - Commitment: Ability to persist despite difficulty and setbacks.
  - Ability = Aptitude x Training x Resources.
    - Aptitude: A person's physical and mental skills and abilities.
    - Training: Managers must train employees to remove their skill gaps and enable them to succeed.
    - Resources: Inadequate resources (hardware, software, access to the appropriate people) can hinder productivity.
- To be productive, employees must be engaged in their work and motivated to work.
- To motivate a subordinate:
  - Offer them autonomy.

- o Increase their span of control.
- o Include them in meetings and discussions.
- o Offer additional training.
- o Offer assignments in areas involving new technology.
- There are four stages of growth for team members:
  - o **Stage 1:** What do I get?
    - ■ **Concerns:** Pay, job role, workspace, computers, commute.
  - o **Stage 2:** What do I give?
    - ■ **Concerns:** The employee's individual contributions (are they excelling, etc.).
  - o **Stage 3:** Do I belong here?
    - ■ **Concerns:** The employee's impact on the workplace.
  - o **Stage 4:** How can we all grow?
    - ■ **Concerns:** Making things around them better.
- Pay increases are only a temporary fix for unmotivated employees; increased pay won't resolve the motivation issue in the long term.
- Depending on their experience, employees have different priorities:
  - o New graduates (< 2 years of experience) prioritize salary.
  - o Employees with two to ten years of experience prioritize job security.
  - o Employees with more than ten years of experience prioritize interesting work.
- Companies can pay higher wages if productivity is emphasized.

8

Providing Feedback

'Feedback is the breakfast of champions.'

—KEN BLANCHARD

On Monday, 19 December 2016, we held our last weekly management meeting of the year. These Monday morning meetings are a weekly ritual where fifteen key managers meet for one hour.

The mood at the meeting was festive. Christmas was in the air; the weather was turning cold. We were getting ready to wind up the year. After another hectic year, our management team was looking forward to the upcoming Christmas break. Instead of discussing New Year resolutions or the mistakes we had made, we decided to focus on what we had accomplished during the year. We wanted to reflect on and celebrate our individual wins.

Participants took turns one by one. They discussed family events (births, marriages), key learning opportunities and project successes. Mullai Selvan was one of the last to speak. He had joined us three years ago after acquiring an MBA from the National Institute of Industrial Engineering (NITIE). He had worked hard and had risen through the ranks. With pride, Mullai explained that the highlight of his year was when I visited Hyderabad and told him I appreciated his work. My feedback to Mullai was based on my evaluation of his project's success. I had admired his results and appreciated his project management skills.

It surprised me that Mullai considered my short interaction with him and feedback to be the highlight of his year.

By providing this feedback to me in front of his peers, Mullai risked being perceived as a sycophant. I was taken aback at first. Our meetings are not about being members of a mutual admiration club. I wasn't sure if he was trying to gain brownie points (managing up) or if he was just starving for feedback. Because Mullai was doing well, he certainly did not need to manage up. Ultimately, I concluded that he genuinely valued the feedback.

As managers, most of us need improvement at giving and receiving feedback. In *Thanks for the Feedback*, Sheila Heen and Douglas Stone argue that most of the time, feedback comes in three forms: appreciation, coaching and evaluation.[1]

Table 8.1: Three types of feedback and the purpose behind them

Feedback Type	Giver's Purpose
Appreciation	To thank, connect, acknowledge, motivate
Coaching	To help improve skills, expand knowledge, build confidence and capability
Evaluation	To rate or rank against a set of standards, align expectations, or share a decision

Mullai's feedback made me realize that I needed to appreciate more people, more often. In my interaction with Mullai, I wished to thank him for his hard work (appreciation). But because I am not liberal with my feedback, my comment to Mullai was based on his project's success (evaluation). I appreciated his project management skills. Looking back, I could have been more personal in my appreciation of Mullai.

Separately, even though Mullai only received the appreciation (of his skills) part of my feedback, I was mentally also evaluating his project performance and comparing it with other projects of similar size and complexity. Consistent with Heen and Stone's observations, in my simple interaction with Mullai, I had incorporated two of the three types of feedback.

As the company has grown, I've realized, individuals risk becoming anonymous. Not many people outside of their immediate team and their supervisor know of them or their contributions. Feedback then becomes quite necessary to make individuals feel comfortable about their standing in the company.

When I interact with my team members, I'm often asked for feedback. It is important as a manager to understand their reasons for asking for feedback. In many cases, they are simply looking for appreciation and recognition of their work. In other cases, they are looking for coaching, advice or evaluation so that they can improve. They want to know how they compare with their team members with similar experience. They also want to know if their view of their standing in the organization is consistent with my assessment of them.

Managers must also understand how subordinates tend to react to feedback. When we receive feedback, we must manage three obstacles or triggers: truth, relationship and self-image or identity.

Truth is easy to verify in the software world. The computer starts or does not start. Mistakes or bugs in software can be independently verified. Data helps us accept the feedback we get. If the facts do not support the feedback, we ignore it.

Our relationship with the person providing the feedback and the trust we've built with her also determines how open we are to feedback. To make sure people don't feel defensive when I give them feedback, I declare my intent before sharing my opinions. Some of my comments are focused on improving people's skills and changing their behaviours. I clarify that as their manager, my interest is aligned with theirs. If the employee is successful, the team will be successful. If teams are successful, the company will be successful.

Self-image or identity is the most difficult part of receiving feedback. When I was a new MBA graduate, it was a humbling experience to join a high-performance team. During the first ninety days at the job, working alongside other new hires, our ability to contribute was limited. We were hired for our potential. To make a real contribution, we needed to accelerate our learning by mastering technical skills, company processes, customer needs, industry competition and self-management. But many of us were not yet aware of the need for these skills.

Our lack of awareness created tension in the team. The existing members did not appreciate the newbie MBAs with a 'know it all' attitude. The new MBAs had yet to develop respect for or earn the trust of existing team members, who may not have had MBAs. Any feedback from them triggered a negative response from us. 'How dare he point out my mistake or question my decision? I'm the one with the degree.' Our naive self-image closed our minds to realistic feedback.

New employees must learn to be open to feedback, but managers must also understand how to provide feedback in an effective manner. Depending on their personality (responsiveness in social style, discussed in Chapter 5), people may be very sensitive to strong words, to tone of voice, or to emotions conveyed in feedback. Managers will do a better job of getting their point across if they are aware of such sensitivities.

Many of us have blind spots when it comes to our work. Like a blind spot in a car, these are issues that are directly in front of us but we are unable to acknowledge them because of our physical or mental blocks. These blocks often relate to negative behaviours that others see but we cannot. When we receive critical feedback regarding our blind spot, we are so oblivious to our blind spot that we are unable to realize that the feedback is applicable to us, as the following example illustrates.

Nearly five years ago, we were starting to handle more complex projects. Because of the nature of the projects, we began meeting with senior managers in our client organizations. We needed to dress more sharply to ensure that our team had a good presence at these meetings. Our human resources person delivered a presentation to our engineers about business casual attire. One of her points was about wearing clothes that fit properly. I enjoyed her presentation to the team. But because I was unaware of my own blind spot, I did not realize until much later that the human resources person was talking about me. I did not register what was obvious to my team members: my own clothes didn't fit properly. As a matter of convenience and probably to save money, I had purchased medium-size shirts when a smaller size would have been more appropriate. I was not aware of my own clothing choices.

Whether your role is as an employee or a manager, it is essential to uncover your blind spots so that you can overcome them and reach your full potential. To find your blind spots, Heen and Stone suggest asking for specific feedback. Do not ask general questions such as 'How am I doing?' or 'Do you have any feedback for me?' These questions elicit superficial and polite responses that may not be useful to you. Instead, focus on specific topics, asking questions such as 'Was I dressed appropriately for the big presentation?' or 'Did I have enough slides for the meeting?'

Clear and Immediate Feedback

A common problem in many companies is that people do not know where they stand—and managers don't have the time to tell them. In my work with our managers and engineers, people routinely ask me for feedback on their individual performance.

With the increased pace of competition across industries, managers cannot wait six months for the biannual performance review cycle to give their feedback. Their input, by that point, is probably too late and may not be relevant.

As our organization has grown quite large, it has become more challenging for me to even know everyone's name. As you can imagine, it is even harder for me to offer relevant feedback to everyone on a daily basis. So, what can I do personally and what do we do at the company level to improve frequency and quality of feedback? And how can fast-moving, high-performance companies provide clear and immediate feedback?

At the company level, we have two approaches that work in tandem to keep the lines of communication open:

1. **Monthly one-on-one meetings with all employees**
   These are fifteen-to-thirty-minute meetings between an employee and his immediate supervisor. One-on-one meetings are a long-standing practice in successful organizations. We started conducting such meetings in our company around 2005. Before we added these meetings to our schedule, it was often the case that our

management team and supervisors arrived at office on a regular Monday to be greeted by an unpleasant surprise—unexpected resignations. Clearly, we had no idea what our employees were thinking, beyond what they had to say about their project work.

Like most companies, we suggested that supervisors conduct one-on-one meetings. The meetings, however, led to a lot of anxiety among subordinates. Managers felt pressured to point out the faults of their team members, and employees felt they were expected to voice their dissatisfaction with the workplace. To avoid conflict, many managers avoided the meetings altogether. Even if the meetings were held, most of the time the subordinates felt their issues were not resolved. The whole exercise was dissatisfying for both sets of participants.

We needed to offer guidance to managers and team members so that the meetings were positive and useful. We came up with boundaries for one-on-one discussions and also suggested a set of talking points that were neutral (non-accusatory) and productive.

We have drawn from Peter Drucker's teachings in planning these meetings. According to Drucker, there are two types of employee dissatisfaction: productive (focused on improving work processes, adopting new technology and training) and unproductive (oriented around salary, administration policies, commute, cafeteria, etc.).

One of the key items we chose not to discuss in one-on-one meetings was salary and benefits.

Both subjects are inappropriate in one-on-one conversations. It is unrealistic to expect any quick changes to be made on such matters because of their impact on budgets and because of the diverse needs of the many employees in the company.

Instead, we've tried to focus on the type of discussions Drucker sees as productive. Team members think up ideas for improving how work is structured. Managers review employee progress towards learning goals and try to align their own goals with the employees' career interests and the customers' needs.

To further enrich these discussions, we ask team members to complete and discuss the Mindset Scorecard (Appendix A) and the Behavioural Indicators (Appendix B) worksheets.

2. 'Stay Interviews'

In India, employers must deal with an employee attrition level that is very high by Western standards. Most of our employees are young. They are not sure what they want to do. As one of my friends said, only in India do people study engineering even though they do not want to be engineers. Many recent graduates join their first company as an engineer while preparing for their management entrance tests.

While there are many reasons why our employees leave (relocation, higher education, job dissatisfaction, higher pay), we, as employers, want to minimize attrition. In *Love 'Em or Lose 'Em*, leading HR expert Beverly Kaye suggests 'stay interviews' which involve the following questions:

- Are you challenged in your day-to-day work?
- What will provide more interest or challenges?
- What will make work life better for you?
- What do you want to learn this year?
- What will keep you here?
- What might entice you away?[2]

We ask our supervisors to look beyond the obvious answers such as 'more money'. We try to extend the conversation by asking, 'What else?'

For most people, answers to these questions do not change from a particular one-on-one meeting to the next. So, instead of asking these questions in a mechanical fashion at every meeting, we encourage supervisors to select a few questions and expand upon them.

Since performance feedback is focused on the past, how can we, as managers, focus more on future performance? Most managers, including myself, are reluctant to dictate to employees what specific behaviour we want them to change. More often than not we avoid performance-coaching-related conversations because we do not know what to say. We are ill prepared for the meetings. We do not have a list of the behaviours that are hampering an individual or the organization.

We do, however, have a list of behaviours specific to our company and which can be used by our team members to improve their performance *automatically*.

In my search for effective managerial tools, I have come across the Positive and Negative Performance Indicators in the seventh edition of *How to be an Even Better Manager* by Michael Armstrong.[3] A slightly modified table used by our company is provided in Appendix B.[4]

Occasionally, I am asked to provide specific feedback to individuals who are not performing well. Some of them disagree with their performance review, performance rating, or associated salary adjustment. Many of us suffer from 'superiority bias', where we feel our performance and skills are better than they actually are.

Instead of getting into an argument with the employees (which frequently results in the less-than-desirable outcome of their leaving the company) I ask them to take the time to rate themselves in the eight areas listed in Appendix B. Because the list details specific behaviours, employees can reasonably and accurately decide if they are exhibiting mostly negative or mostly positive behaviours.

In my experience, most people are genuinely interested in improving their performance in the short term and certainly in the long term. A simple review of their rating helps them share with me the future behaviours they can focus on to improve their performance. Usually, employees take a day or two to complete their self-assessment, which further calms them down (the result would be the opposite if they had a heated argument with me, where there may be only one 'winner'). With their mostly objective assessment, they can return to their work with a renewed focus on desirable behaviours. A few individuals recognize that most of their behaviours are negative and themselves choose to leave the company shortly after the self-review. Either way, they are greatly helped by the self-assessment of their behaviours.

Early on, we made the mistake of sharing this positive and negative indicator method only *after* there was a problem with an employee. Most of the good performers already had positive behaviours that they had learned by observing others. Most of the bottom performers (the lowest 10 per cent) were not interested in improving their performance. The challenge for most of us as managers is to educate the middle 80 per cent who are motivated to improve their performance but do not know what desirable behaviours are expected. So now, during our new employee orientation itself we inform new recruits about the positive behaviours that will result in them achieving long-term success.

To Criticize in Public, or not?

Patrick Lencioni, a leading management consultant and bestselling author of *Five Dysfunctions of a Team*, describes the need for managers to focus on the health of an organization. Lencioni says that when there is a high level of trust, he prefers that leaders correct or criticize erring actions or undesirable behaviours in public as soon as it is practical to do so to maximize learning. In his company, the entire organization benefits from such an approach because the leader does not have to repeat the same information to multiple people privately. The entire organization gets the message first-hand, clearly and without ambiguity.[5]

If you look at an industry or company that is in a period of rapid change, many of their leaders follow the public feedback approach. Examples of such leaders are Jack Welch of GE, Bill Gates of Microsoft, Steve Jobs of Apple, and now Jeff Bezos of Amazon.

While I don't necessarily condone or endorse these leaders' operating style, there's no arguing that these leaders got things done. Many of us have, after all, had experience with public feedback.

Public feedback takes place naturally in the family—the earliest group to which we belong. For example, a sibling or family member may point out another family member's mistake without creating long-term ill will. This is possible because of the high level of trust inherent in a nuclear family.

However, this style is not natural for everyone and will not work in all situations. In a high-trust environment, such as Microsoft Corporation or our own company, I have seen this approach work. In our company, due to continuous delivery and daily feedback from clients, it is difficult to sugar-coat or hide mistakes. We want daily feedback from our clients so that we can correct our mistakes and deliver exactly what they want. We pass that feedback along to our teams in as direct a manner as possible so there is no mistaking what needs to be done. Nonetheless, what works in MAQ Software may not work in every firm. If you are operating in an environment where you are still building your team's trust, everyone is probably more comfortable with private feedback until you have built a feeling of safety.

How to Handle Feedback?

In June 2014, the *Wall Street Journal* (*WSJ*) wrote on the subject of employees not being given enough practice in receiving negative feedback. Many employees are used to receiving top marks in examinations, breaking records and getting very positive feedback from parents. Accepting negative feedback is a useful skill that, according to the *WSJ* 'requires practice, humility and a sizable dose of self-awareness'.[6] The *WSJ* also said, '. . . the ability to learn from criticism fuels creativity at work, and helps the free flow of valuable communication.'

As shown in Table 8.2 below, the article advises people, when confronted with negative feedback, to not get angry, cry, deny or blame others. This is easier said than done, perhaps.

According to Heen and Stone, authors of *Thanks for the Feedback*, there are usually three reasons why people react badly to feedback.[8] First, the criticism may seem wrong or unfair. Next, the receiver may disrespect or dislike the person giving the feedback. And last, the feedback may hurt or rock the receiver's self-image or security.

Table 8.2: How to give and take negative feedback

Don't	Subordinate's Response	Manager's Response
Get Angry *'You're wrong!'*	Shift from 'Why?' to 'What?' Ask your manager for specific feedback: 'I may have misunderstood. Can you give me some examples of what you're saying?'	Don't get frustrated. Offer specific feedback: 'Here are a few examples of what I'm telling you.'
Cry *'I can't believe this.'*	Compose yourself. Apologize for crying. Schedule another meeting: 'Can we meet to talk about this later?'	Don't focus on the crying. Offer to schedule a new meeting: 'Let's discuss this at another time.'
Deny It *'No, I don't think so.'*	Let your manager know that you'd like to better understand where they are coming from: 'I'm surprised by this. Can you give me some examples?'	Don't question the subordinate's credibility. Help him understand where you're coming from: 'Perhaps I am not clear. Let me be more specific.'
Blame Others *'This wasn't my mistake.'*	Do not shift blame, focus on your actions. Ask your manager what you can do differently: 'I had not looked at it that way. Could you tell me more about how you see that?'	Don't question the subordinate's loyalty. Focus on what they can do better: 'Let me explain specifically what you can do better.'

Source: Adapted from the Wall Street Journal, *18 June 2014*[7]

As managers, all of us should show tact and empathy when delivering feedback. Employees appreciate regular and direct feedback, even if it is negative.

Who Is in Control?

> '*Whether you prevail or fail, endure or die,*
> *depends more on what you do yourself than on*
> *what the world does to you.*'
>
> —JIM COLLINS

Psychologists use the term 'locus of control' to refer to the amount of influence people believe they have over their environment. A person with an *internal* locus of control believes he can influence events and outcomes, whereas a person with an *external* locus of control believes outside forces control everything.

Occasionally, I am asked by our management team to meet with team members to discuss their grievances. In most cases, the person meeting me has high potential and is a valuable employee. The employee's manager wants to retain the person and resolve issues with him.

When I meet with the team member, I listen for 'I' statements. For example, 'I do not understand' or 'I have failed to do this'. If the team member is not using 'I' statements, I recognize the person does not have an internal locus of control.

Often, the team member is agitated. He blames other people and situations outside of his control. As soon as I recognize that the person has an external locus of control, I realize no amount of my counselling or coaching will help the person change. I end the meeting in a few minutes.

Individuals with an internal locus of control believe their own actions cause the events in their lives. When a problem arises, they ask *what* they can do differently instead of *why* the problem is happening to them. If a team member has an internal locus of control, I can usually work with him to suggest solutions to his problems.

Depending on one's locus of control, the same situation may be viewed in two different ways. Someone with an external locus of control may say, 'The client doesn't understand.' A person with an internal locus of control will say, 'I need to explain this in a better way.' A person with an external locus of control will say, 'I don't have the time.' Someone with an internal locus of control will say, 'I did not prioritize.'

Eventually, each team member must learn to have an internal locus of control. If an individual is always placing blame on external factors, he will not grow as an employee. Such an individual can be frustrating to manage—but they far outnumber the proactive employees that have an internal local of control. Many externally focused individuals end up on a slow track and do not last long in our company. Growth and progression depend on taking ownership of one's actions and moving forward with purpose and confidence. Without these characteristics, one cannot advance.

Chapter Summary

Key Points

- Feedback comes in three forms:
  - **Appreciation:** To thank, connect, acknowledge and motivate.
  - **Coaching:** To help improve skills, expand knowledge, build confidence and capability.
  - **Evaluation:** To rate or rank against a set of standards, align expectations or share a decision.
- As companies grow, managers must give feedback to make employees more comfortable about their place within the organization.
- There are three obstacles to feedback:
  - **Truth (or rather, lack of it):** The veracity of the feedback.
  - **Relationship of receiver to giver:** Whether we trust the person giving the feedback.
  - **Self-image or identity:** Whether the receiver is open to the feedback.
- Limited feedback frequency in large organizations creates timeliness problems.
  - In fast-moving industries, biannual performance reviews risk being feedback that is too late or not relevant.
- To improve frequency and quality of feedback:
  - Conduct one-on-one meetings with each employee every month.

- o   Conduct 'stay interviews'.
- To improve their future performance, encourage employees to conduct an objective self-assessment and review it with them.
- Public criticism within an organization:
  - o   Allows the leader to not have to repeat the same information to multiple people privately.
  - o   Is effective in an environment of high trust.
  - o   Is beneficial in a setting where there is continuous delivery and daily customer feedback.
- The ability to learn from criticism fuels creativity and helps the free flow of valuable communication.
- People react badly to feedback when:
  - o   The criticism seems wrong or unfair.
  - o   The receiver disrespects or dislikes the person giving the feedback.
  - o   The feedback hurts the listener's self-image or security.
- Employees become less defensive if they receive regular and direct, tactful feedback.
- In order to advance in the workplace, one must maintain an internal locus of control, accepting that one has control over one's actions and that one's actions are not controlled by the external environment.

9

Can I Retain the Right People?

'Unless the job means more than the pay it will never pay more.'

—H. BERTRAM LEWIS

Over the last seventeen years, my team at MAQ Software has structured our project-based organization loosely around two implicit groups. One is a core group of managers and engineers. They represent about 30 per cent of our staff at any given time. This group is responsible for managing and delivering multiple projects during the year. They are supported by a flexible (flex) team of engineers who work on these projects. These engineers represent about 70 per cent of the staff hired in the past two to four years.

Our core team stays fairly constant, with attrition matching the industry average. The flex team is relatively transient, working on short-duration projects. These engineers will try their hand at multiple companies and professions before they turn thirty. For some engineers, we are their first employer. These engineers have no intention of staying with us for very long. Based on my own experience, I believe they are seeking clarity about what they really want to do in life.

As a result of this churn, we have hired more than 2000 engineers in India over the last seventeen years. Most of them started off being part of the implicit flex team. More than 50 per cent of our engineers leave the company within the first two to four years of their joining.

To a typical manager in a Western machine organization, this rate of attrition is alarming. We are effectively a new company every two years. Except for the core team (30 per cent of employees), nearly everybody else is new in our innovative project-based organization.

As the head of the company, it is easy for me to rationalize the turnover as arising from external environmental factors and matters beyond our control. Some of these factors include demand for engineers in the overall economy, supply of engineering graduates and availability (or lack of availability) of the type of challenging projects employees want. Many engineers have left our company to pursue higher studies within the first few years of their employment, just as I left Frigidaire after my first few years there to pursue higher studies. Other people leave within the first few years to relocate to a city closer to their hometown. At our Hyderabad location, we lose a lot of employees to companies in north

India because they want to be closer to their hometowns in Uttar Pradesh or Rajasthan. Many other employees leave after a few years (after they have mastered certain skills) because they qualify for higher-paying jobs at other companies.

As an employer, we have learned to accept and staff our projects around these realities. I am well aware that for MBA graduates, the pressure to accept a job while still on campus is very high. Many MBA graduates carry a significant loan burden from financing their education, as I once did. Additionally, finding an entry-level management trainee job as a recent graduate can be hard. Hiring managers are sceptical about candidates who were not hired while in their MBA programme. Given these factors, MBA graduates are under tremendous pressure to choose a job quickly. As a result, they often accept *a* job while on campus but keep looking for other opportunities. Their eventual goal is to find a job where they will do the work they like and in the location of their choice.

In my experience with our company as well as from my discussions with MBA graduates, about 50 per cent of them change employers within a year or two of their first employment. We have found that fewer than 25 per cent of MBA graduates consider their first post-MBA employer as their ideal place of work. Many employers (including us) plan for this contingency. Unless the company is growing by more than 100 per cent year-over-year, we may not be able to offer opportunities for all our MBA graduates to be promoted. Our organization is also increasingly flat; this means we need fewer mid-level managers. Pursuing assignments in a different domain may be another attractive option for ambitious engineers to build strong capabilities.

Most new managers do not realize that retaining good people is a part of their job. In reality, many of these managers are rated on the attrition levels in their teams. As managers, when one of our direct reports leaves, there are several repercussions. We may, as supervisors, feel disappointed and rejected. More importantly, the work the former employee was doing does not go away. As supervisors, we are still responsible for the work assigned to the unit or team. We have to pick up the work and train a replacement.

Not all attrition is bad in every setting. Mid-sized organizations do not have enough buffer to accommodate and promote non-performers. Mid-sized employers may welcome the departure of poor performers who don't contribute to the bottom line. It saves managers from having to lay them off, which can upset other employees. In large organizations, even poor performers can go unnoticed and this will not significantly impact company results.

There is healthy attrition and there is unhealthy attrition. Of course, employers are concerned about unhealthy or undesirable attrition, where some of the top performers are leaving to work for other organizations (hopefully not a competitor!).

In my experience, many managers avoid conflict when it comes to their own teams. Hiring and training a new recruit is difficult and time-consuming. There is no guarantee that the new hire will be better than the current non-performer. Terminating a person (even a non-performer) also creates a sense of insecurity in the team. As a result, managers delay tough decisions, such as removing non-performers, in the hope that things will improve over time or that the non-performers will go away on their own.

To maintain decorum and protect the dignity of non-performers, most managers choose not to publicly identify or announce them. But team members have a good idea of the skills and contributions of other team members. They do not, however, want their peers to lose their job involuntarily, even when they are doing the non-performers' work for them and cleaning up after their mistakes.

If a non-performer leaves the company voluntarily, that is *good* attrition for the organization. Chances are that the concerned individual will get an opportunity somewhere else where he can put to use his unique talents more productively.

Over the years, we have had to release a handful of people. In all those cases, the individuals concerned landed much better opportunities than what were offered by us.

We also stopped endlessly discussing the non-performance of that individual. The management team was now freed from the unnecessary burden of justifying their non-performance to our clients and co-workers.

Another technique used by companies is 'punishment posting' for low performers. This is done in the hope that the transferred employees will resign from the company of their own accord.

Early in my career at Frigidaire Company, we purchased design workstations from IBM. An IBM sales representative and an IBM systems engineer were assigned to the workstations. Once the sale was made, the systems engineer was our technical support and source of information. Because IBM was cutting jobs, it moved one of its engineers to one of the less desirable locations to support our company. The systems engineer understood what the move meant; he was essentially demoted. As a result, he was not very motivated at work. He was spending his years waiting for his retirement and pension. As a customer, we had to bear the brunt of his incompetence and poor customer service. Later on, there were additional layoffs by IBM. I am not sure if he survived the additional cuts.

On the other hand, the loss of good performers is a huge expense for companies. As managers, we hold ourselves accountable for retaining good performers. As a company, we are concerned when any of our great performers leave, regardless of their seniority or job title.

What can a manager do to avoid losing great people? Sometimes it isn't possible to prevent a top performer's departure. Some employees leave for higher education, others go abroad. I have been surprised many times when one of our key performers has unexpectedly resigned.

Most large organizations have regular succession-planning exercises at multiple levels. Even then, there are protracted searches for key positions in many of those companies. For smaller companies, usually a crisis is at hand when a key employee leaves. The manager's manager is usually the only person who can take over the vacant role.

Besides offering competitive compensation, interesting work and recognition, what can a manager do to retain great workers so that these resignation crises don't take place? Succession-planning exercises can only take you so far. To retain great people, Beverly Kaye and Sharon Jordan-Evans, authors of *Love 'Em or Lose 'Em*, suggest that managers 'ask people'.[1] They instruct managers to conduct stay interviews with their direct reports. The authors promote the idea of asking several open-ended questions aimed at discovering what employees find satisfying and dissatisfying about their jobs. In addition, they suggest gathering ideas from the employees about how the manager and the company can retain top performers. Here are some examples of 'stay interview' questions:

1. What do you look forward to when you come to work each day?
2. What do you like most or least about working here? What keeps you working here?
3. If you could change something about your job, what would that be?
4. What would make your job more satisfying?
5. How do you like to be recognized? What talents are not being used in your current role?
6. What would you like to learn here?
7. What motivates (or demotivates) you?

8. What can I do more of or less of as your manager?
9. What might tempt you to leave?[2]

By using these questions as part of our one-on-one meetings, managers identify issues that are within their control. Many employees want to be able to learn and work on a specific technology. Managers must look for opportunities that match the interests of employees with project-staffing needs. In some cases, employees are looking for flexibility in timing beyond core office hours.

Most of us are hesitant to conduct stay interviews because we are afraid that the better performing employees may plan to leave. Avoiding the topic will not prevent the employees from leaving. If a person is planning on leaving, we can only delay their departure or change their minds in 10 per cent of cases. We have found that once people have made up their mind to formally resign from the company, we are rarely effective at getting them to stay with us for any extended duration.

Usually, there are several factors underlying their decision. One is salary. In such cases, the manager can easily change an employee's compensation. But by the time the manager knows that an employee is resigning, it is too late to offer a raise, so we almost never make a counter-offer. Employees already feel frustrated that they had to go out and get a higher-paying job elsewhere to get their manager to recognize their value to the company. If that's the case, they might as well leave since they have done all the work of finding a new job. And if other factors, such as the work the employees are doing or the company culture, have contributed to their decision, most managers cannot change that. Also, in such cases, money is not usually sufficient to retain the employees.

So how can managers prevent employee dissatisfaction before it becomes a problem? One effective means is to ensure that employees are properly trained. As discussed in Chapter 6, training allows them to feel comfortable in their job duties and more invested in the company.

Chapter Summary

Key Points

- Project-based organizations deal with high employee turnover, but managers must work to retain good performers.
- Not all attrition is bad; mid-sized organizations can't afford to accommodate non-performers.
- Refusing to confront underperformers hurts the company and its customers.
- To retain good performers, managers should conduct stay interviews to directly ask good performers about their concerns and expectations.

10

Why Are We So Busy?

*'Time is what we want most,
but what we use worst.'*

—WILLIAM PENN

As managers, we struggle to find time for all the things we want to do at work and in our personal lives. Recently, *1843* magazine (published by *The Economist* group), carried an article by Ryan Avent titled 'Why Do We Work So Hard?' The article discusses changes in the workplace, and how, in 1930, John Maynard Keynes predicted that workers in wealthy societies would eventually put in only ten to fifteen hours of work a week. Reality, of course, has not turned out that way. It seems as if with each passing decade we're becoming busier. And yet, as the article alluded, we continue to choose industries and professions that are time-consuming. We enter these industries because we enjoy the professional work and the rewards associated with it, despite at times feeling overwhelmed. 'The problem,' the article says, 'is not that overworked professionals are all miserable. The problem is that they are not.'[1]

When I was completing my MBA, the highest-paying jobs were in management consulting and on Wall Street. It was not unusual for management consultants to travel every week on assignments. Similarly, many Wall Street jobs require eighty hours or more of weekly work to close important deals. Many of my classmates coveted such jobs for their high pay and large impact. I doubted that I was qualified for those jobs, so I did not apply for a single management consulting or finance job. But if I had applied and won such a job, the associated lifestyle and intense pressure at work might have impacted my health and marriage poorly. Instead, I chose to seek a corporate marketing position in a high-growth industry (at Microsoft) at significantly lower pay.

Many of my friends decided to raise their families in smaller company towns (e.g., Bhilai) or university towns (Kharagpur). Life is more relaxed in these towns. Everyone knows everyone. Fewer people are stressed from time pressures. Job opportunities in these towns, however, are often limited to a single company. Also, the company may not provide great employment opportunities for two earners in the same family.

I grew up in a two-income family in a small town. Unlike many of my neighbours, both my parents worked. Though the average commute was only ten minutes, my parents were much busier than families where only one parent worked.

Many in my family are physicians. All of them became doctors by choice, partly for the nobility of the profession and partly to attain higher stature in society. All of them chose to work seven days a week to keep their income levels high. Some of their children who did not want to work every day chose medical specialities that did not involve weekend work or dealing with emergency cases. Some of them pursued jobs in corporate hospitals with fixed salaries and limited hours.

In technology firms, employees and managers must grapple with similar trade-offs. Similar to the medical profession, attaining higher status and pay often requires long hours. For some people, putting in those hours is worth it. For others, a long workday is too big a price to pay.

Long hours at work contribute to packed schedules, but so do our personal decisions. Being aware of this can help those who aspire to attain management positions and those who have just stepped into their first job as a manager. If we are aware of where our time commitments are coming from, we can avoid getting stressed out by the strain of too many commitments.

Labour economists in the US have been studying workers' time usage for many decades using the Time Use Survey.[2] Economists divide individuals' time use into the following categories: education, personal care, shopping, leisure (including TV, WhatsApp, Facebook), sleep, work, commuting, eating, housework and caring for others. The findings, while specific to the US, are relevant for India too. The challenges posed by the lack of time in our lives fall into three broad categories:

1. Society-imposed time pressures
2. Work-related time pressures
3. Self-imposed time sinks

Society-Imposed Time Pressures

'I can think of nothing less pleasurable than a life devoted to pleasure.'

—JOHN D. ROCKEFELLER

In both quality and quantity, our leisure time has tremendously improved. Many of us are not aware—or have forgotten—that not too long ago, we worked six days a week. On 21 May 1989, our late prime minister Rajiv Gandhi reduced the number of working days to five days for central government officials. With the globalization of our workforce, many new companies in India introduced a five-day week system. While many industries, including construction, still work six days of the week, most Indian companies are generally shifting towards a five-day week. This work schedule offers us two-day weekends, which equate to 104 weekend days a year for leisure. Additionally, we take a vacation and holidays.

Despite our fewer working days, we are today expected to fulfil many more obligations than we had to even ten or fifteen years ago. These obligations relate to transportation, travel, health, entertainment, shopping and social media, among other things. Our choices regarding how we use our time are greatly influenced by the broader society, co-workers, friends and family.

Transportation and Travel

Most of us feel a social pressure to own a vehicle. A vehicle provides us new freedoms and saves us time on our daily work commute. Vehicles, however, also add to our time constraints.

When we own a vehicle, we end up travelling more for social activities. Our friends and families assume we will attend functions, outings and weddings they invite us to. We may be expected to shop at an out-of-the-way mall just because we can drive.

Vehicle ownership also requires keeping track of multiple official documents, such as registration licences, car insurance and driver's licences. Car insurance claims and occasional repair challenges may be necessary if our vehicle gets involved in an accident. Dealing with these official documents requires time. In the best-case scenario, staying up to date on mandatory registrations consumes one to two days every year. Vehicles also require regular servicing and repairs, which at a minimum require up to two days a year.

Again, air, train and road transportation options have expanded significantly over the last twenty-five years. Most of us can afford these choices. As a result, many of us attend family and friends' functions, such as engagement celebrations and weddings more often than we did before. Just fifteen years ago, these possibilities were prohibitively expensive or required us to take at least one week off from work.

As discretionary income levels increase, more people participate in religious tourism. From Mumbai, it is easy to travel to Nashik for a weekend trip. From the Delhi-NCR, road trips to Mathura have become accessible and affordable for family gatherings. Many of us have gone on more pilgrimages before turning thirty than our parents did in their entire lives. While most of us appreciate enjoying a richer social life, it does place time pressures on us that we didn't have before.

Health

Life expectancy has increased in our society, which is indeed desirable. Medical advances allow many of us to live healthier and longer lives. I know many people in their thirties and forties who have completed marathons. Fifty years ago, Indians of this age rarely participated in marathons.

Due to medical advances, however, many of us now have additional obligations, such as helping our aging relatives. We are also under social pressure to make time-consuming investments in our health. Visits to physicians for preventive tests and check-ups can occupy half a day. Many of us spend hours every week on health improvement activities, doing yoga, working out at fitness facilities or participating in sports programmes. These pursuits help us stay healthier, but they take time as well.

Entertainment

On the entertainment front, modern life offers us an incredible range of options. When I ask people about their weekend plans, they almost always mention a variety of cricket match formats and global sporting events. While others mention very exciting—almost real-time—regional, national or global TV shows. Such entertainment options were unavailable when I was younger. While they give us new ways to enjoy ourselves, they can cut into the time we once spent on other things.

As a teenager growing up in the 1970s in Shahjahanpur, a small town in Uttar Pradesh, I had limited ways of spending my leisure time. Most of the families in my locality could not afford a record player, much less a TV. Instead, we listened to news and music on All India Radio. We had, apart from the daily news, Narottam Puri providing us commentary on the five-day cricket test matches.

In our town of several lakh residents, there were only three cinema halls, each with only one screen. The cinemas played the same movie for weeks together instead of changing them every Friday. We could either choose to watch popular movies repeatedly or nothing at all.

Most parts of India did not receive television broadcasts until the early 1980s. In 1981, to ensure the entire country could enjoy the 1982 ASIAD games, prime minister Indira Gandhi spent Rs 125 crore to set up low-power transmitters. Around that time, reduced import duties and other incentives also made colour TVs more easily available in India.

People living in the metros could look forward to the two movies screened every week on the government Doordarshan (DD) TV channel. The movies aired on Wednesday and Sunday evenings. Other than these two weekly movies, there was little reason to turn on the TV.

As the years passed, advances in communication technologies brought cable television. These days, most people spend at least two hours every day in front of a TV. The current breadth and quality of TV programming offers us countless choices, enticing us to spend more time watching TV. In many homes, the TV is always on, playing constantly negative news. Watching TV eats up a significant amount of time in the present day.

With the advent of the Internet, and now YouTube, even more video content is available. Technological advances have provided us all kinds of ways to spend our time.

For live events, the government and private entities have built many new stadiums, offering us a variety of entertainment with quality sound and video, and at varying price points. Many of us enjoy these shows. Nonetheless, added to our television time at home, they can fill up our schedules quickly.

Shopping

'Let's go shopping' is music to many ears. Shopping has become a weekend ritual of modern life. Visiting shopping malls, with their stores, restaurants and movie theatres has become a new pastime. We meet our friends—some special and some not so special—in air-conditioned and spacious shopping malls. As if shopping were a treasure hunt, we seek and find pleasure in bargains. We socialize and entertain ourselves, spending our time and money at these malls. Like the hours we spend watching TV, this is time we could potentially be investing in other activities.

Social Media

Social media, a relatively new temptation, also devours our time. Facebook, founded in 2004, allows people to connect with long-lost friends. Most of us did not open Facebook accounts until sometime after 2010. Just five years ago, we did not spend any time on Facebook updates or on sharing photos. Now, most Facebook users in India spend at least thirty minutes every day on the social media website, accessing it from desktops or mobile phones. Some of this time is not dedicated solely to Facebook. Many people use Facebook while eating or watching TV. Those who do not use Facebook are routinely reminded by their friends, co-workers and family to check their statuses or view their photos.

Facebook has even made its way into the workplace. Many engineers replaced Yahoo messenger with Facebook messenger on their desktops. Now many young people cannot imagine life without Facebook. They believe that Facebook should always be available to them.

WhatsApp, now a part of Facebook, is a recent phenomenon. Due to its low cost and compatibility with not-so-smart phones, the app has increased engagement in India over the last three years. Today, WhatsApp is a good source of chain messages containing jokes, gossip and information.

Many of us also have accounts on Twitter, Snapchat, Pinterest and now, Periscope, that link us to other entertaining sites, providing us with even more pleasurable entertainment.

Many intelligent people use these social media tools to integrate their professional interests into their online socializing. For merchants, Facebook and LinkedIn are good ways to promote their causes, goods and services to a broad network of connections. For buyers, Facebook pages and 'targeted' advertisements are an efficient source of information about the goods and services on offer. I can admit to using Facebook links to evaluate products and services.

All the social sites we use have made it easier for us to stay connected with people, but they take away from the time we used to spend doing other things.

A Bank Never Sleeps

Not so long ago, most of us relied on cash payments using rupee notes (bills). We had at the most one bank account, which we used sparingly. Now, most of us *need* three to five bank accounts. One account is for our salaries, which are paid as direct deposits from our employers. Getting lower mortgage or auto loan rates may require us to start another bank account. We need accounts for two to three credit cards to take advantage of beneficial offers. We need another account and possibly a mobile wallet or other apps for online shopping.

Having all these accounts requires maintaining multiple online user names and passwords to manage the flow of money from one account to another. While online access is great, this self-service option requires us to spend a few hours every week tracking our transactions. Occasionally, we experience billing errors and fraud, which can easily take up a day or two of the year.

Modern city life offers myriad ways to spend our leisure time. Most people living in Tier-3 cities and rural areas do not have these options. They rarely complain they lack time.

Going back to the limited options of the past is almost unthinkable for any young person of today. Technological advances enable many of us to spend our time in fun and enjoyable ways. These advances seem to accelerate in line with Moore's law. Computer processing power doubles nearly every two years, resulting in new ways of using microprocessors, which inevitably uses up more of our time.

Many adults expect and rely on these choices for a satisfying life. These privileges, however, all come at the expense of our time. At some point anyone who hopes to build a fulfilling career and enjoy a rewarding family life will need to make their choices. While it is great to enjoy modern pleasures in moderation, it is sometimes important to make a conscious decision to unplug and think or enjoy the simple pleasures of an in-person conversation.

Work-Related Time Pressures

One of the reasons most of us feel more pressured for time is because of poor decisions related to time management within our companies. In some situations, this is beyond our personal control. In many others, we have some power to influence how time is spent at the company. A conscious awareness of where time tends to get wasted at the company can help managers improve everyone's life at work.

Budgeting Time

Managers spend their subordinates' time, sometimes unwisely, in a company. In most companies, managers must justify the expense before spending company money. Firms commonly use financial budgets and audits as tools to direct activity towards company priorities.

However, managers do not usually budget or audit their time or their subordinates' time. If you want to become a great manager, it is essential to impose some discipline on how you manage your time and others' time, even if your organization does not require this. In 'Making Time Management the Organization's Priority', McKinsey experts suggest treating employee time as a 'finite resource', just like capital. The authors suggest that companies should tackle time problems systematically, rather than leaving the issue to individuals.[3]

A *Harvard Business Review* article, 'Your Scarcest Resource', echoes the position of the McKinsey experts. The article identifies meetings as a big reason for lost organizational time. 15 per cent of an organization's time is devoted to meetings. This percentage has been steadily rising since 2008. Even worse, the effectiveness of meetings is declining. Managers must work on improving the effectiveness of their meetings to preserve their organization's time capital.[4]

Managing Meetings

Due to their positional power, managers can call for meetings with subordinates at their (managers') convenience. Early in my career at MAQ Software, I did not have pre-scheduled meetings with our team. Instead, I would hold ad hoc meetings. Most of them were story sessions in which I rambled on about issues that were important to me. As our company grew and work pressure increased, we started to hold structured meetings. Forced to use our meeting time more judiciously, I became a more effective manager.

Meetings that run past the allotted time are a common problem at companies. A few years ago, we asked one of our senior managers to preside over our quarterly employee meeting. Most of us are excellent storytellers, and he was no exception. A great orator with an ability to engage an audience, he entered into storytelling mode with 200 people. That day, those 200 people each spent four-and-a-half hours at his session. Because of the manager's positional power, most of the attendees felt they could not leave the session. Many employees could not finish their work for the day after the meeting. While such incidents are not common, even one such meeting uses up precious organizational time. Now, our managers know that meetings must start and end on time, even if some items remain unaddressed.

One thing I learned over time is that before scheduling a meeting, I need to consider the hours we would have to invest in planning it and decide if they are worth it. One of our biggest meetings is our quarterly employee meeting. It is supposed to run for just ninety minutes. But organizationally, the meeting consumes a great deal of time. If 200 people attend, the company spends more than 300 hours (200 times 1.5 hours). In addition, three to four key people spend two weeks getting ready for the meeting. The infrastructure and support teams spend hours preparing the room for the meeting and clearing the room after we finish.

While the quarterly employee meeting is important—it is where we make sure our team is aligned on key strategic objectives—we can't hold such meetings routinely.

Bringing Clarity to Meetings

Running efficient meetings is difficult, but they are critical to a company's success. Meetings can help synchronize team members, increase morale and result in better and faster decisions. When run poorly, however, employees find meetings painful, boring or just pointless.

Confusion over what type of meeting is being called creates ambiguity about each attendee's expected role at the meeting. The problem becomes worse when several types of issues are thrown into one meeting. Meetings should be limited to clear purposes, such as:

- Informational—someone (usually the manager) provides information that is better shared in person than by email.
- Brainstorming—no clear outcome may result.
- Problem solving—many participants (perhaps different subject-matter experts) provide expertise.
- Decision-making.
- Morale boosting or group meetings.
- Observing or just listening in meeting.
- Debating.
- Voting.
- Weighing in.

Managers can create clarity by sharing agendas in advance for their meetings. Some experts, such as *Death by Meeting* author Patrick Lencioni, suggest that creating clear meeting agendas can make meetings much more efficient.[5] Other experts agree, but also insist on creating follow-up-action items before and after meetings. Still others recommend regular meetings with open agendas. During these gatherings, attendees decide the agenda at the beginning of the meeting.

With the Agile engineering approach, the business world is shifting to daily stand-up meetings that should last no longer than fifteen minutes. Unfortunately, most department managers convert daily stand-up meetings into status and problem-solving meetings, which can last up to one hour. Most of us lack the discipline to ensure that our communication is crisp and effective.

Problems with Remote Meetings

With the globalization of work and improvements in communication technology, many companies now rely on conference calls and online meetings. These communication options make it cheaper and easier to hold meetings with employees in other countries.

Conference calls and online meetings may be easy to attend, but they facilitate many undesirable behaviours from remotely distributed attendees. All our managers have observed our remote participants responding to emails, texting, checking Facebook updates, surfing websites, eating, driving and doing housework during remote meetings. Keeping meetings brief and well-focused is the best way to prevent team members from becoming distracted. Being trapped in a rambling teleconference is just as much a waste of time as being locked in a conference room.

Optional vs Mandatory Meetings

Many people are unclear as to whether meetings are optional or mandatory. Depending on the organizational culture and the host, even optional meetings become mandatory because subordinates perceive managers' suggestions as orders. Managers can address this issue by clearly stating whether a meeting is truly optional.

Shadow Work

Most companies now require employees to handle administrative items on their own. For instance, in my first decade of work, administrative assistants (formerly called secretaries) handed my pay cheques to me in person. Now, employers offer self-service portals. If we want to review our pay and vacation balances, or get a copy of pay slips, we can visit the self-service portal anytime, anywhere. Similarly, we can review our pensions or provident fund plan balances through a website. For arranging travel, we can now use a convenient employee travel portal to reserve airline tickets and hotel rooms. Employees must also spend time preparing and submitting expense reports using online software. Even meeting scheduling takes place online, through our public calendars.

In the past, administrative assistants typed and circulated memorandums (memos). Now, workers are expected to type and send their own correspondence. In June 2015, *Fortune* reported that 80 per cent of surveyed Fortune 500 CEOs handled their own email.[6]

In my third year at IIT Kharagpur, during the Durga Puja and Dussehra festival break, I decided to stay on and attend a typing school. My fellow students trained other students to become career typists (or stenographers). Realizing that computers were coming to a desk near me, I felt it was a good use of my time to learn to use all ten fingers while typing. My parents were surprised that I chose to spend my vacation learning to type. My parents told me that as an IIT graduate, I would be assigned a secretary to type my correspondence.

As it turned out, secretarial jobs soon disappeared from the workplace and the time I spent learning to type was well worth it. In my career, I've always had to type and read my own correspondence and memos. This added a significant time commitment to my daily tasks, but at least I could do it efficiently.

Self-Imposed Time Sinks

Leading management expert Peter Drucker stresses the importance of time for executives. He says time is the only resource that cannot be reclaimed. Yesterday is gone forever. We have only twenty-four hours in a day. Unlike other items, we cannot buy or trade additional hours.

Throughout most of my adult working life, I was not mindful of the use of my time during and after work. Maybe I was inattentive to my time because I did not hold senior positions. Maybe the organizations I worked for were overstaffed, with too many people for too little work. I usually had enough time. But, like many co-workers, I lacked awareness of how I spent my time.

During my MBA programme, I was focused on learning functional skills such as cost accounting, corporate finance and marketing. As a result, I did not come across Peter Drucker's seminal book, *The Effective Executive,* until later in life. In the book, Drucker advises executives to learn and measure how they use their time at work (*know thy time*).[7] I have since found Drucker's advice invaluable, especially in a fast-paced growth environment.

In his study of managers, Mintzberg discusses the characteristics of effective managers. For productive managers, free time is made, not found. Mintzberg says that effective managers *gain control of their own time by turning obligations into advantages and by turning those things they wish to do into obligations*. The following examples show how experienced managers follow Mintzberg's advice.

Example 1

I regularly visit many business schools as part of our MBA campus recruitment effort. During my visits, I speak to MBA students about career planning and the IT industry. I also meet with the relevant faculty members. I use the visits as an opportunity to learn about recruitment strategies and salaries offered by our competitors. I read the student notice boards to increase my awareness of student and company activities at the institute. In my interactions with students, I learn about their current courses, their mindsets and their aspirations. This first-hand knowledge allows me to tailor my discussions when these students join our company.

By doing my homework on the new recruits, I can provide better inputs to our management trainee programme. These simple activities increase my effectiveness as a manager.

If I were to view these campus visits as a mere work obligation and not as an advantage to sharpen my job performance, I would be unhappy at the extra travel and time away from my desk. I have made more than 100 visits to engineering and management campuses over the last seventeen years; I cannot recall a single trip I consider a waste of time. The campus visits resulted in better candidates applying for positions with our company. As a result, the quality of our team improved.

Example 2

Some may think the ability to decide what we wish to do with our time is only available at senior levels. That is because subordinates are told what to do most of the time. While it is true that seniority brings increased latitude to the range of activities and obligations one can choose from, higher positions also come with increased expectations. As Mintzberg mentions, unless managers deliberately convert what they wish to do into obligations, their effectiveness will be limited. Managers will not be able to free time to do what matters to them.

While completing my MBA at the University of Michigan, I worked part-time at the school's Intellectual Properties Office (IPO). I was trying to broaden my skills and experience beyond engineering. I was paid a student salary, which was minimal.

Due to my marketing background, my assignment was to sell and license automobile simulation software (called AutoSim then) to companies. Once I narrowed down my list of potential CAD/CAM and analysis companies, I contacted them by post, fax and telephone. In my research, I discovered that Hewlett Packard (HP) had a CAD/CAM division in Stuttgart, Germany.

In an unrelated development, one of my International Business classes required me to travel to Germany for a week to visit GE Lighting factories. Recognizing that HP's CAD/CAM division could be a potential licensee of the AutoSim software, I contacted the division's engineering manager. I set up a meeting in Stuttgart, making a one-day side trip for the appointment.

My supervisor at the University of Michigan was not expecting me to visit HP in Stuttgart as part of the job. The IPO did not have the budget to pay for my additional trip to Stuttgart. Regardless, I wanted to sell the software licence and increase my knowledge of business in Europe, so I made the trip. While I did not succeed in licensing the software to HP, I had gained exposure to a company in Europe and had gone beyond where my expected study trip could have taken me. If I had considered my additional trip to HP a burdensome job obligation, I may not have been as successful or effective in growing my knowledge (which was the reason I took the class).

Example 3:

A more recent example relates to the launch of my book, *What I Did Not Learn at IIT* in November 2013. After completing the book, I contacted the IIT Kharagpur Alumni Association in Delhi to check if they would be willing to host an alumni event around career planning. As part of the event, we would also formally launch my book. The book publisher also happened to be based in Delhi, so it made sense to do the event there. With some effort, the IIT Kharagpur Alumni Association hosted the event at the very prestigious India International Centre (IIC) in New Delhi.

I mentioned the book launch to Rakesh Tyagi, one of our managers. He is from Delhi, and had planned to be on vacation in the city around the same time. Once he learned about the book launch, he asked if he could attend. He even volunteered to record the event.

As head of the company, I was delighted to see Rakesh's enthusiasm. He would have the chance to visit the prestigious IIC, a venue frequented by the New Delhi elite. In addition, we could spend time together, which is difficult to do in the midst of our daily routines. He learned about book launches and met the IIT alumni. In my opinion, Rakesh successfully converted a day of his vacation into an obligation.

Is my assessment correct? To this day, I am not certain if he considered attending and recording the event an obligation. I never expected him to use up one whole afternoon from his hard-earned vacation time to attend a book launch. He could have used the time for many other social activities. Nonetheless, he was happy to show up at the launch. He took advantage of a company-related event happening in his area. After the event, he thanked me for allowing him to be part of the launch. Years later, I am grateful to Rakesh for taking the time to attend it.

These examples illustrate that it is always possible to turn things we wish to do into obligations and vice versa. By deliberately adopting the mindset Mintzberg describes, we increase our effectiveness.

Schedule Time

So how does a manager turn an obligation into an advantage? One way to find time is by scheduling appointments in advance so that other urgent activities can revolve around these pre-arranged commitments.

Early in my marketing career at Microsoft Corporation, I worked with a senior R&D manager in one of the HP divisions. We worked together, reviewing software-related changes we planned to make over the next few months. He suggested fixing a meeting six months in advance. After nearly twenty years, I still remember the conviction in his voice when he said: 'If we schedule the meeting, it will get done. Just go ahead and schedule the meeting.' Surely enough, the meeting got done and other activities were adjusted around the pre-set schedule.

Using Discretionary Time

Most operating managers begin their workday knowing they have limited control over the activities that will advance their missions. Strategic use of discretionary time can alleviate this problem.

For instance, in the daily stand-up meetings I mentioned earlier, participants are required to share three things they did the day before and three things they plan to do the current day. This simple approach has helped us unblock team members and encourage communication, freeing up time and increasing productivity.

Managers play an important role in modelling behaviour in these meetings. The type of activities managers choose will influence the choices subordinates make about how to use their time.

How should meeting participants choose their three daily activities? The late Stephen R. Covey answers this question in his book, *The 7 Habits of Highly Effective People*. He explains that most of our activities fall into one of four quadrants:

I. Urgent, Important
II. Not Urgent, Important
III. Urgent, Not Important
IV. Not Urgent, Not Important

These quadrants are illustrated in the table below:

	Urgent	Not Urgent
Important	**I** • Submit a sales proposal to a client • Respond to an inquiry from a journalist • Manage cash flow (collecting and spending money) • Handle customer complaint about quality • Recover from a computer system failure • Fix software bugs in production software • Visit a hospital for medical emergencies • File annual taxes • Handle last-minute changes to product specifications	**II** • Coach employees (monthly one-on-one meetings) • Learn emerging technologies • Attend professional networking events • Participate in strategic meetings • Attend meetings that require your input • Exercise • Spend quality time with family and friends • Create budgets
Not Important	**III** • Attend meetings that you will not contribute to • Social interruptions by co-workers (Ex: 'Let's get coffee' – but for unimportant issues) • Check email constantly • Answer all phone calls when focusing on a project • Respond immediately to Facebook posts, texts, and instant messages • Firefight issues that fall under a subordinate's responsibilities • Resolve minor team disagreements	**IV** • Many use activities in this quadrant for entertainment and to manage stress • Visit social media sites such as Facebook, Google+, and Twitter • Watch TV soap operas (serials) • Play video games • Gossip • Read recreationally

Figure 10.1: Covey's time management matrix[8]

Most of us live our lives in crisis mode. Our days start with urgent work of little value and interruptions (Quadrant III). By the time the day ends, we are completely exhausted. We cannot wait to escape the workplace and hit the road. We are further exhausted by the traffic, with everyone trying to get home at the same time using the same trains and roads. We are spent by the time we reach home. We use any remaining energy to alleviate our stress and look for entertainment, such as watching TV (Quadrant IV).

Instead of falling into this pattern, we must focus on spending most of our time on 'not urgent but important' items (Quadrant II), as Covey advises. For example, if we take time to organize our schedules to include regular exercise, we can avoid some medical problems that may result in unplanned visits to the doctor. Quadrant I activities are urgent and important and need to be handled immediately. We must handle them as part of our normal business. For many of us, our job depends on them. With a proactive approach, however, we can train ourselves to work on the important activities before they become urgent.

Based on our experience at MAQ Software, we found examples of activities in each of the four areas that are relevant to our industry. The examples are listed in each quadrant of Figure 10.1. Reviewing these examples may help us identify ways of transitioning our focus to Quadrant II activities.

If we analyse our daily work as managers, most of us work on urgent activities as soon as we enter our office; this is also known as 'firefighting' or 'crisis management'. Preventing this from happening every day takes planning.

Covey advises executives to focus on *important* activities to reduce 'urgent but not important' (Quadrant III) activities. These important activities or initiatives move the organization forward and reduce anxiety for its managers.

Integrate Work and Life

'The master in the art of living makes little distinction between his work and his play, his labour and his leisure, his mind and his body, his education and his recreation, his love and his religion. He hardly knows which is which. He simply pursues his vision of excellence at whatever he does, leaving others to decide whether he is working or playing. To him he is always doing both.'

—J.P. SPARK

It is commonly thought that work–life balance means working less. That is a myth left over from the factory days, when workers put in long hours for very low wages.

The idea of work–life balance can be better pictured if we think of leading an integrated life, viewing family, work, community and health as part of the same picture, not as opposing forces. My own life includes work, family, social service and my health. As a professional, I must integrate every part of life into my schedule. To balance my life, I decide how much energy I will spend on each of the four areas of my life.

When I was unemployed, I was desperately seeking to add work to my life. Once I got a job, I worked hard to add family to my life. Next, along with my family and work, I added social activities. As I got older, my health became a larger focus area and consumed more of my time. I continue to actively seek to integrate all four areas of my life.

As job opportunities have increased around the world, we are all presented with choices about how we integrate the elements of our lives. In the context of companies, most people are looking for work–life balance, which typically means they want their supervisor to reduce their work. But supervisors can hardly give what they do not have. Given the realities in most industries, supervisors are being asked to do more work with fewer people.

It is important to consider such realities when making career choices. As professionals, we get to *select* industries and *choose* job roles. Not all jobs are equal in work intensity and level of compensation. Some industries and job roles are more demanding than others. We can decide what level of effort at work is compatible with our lives. There is no right or wrong answer. What is right for me may not be right for you.

In my experience, senior-level jobs are demanding in terms of time. Most of these jobs require regular travel to meet customers, suppliers and business partners, and to recruit candidates. Travel is time-consuming and requires extra effort. Whenever possible, I combine business travel with visits to my extended family. They are happy to see me. As a side benefit, I get to avoid hotel food and enjoy healthy, home-cooked meals.

The choices you make about your career cannot be made in isolation. Spouses and extended families of senior managers often make many sacrifices to support the managers' work demands. This is a side effect of the senior manager's demanding schedule that should be considered when weighing job options.

Many dream of getting a cushy job with a low workload. It is best not to pin your hopes on this. Even if we find a cushy senior-level job with limited responsibilities, chances are the job will not last for long. With the rapid pace of change in technology and with globalized economies, inefficient companies are wiped out quickly. When the company goes, the cushy job will go with it.

As Jack and Suzy Welch mention in their book *Real-Life MBA*, work–life balance is a myth; there is only work–life choice.[9] If we aspire to reach senior management roles, we must put time and effort into our work. Sometimes we choose to work at the expense of life (family and leisure). The Welches note that in any competitive business, management should promote the most hard-working candidates, regardless of gender. Some of these individuals choose to have no life outside of the office so that they may focus 100 per cent on work. That choice may or may not be right for you.

Jeff Bezos, founder and CEO of Amazon.com and many other companies, likes to use the word 'harmony' instead of 'balance' to describe work and home life.[10] He explains that it is difficult to be happy at home when we have had a bad day at work. Similarly, if our home life is filled with stress, it is unlikely that we are making much progress at work. He explains that stable industries may be appropriate for some people. For other people who thrive on new challenges, dynamic and fast-moving industries are more energizing. Like many people in the software industry, I would be unhappy and bored at work if innovations were not happening, but I recognize that this comes with a cost: long hours.

The Four Life Domains

All of us must pay attention to the four domains of our lives. The first domain revolves around ourselves, which includes our physical, mental and spiritual health. The second domain involves our professional lives at work. The third involves our immediate and extended families, including our parents, spouse and children. The fourth domain involves the broader community, such as alumni associations, the temple or the community, where one may be doing voluntary work.

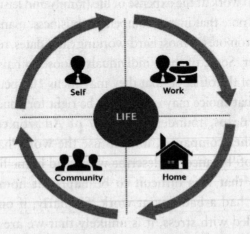

Figure 10.2: Friedman's work–life integration

Professor Stewart Friedman at the University of Pennsylvania has been teaching and writing about work and life integration for over thirty years. In his September 2014 *Harvard Business Review* article, 'Work + Home + Community + Self: Skills for integrating every part of your life', he observes that most people describe themselves as 'overcommitted', 'stressed out', 'frazzled' or 'stretched thin' in their lives.[11] These descriptions are used regardless of the age, gender, profession (executives and stay-at-home parents), or geographical location of the person in question. On Friedman's website 'www.myfourcircles.com', anyone can take a free test to assess their life integration.

Friedman found that virtually everyone is struggling to find meaningful work and a great family and social life. Based on his research and interviews with thousands of executives, he found that instead of making trade-offs in the four aspects of our lives, we should integrate them through pursuit of what he calls *four-way wins*. This improves one's performance in all four life domains.

Friedman found eighteen specific skills that help individuals gain clarity and improve their work–life integration. As part of his Total Leadership programme, Friedman groups those eighteen skills under three heads: authenticity, integrity and creativity.

Cultivating 'authenticity' skills requires executives to be 'authentic' and 'clear' about what is important to them.

The second group of skills, 'integrity', challenges us to view ourselves in different integrated roles. Honing these skills allows us to 'clarify our expectations' to those whom we interact with.

We can use our resources to integrate and transfer our knowledge and skills. For example, early in life I realized that education is a great equalizer. All of us can increase our income and standard of living with education. Over the past twenty-five years, one of my life goals has been to help people gain an education so they can increase their income potential. When I visit my relatives, all of them seem concerned about their children's education and career prospects. I share Khan Academy videos with friends and extended family. I take it further by evangelizing the flipped classroom model to start a conversation about how the shortage of teachers can be overcome. Some of these active learning techniques I picked up as part of my work at our company.

The third area of skills, 'creativity', revolves around being innovative by 'focusing on results, rather than the amount of time and energy' spent.[12] Last year, we wanted to maximize our engagement with communities in India. Utilizing crowdsourcing, we invited our executives to nominate non-profits that are doing good work. In our first year, we found at least ten new organizations that could advance their missions with a little help and guidance from our company. Our company may not have discovered these organizations without this group effort.

Many people in our company are short on time. Some, however, find time for exercise and benefit from being fit. Even simple solutions like choosing to take the stairs instead of the elevator can improve one's fitness levels. I myself use the office stairs to integrate physical activity into my work routine. Additionally, some of us stand during our meetings, sometimes for up to one hour, to increase our daily physical activity.

Recently, a journalist interviewed me regarding our company's fifteenth anniversary celebrations. In the interview he asked me, 'What are you most proud of in your life?' I was not prepared for such a broad question. Many people would answer their children, job, or parents. After some deliberation, I told him that I am proud of the balance I have achieved in my life. Achieving balance is not easy and is not a given for anyone. With age, I have gained the confidence to focus on a few ideas or values that matter the most to me. I have tried to cut down on non-essential activities in all four aspects of my life, including work.

Most of us aspire to find balance in our lives. With time, we can gain clarity on our life goals. With deliberate effort, I have been able to integrate my four life domains to improve my performance in each. I am still working to further improve the balance I have achieved.

Chapter Summary

Key Points

- As our standard of living increases, personal activities demand more of our time and attention.
- Managers have more demands on their time than ever before:
  - o Efficient managers budget time in the same way they budget financial resources.

- o For effective managers, free time is made, not found; they convert obligations into advantages.
- To avoid wasting time, meetings should have a clear agenda:
  - o The purpose of the meeting (informational, brainstorming, problem solving, etc.) should be determined beforehand.
  - o Attendees should be clearly informed whether a meeting is mandatory or optional.
- Managers should focus on tasks that are *important* and *not urgent* to prevent time-consuming, urgent problems in the future.
- Work–life balance is a myth; all areas of your life must work harmoniously together.
  - o You must choose a career path that complements your home, community and life goals.

11

Issues New Managers Face

'The secret of success is to do common things extremely well.'

—JOHN D. ROCKEFELLER

Getting promoted to manager can be very exciting. We feel recognized for our track record of superior performance, loyalty to the company, and, in some cases, loyalty to the boss.

But becoming a new manager can be a little frustrating too. After interviewing new managers in the financial services industry, Harvard Professor Linda Hill found that they are surprised by the 'negativity' associated with managerial work. In *Becoming the Manager*, she notes that most of the time employee contact with managers is about problems. These problems may be trivial (such as a printer not working or a bad Internet connection), or they may be more serious (such as problems with customers). The problems are compounded by the fact that many subordinates are not as motivated at work as the manager is, and do not have as much experience as the manager does. They rely on the manager's superior skills and judgement to solve their challenges.

New managers must handle multiple constituencies: superiors, subordinates, peers and, in many cases, customers. These constituents have very specific needs and expectations from the new manager:

- Superiors are tasked with improving the output of the team led by the new manager.
- Subordinates want the new manager to provide them the required resources (budgets, equipment, approvals, visibility, etc.).
- Peers want cooperation and input on issues concerning their departments.
- Customers want the new manager to solve their problems (usually by doing more for less).

When new managers are promoted from within a team, they must manage conflicts involving *loyalty*. Perhaps you have been in one of the roles in the following example:

> Before the manager was promoted, all team members were loyal to one another. All of them shared common concerns about the management. They shared a common approach and saw the same possible solutions to their problems. Now, one of the team

members has been promoted. He is now managing his former friends. The new manager is expected to be loyal to his superiors. The new manager works closely with his superiors on projects that may not have been announced to everyone yet. His friends, now also his subordinates, expect him to share with them all the details that are discussed in the management meetings.

This situation, of being pulled in two different directions, is a constant in the world of management. Fortunately, there are solutions to these challenges, and to other common ones, if one is well prepared for such situations.

Here are a few of the other issues faced frequently by new managers:

- **Being considered outsiders.** Usually, new managers are either promoted from a group of individual contributors or brought in from outside the team (i.e., from within the company or from outside it). When they are from outside the team, they must learn the company culture and earn the trust of the existing team before they can 'boss' anyone around. The challenge is difficult because they must learn the job of their subordinates as well as their own.
- **Envy.** Former peers often struggle when a team member is promoted to manager.
- **Isolation.** It is lonely at the top. The new manager must learn to deal with isolation since he is not one of *them* (subordinates).

- **Being a role model.** Managers must also get used to being viewed as a role model by their teams. It is important to be the 'subordinate' you want to have. As managers, we often criticize our team members for bad behaviour that we ourselves display. Team members are quick to recognize and copy the behaviours of their managers. Managers have to learn to lead by example.
- **Trust.** If the new supervisor is promoted from within the team, usually he is the most skilled and productive person on the team. Even though they have superior skills, new managers need to resist the pressure to complete tasks themselves. They may believe it is easier to do the work themselves rather than trust someone else who is not so skilled or motivated. *Why waste time training someone else,* the new manager thinks, *when I can do it faster myself?*

   Even if the new manager can himself do the work—faster and better-quality work—that doesn't mean he should expect a new team member to match him in proficiency. I have learned to be patient with new team members who are still learning the job. If I try to do all the work myself, I will ultimately create a bottleneck at the workplace. It is far better to give the team time to develop their skills so that we can all work together efficiently to complete projects.

   There is a flip side to this. Some managers mistakenly delegate everything quickly because they are taught the mantra of delegation. Depending on the team, too much delegation may not be advisable or possible, as there is a possibility that team deliverables might suffer. Managers need to learn to assess their team's capabilities to deliver what is expected of the team and know when it is necessary to step in.

- **Lack of trained talent.** It is rare to be put in charge of a team that is fully trained. Training is a new manager's critical responsibility. He may need to train the team in the absence of a formal corporate programme for it.

- **Communication challenges.** Despite flatter organizations and easy access to email, managers must often communicate with their teams in person. People need to hear certain information from their managers directly, if possible.

   Managers get new information mostly from management meetings or from emails sent out to select managers. They need to use their discretion when sharing with their subordinates the information they get. On the other hand, managers need to share information, especially bad news, with their superiors as quickly as possible. The manager's superiors expect him to deliver the bad news quickly so that alternative arrangements can be made to promptly tackle the situation. To 'manage up'—promptly informing their superiors of any new developments—is one of the manager's responsibilities.

- **Building strong relationships.** New managers need to know their team members. More importantly, they need to know each individual's strengths and superpowers. Managers need to understand their team's capabilities and their team's velocity in order to manage their output and external commitments.

Many managers rely on the perceptions of the previous manager about individual team members and deal with the team accordingly. Some of these perceptions may be incorrect. As a new manager, it is often wise to freshly assess each individual in the team. Most employees want their manager to show interest in them as a person (e.g., mentor them on their career, personal issues and growth). This can be valuable. Many good managers choose to invest time in developing their key players.

- **Developing soft skills.** It is very important to demonstrate emotional intelligence as a new manager. Showing empathy for an individual when the time calls for it can strengthen a team. At times, a circumstance may require you to slow down your efforts and allow team members a chance to come back into their own. This balancing act (meeting team needs versus project deliverables) is likely to be a weekly challenge.

- **Prioritizing.** Quite often, companies have a broad vision for their future. They have thought about long-term and short-term goals, and they expect a manager to consider these goals when prioritizing their day. It's important for managers to keep in mind the broader organizational initiatives as they complete immediate project deliverables.

- **Motivation problems.** Some new managers may ask, 'Can't you solve your motivation problems by hiring the right people?' Even if we hired no one except the top 10 per cent of our engineers, it would not solve all of our motivational issues.

Not every team member is driven to make a contribution to the company. Some make a good impression in job interviews but show a lack of initiative once hired. Technical proficiency in a university does not always equate to being a good engineer at work, especially when the company is in the early stages.

Part of being a good manager is learning how to inspire team members who are not driven to do their best work. This requires a good understanding of human psychology.

If our company is indicative of the broader industry, most employees do not feel appreciated or recognized for their contributions. Like most managers, I am still working on meeting this innate human need. As the French philosopher Voltaire once said, 'Appreciation is a wonderful thing. It makes what is excellent in others belong to us as well.' Looking for ways to show your appreciation can go a long way towards getting inconsistent team members to improve their output.

- **Working efficiently.** In many organizations, we must do things that are unproductive or repetitive. Drucker calls these tasks 'productive dis-satisfiers'.

Teams look to the manager to, at the very least, improve the quality of their work life. As managers, we can reduce or eliminate some of these tasks. In many cases, the dis-satisfiers can be done away with or automated. If not, they can be completed by a different person or by another team, which is internal or external.

When I faced these issues for the first time, I was not mature enough to handle them without becoming intensely emotional. I would get depressed and angry and handle them poorly. As a result, I created unnecessary drama and anxiety in our teams.

Experience is a great teacher. Being forced to experience these problems first-hand, I developed resilience and learned to control my emotions.

I hope many new managers can spare themselves this emotional upheaval by becoming aware of these issues by reading about them before they actually encounter them. As managers gain experience, they develop emotional resilience and are able to manage these issues without a lot of drama. The art of management is always changing and it is a constant learning process. With patience and perseverance, it is possible to overcome many of these challenges.

Chapter Summary

Key Points

- New managers must manage:
  o Superiors who need to improve the output of the new manager's team.
  o Subordinates who need the manager to supply the required resources.
  o Customers who want the manager to solve their problems.

- Managers promoted from outside the company must earn the team's trust before they can adequately lead.
- Managers promoted from within the company must deal with the egos of former peers.
- Managers need to communicate in an authoritative yet empathetic/respectful way.
- Managers need to align their priorities with company goals.
- Managers need to mentally prepare for the negativity associated with being constantly confronted with problems.

12

My Notes on the Business of Life

*'Follow effective action with quiet reflection.
From the quiet reflection will come even more
effective action.'*

—PETER DRUCKER

The most successful people I know share one thing in common: they lead intentional lives. They are deliberate regarding everything they do—how they cultivate relationships, how they maintain their health and how they spend their time. One of my key intentions has always been to seek out learning opportunities. Over the past few decades, this intention has led me to realize the following lessons on the business of life.

- The longer you live as an independent, single adult, the harder it becomes to adjust to a new person in your life. When we are in our mid-twenties, we do not think much about delaying marriage. Delaying marriage by a few years into our late twenties has its consequences. We are older when our kids are born. They finish college when we are in our late fifties. We risk running out of life energy.

- For most of us, two incomes are better than one. As our lifestyle aspirations have increased, it is easier to afford more and save more with dual incomes. Both my parents worked. As a lawyer in private practice, my father was self-employed. My mother's monthly salary smoothed out the cash flow issues of uneven income from his self-employment.

  In my family, because both my wife and I work, my children have two professional role models. As a couple, because of our jobs, we have a lot of interests in common, including professional and business matters, which we discuss a lot.

- Marriage and careers can be complementary or can give rise to conflict. A lot depends on the spouse with whom we choose to spend our lives and how we integrate our work and family.

- I've found that high performers seek out and associate with other high performers. In my workplace and socially, I seek out positive people. Many of them are also high performers. They are full of creative energy and possess a positive mindset. By avoiding or limiting my interactions with cynics, my mind can absorb positive information and focus on new opportunities. TV networks are constantly delivering negative news. I avoid these hysterically negative news networks.

- I have learned that I must be careful with my behaviours and actions. If I want team members to report to work on time, I myself need to come to the office on time. If I desire good subordinates, I must be a worthy subordinate myself.

- Fun jobs for life are rare. I've realized it is an uncommon blessing to find a perfect job where everything is in harmony. This includes the daily commute, pay, boss, co-workers, projects and the economy. Most of the time, I had to work in less-than-perfect situations because I was also less than perfect. It takes years to discover our 'genius' and to get paid for being in our 'genius' zone. Once I become good at something, it becomes my passion. A great job becomes a self-fulfilling prophecy.

- Life in large cities, despite the traffic, is better than in a smaller city. There are more job opportunities for career couples. Large cities offer access to facilities that are not available in smaller cities. I lived the first three decades of my life in small cities. There are more life options in the larger cities. Despite all the problems related to urbanization, cities have won. As author and urban expert Edward Glaeser puts it, '[Cities] are proximity, density, closeness. They enable us to work and play together and their success depends on the demand for physical connection.'[1] Inevitably, large cities bring us closer to each other.

- All business models and job roles come with an expiration date. Our best insurance is to stay fit professionally by 'learning' continuously. I see many LinkedIn profiles of people who have switched companies and roles every decade, some by choice and probably some because of economic forces.

- I have learned the hard way not to confuse 'positional' power with my individual 'expertise' power. While being assertive is good, I have made the mistake of being arrogant when I was holding certain jobs. As soon as I left the company, many people stopped returning my phone calls. I mistakenly thought they were interested in talking to me. Well, they *were* interested in talking to my company. Because I was no longer in that position in that company, they did not need to humour me anymore.

- I have realized that I am dispensable, regardless of what I thought about my being 'indispensable'. When someone leaves, others step up and the work group evolves to absorb the space created.

- Companies in our networked economy rely on other firms to complete projects (e.g., handling fulfilment of goods, answering calls, legal and accounting work, and, of course, software development). As a new manager, I used to focus and operate as if I was a buyer who needed to always win (heads I win, tails they lose). However, I have realized that we must create a win-win situation for our partners who may be our suppliers. Good partners are rare. For us to attract and retain a good partner, we must be a good partner first. Many of us do not realize that our promotion increasingly depends on how well we work with external partners to deliver superior results. Maintaining good relationships is good business.

- I have learned to not worry about 'fads' or timing. I act with economic prudence when there is a business need. By taking a longer-term view (usually a decade), I can help improve our company decisions.

- With age and experience, I have become more comfortable with being 'authentic'. I have realized that I will never be all things to all people, all the time. I have become more consistent with my lifestyle choices, behaviours and interactions with my friends and colleagues. In the context of business decisions, many times I was urged to follow the somewhat unsustainable practices of other organizations. Instead, I found it useful to lead from my authentic self and with confidence. Over time, being authentic worked out.

- Customers are smart. If we offer superior products and services consistently, customers will stay. We have worked hard to lead with superior delivery to maintain the sustained growth of our company. During my marketing career, I saw first-hand that a superior product and service beats marketing. Even a good product or service needs to be marketed and sold. But no amount of marketing and sales effort can overcome a poor product or service.

- Initially, we accept an employment because it is the best opportunity or sometimes the only job that is available to us. As time passes, our expectations from our employer change. Eventually, we suffer from unproductive dissatisfaction—we complain about compensation, parking, the cafeteria, etc. Soon, negativity sets in and we complain about our employer to anyone who will listen. These somewhat public complaints and negative talk get back to the employer. I have seen so many of my friends lose their jobs in this way. My friends were unhappy with their employer about everything. I often wondered, 'If everything is so bad, why are you still there?' Eventually, their employer ensures that their future is not with the company. In many cases, they ended up in what appear to be worse positions.

- Exit gracefully. Over the years, there have been times when I left my manager and my employer to pursue a different opportunity. I did my best to ensure that I did not burn any bridges with them. When someone leaves a company, the manager and their existing employer feel rejected. Even if I had got an enviable opportunity, I stayed humble and in touch. In many cases, I had to go back to my previous manager for support that I did not anticipate I would need.

Admirations

'As we express our gratitude, we must never
forget that the highest appreciation is not to
utter words but to live by them.'

—JOHN F. KENNEDY
Thirty-fifth President of the United States

For the last twenty-five years, Microsoft Corporation and its software helped me realize my full potential. I admire Bill Gates for enabling billions of people to realize their full potential through use of his software. I am awed by your intellect, business acumen, hard work and passion for making our world a better place.

What is more inspiring than your business success is your commitment to give away your wealth during your own lifetime through the Bill and Melinda Gates Foundation. Your charter— 'All lives are created equal'— your focus and your knowledge of health care priorities in India leave me amazed. Our world needs more leaders like you, now more than ever.

I admire Satya Nadella for paving the way for aspiring professionals with a technical background to head one of the largest and most powerful corporations in the world. I am amazed at how you learn so much in such a short time, balancing so many competing priorities.

I am inspired by Arjun Malhotra, one of the illustrious alumni of IIT Kharagpur. I first met Arjun in 1985. As a student editor of the *Mechanical Engineering Society Journal*, I needed to raise funds for printing the annual magazine. Prof. M.A. Faruqui of the mechanical engineering department asked me to stop by at his office to meet Arjun, who was with HCL Computers at the time. I requested Arjun to help fund the magazine. It took him less than a second to agree. More importantly, he followed up on his promise, ensuring that HCL sent the payment. He could have easily blown me off or not followed through. Countless people like me have benefited from Arjun's leadership and generosity.

What is more inspiring about Arjun is how he funded many initiatives at IIT Kharagpur, none of which bears his name. In the early 1990s, he set up the Professor G.S. Sanyal School of Communications at IIT Kharagpur to recognize one of his best teachers. Arjun and his wife Kiran established the Professor M.N. Faruqui Innovation Centre at IIT Kharagpur to recognize one of our best teachers there. Not many of us would donate millions of dollars without seeking credit for it.

Even today, Arjun helps others. Despite his busy schedule, he made time to write a foreword for this book. Many coming generations will be inspired by Arjun Malhotra and his selfless acts. Thank you, Arjun, for being a role model for all of us. I want to be like you when I grow up!

I am forever indebted to the Sahai family in Webster City, Iowa, for cheerfully letting me go off to Michigan to complete my MBA. Because of you, my Iowa years were wonderful. I am yet to give up on my plan to return.

I admire one of my first managers, Robert Wintersteen, at Frigidaire, for helping me recognize my potential. I thank you, Bob, for supporting my aspiration to pursue an MBA. Thank you for staying in touch.

I am grateful to many friends at Michigan who helped me succeed in the MBA job market. They include Michigan alumni Serena Allen Glover, Bhanu Singh, John Pollard, Darin Quest, Samir Bagri, Munish Hingorani, Anil Khurana and Rajiv Ranjan. Without your intervention, I would have remained unemployable. I am grateful to each of you.

Thank you, Shirish Nadkarni, for offering me the opportunity to work in my dream job at my dream company. You taught me to focus on customers and de-escalate internal turf wars.

I admire my wonderful colleagues, friends and managers at Microsoft Corporation. David Malcolm, Pat Fox, Stan Sorensen, Keith White, Rich Tong, Russ Stockdale, Bart Wojciehowski, Enzo Schiano, Audrey Watson, Paul Mitchell, Solveig Whittle, Stacey Breyfogle and many others. Thank you.

I admire Thomas Rizzo and Stacy Eckstein for their friendship. It still astounds me that Thomas wrote so many books while working full-time.

I thank our friends Raju and Kavita Gulabani, Dilip and Varsha Naik, Sanjiv and Rajani Rastogi and Rajesh Bansal for their guidance and support over the years.

I am grateful to Verne Harnish and his team at Gazelles for helping us improve our management practices. We were slow to implement their suggestions. When we did, we were grateful.

I thank all the entrepreneurial managers who took a chance with us and managed a fledgling company in its initial years. Your conviction and winning spirit kept us in business. Sometimes I've wondered if you were naive or if we were really on the right track. I am grateful to Darin Quest, Vikram Kumar, Ranvir Singh, Girish Kundlani, Ronojoy Chatterjee, Nilesh Dias, Neha M. Bajpai, Rojan George, Vikas Adke, Anurag Bajpai, Ranbeer Makin, Piyush Trivedi, Farzeen Kochhar, Prakriti C. Sinha, Chayanika Mishra, Sunny Dhuri, Oliver Huslid, Ram Kumar Chandrasekaran, Kartik Shah, Ganeshan Iyer, Joshua Krawitz, Frank Anderson, Amit Ravat, Amit Mirchandani, Arun Kamboj and Girish Nair. All of you taught me a lot about management and entrepreneurship. Even though you never doubted it, in the first ten years our company's survival was tested everyday with every software build. Because of your confidence in the company, I never had self-doubts either.

I am immensely grateful to Vishal Prabhukhanolkar, Naveen Kumar Pallayil and Amrish Shah for giving me the time and space to work on this book. Your insights and actions brought clarity to my thoughts on management.

I admire many of you who run the company every day. I have learned everything I know about management from you. I thank Rakesh Tyagi, Rakshit Gandhi, Vijaya Gowrisankar, Ninad Patankar, Prasad Koli, Vimal V. Rao, Saurabh Srivastava, Ashish Goel, Megha Desai, Nitin Shinde, Rohit Jha, Sandeep Yadav, Sunny Mistry, Archita Joshi, Aquil Arif, Devin Anderson, Ashim Narula, Sagar Shah, Dimple Doshi, Srinivas Kandula, Keshav Polepalle, Wilson Peter, Pratik Agrawal, Nikhil Darjee, Abhishek Mahapatro, Anh Ta, Naveen Babu Dullur, Shraddha Chatpalliwar, Darpan Gupta and Avinash Kumpati.

I was humbled to find out that Aseem Marwaha from eLitmus and Sunil Goyal from Sopra Steria Group distributed thousands of IIT book copies to new engineers. I am grateful for your support.

I thank Penguin Random House for publishing this book. I am grateful to Radhika Marwah, my editor at Random House, for agreeing within just a day to publish my first book. Without your encouragement and support, I would have stopped writing after my first book. Your guidance helped me develop a better book than I could have imagined. I appreciate Caroline Newbury at Penguin Random House for her marketing efforts and for supporting the book. I also thank Kripa Raman and Indrani Dasgupta for putting a final polish on the book through their critical reviews and edits.

I thank my editor-in-chief, Malina Iida for her reviews, her constant questioning and holding me accountable for clarity. I am still learning that the editor is always right. I also thank Elaine Pofeldt, Thomas Cloud and Alex Ferguson for helping me review many drafts of the book. They relentlessly questioned every phrase and word I used to ensure they made sense. I am sorry that it took so long to compile all the words. The book is done now.

Many of my friends at IIT and Iowa State University helped me shape my thoughts on life and management. I thank Guha Seshadri, Partha Pratim Goswami, Deepak Lumba, Shiva Shenoy, Gopi Somayajula, Sudhakar Reddy, Sanjay Mehra, Pankaj Gupta, Ajit A. Phadke, Sandipan Deb, Debabrata Dey, Aditya Nath Jha, Shailendra Kumar, Prasad Vemuri, Chakresh Jain, Joyjit Nath, Rajiv Khemka, Rajesh Singh, Asim Parekh, Manvendra K. Sinha, Rakesh Gupta, Prashant Singh, Veerendra Jaitley, Arun Thomas and Manoj Chugh.

I admire my parents for looking forward to reading my written words with pride. I thank my siblings— Sanjeev and his wife Chhavi, Pankaj and his wife Rita, Mudita and her husband Mohit—for their affection and support. I am happy to acknowledge my nephews and nieces who refuse to admit that they read my book.

To Arpita, my wife and partner, despite being seemingly my opposite, for providing harmonious balance in the business of life, just like Yin and Yang. I lucked out.

I thank my harshest critics, Jay and Shelly. As the Nobel Prize–winner Pearl S. Buck has said, 'The young do not know enough to be prudent, and therefore they attempt the impossible . . . and achieve it, generation after generation.' I hope that you attempt the impossible and achieve it.

'The only thing that we can be sure of the future is that it will be absolutely fantastic.'

—Arthur Clarke in 1964

Appendix A

10x Mindset Scorecard

Building a Future Bigger than your Past

'If you get up in the morning and think the future is going to be better, it is a bright day. Otherwise, it's not.'

—ELON MUSK

Our mindsets determine who we are, how we live and who we become. According to Stanford psychology professor and researcher Carol Dweck, 'The view you adopt for yourself profoundly affects the way you lead your life.'[1] People with a growth mindset believe they can develop the qualities necessary for success and are willing to put in the effort required.

The Mindset Scorecard below lists eight mindsets in various stages of development. To complete the Scorecard, review each of the eight mindsets and find a score that is the closest reflection of you.

Although mindsets may be interdependent, for ease of scoring select a score (1–12) for each mindset independently. To my mind, there is no ideal score. We are all works in progress.

Growth Mindsets	1	2	3	4	5	6	7	8	9	10	11	12	Current Score (1–12)	Future Score (1–12)
Personal Success	*I envy my friends who have 'better' jobs. I feel sorry for myself for not getting a better job. I dislike coming to work. I will change jobs as soon as possible.*			*I am satisfied with my current job for the time being. I worry whether I can keep up with the pressure to learn and change quickly.*			*I am happy with my position and my career direction.*			*I have the best job in the world. I always find something new and interesting to do. I cannot wait to get to work.*				
	I feel poor since I spend more money than I earn. I blame my employer for not paying me enough and for my having to relocate to a new city. I feel guilty that my family has to send me money, even though they have the money.			*I am always stressed since I do not have enough time for all the things I want to do. I feel a lot of pressure from family and friends to spend time with them. I spend a lot of money going out with my friends, which I later regret. I do not know how to manage all areas of my life (work, health, family, friends, community and spirituality). I am hoping that with time, things will improve.*			*I have achieved success in my life. Work is an important part of my life. I understand there is no guarantee of success even with hard work, but without hard work, failure is guaranteed.*			*I have great health. I am improving my exercise and meditation practice (am in the top 5 per cent of population my age). I do not think about money every day to maintain lifestyle. I am optimistic about my future.*				
	I feel sorry for myself because I do not have the success I deserve.						*I have money for a comfortable family life. I am confident of my abilities to persist (grit). Every day, I go home with a great sense of achievement. My health is good. In the last 365 days, I exercised and/or meditated on 292 days (80 per cent of the days).*			*I am inspired by the tremendous opportunities being enabled by the advances in technology. I always aim to make myself better.*				

Growth Mindsets	1	2	3	4	5	6	7	8	9	10	11	12	Current Score (1–12)	Future Score (1–12)
				I am yet to achieve success. I am frustrated that I do not know how to help myself.			*I have many friends at work and outside work. My family members are proud of my achievements.* *I am satisfied with my impact and my success. I do not know what more could be done by me.*							
Learning	*I completed my college degree. I already have a job. I am satisfied with what I know. I am still learning syntax and software tools. I am overwhelmed by all the areas that I need to know. I feel that my team and my supervisor are not training me properly.* *I do not have any interest in reading books.*			*I received my college degree from a good college/university. I am irritated that technology is changing too rapidly for me to keep up with. I am not able to compete with my co-workers.* *Life is too busy to find time to learn anything new. I want to work in a stable industry that does not require new training every week.*			*I am constantly learning and improving my knowledge and skills. MOOCs and vendor certifications allow me to learn and prove my technical competence. I continuously develop expertise on emerging technologies. To master new skills, I volunteer to teach team members. I am developing expertise in upcoming areas. I am committed to lifelong learning.*			*I am always pushing myself to acquire radically different capabilities. I am committed to growing my capabilities in technical and non-technical areas. I am always exploring new learning sources and faster ways to learn. My interests and knowledge are aligned with the company vision. As a result, I enjoy and can easily complete the company's assigned learning objectives.*				

Growth Mindsets	1	2	3	4	5	6	7	8	9	10	11	12	Current Score (1–12)	Future Score (1–12)
				I have not read any books in the last year due to lack of time.			*I read at least twelve books last year to gain actionable insights.*							
Delivery	*I need to be told what to do and how to do it. My work must be reviewed by someone else prior to being sent to the client. My work is often late. I make many mistakes. I do not think about quality. My team leader must remind me to complete work items. I do the minimum that I can get away with. I have fewer responsibilities now than when I began work. I do not understand how work gets done here. I am conflicted about the delivery approach (Agile with fast speed vs Waterfall with reliability). I am confused about which delivery approach is better.*			*Once I am told what to do and how to do it, I complete the work. My work must be reviewed by someone else before it is sent to the client. I complete about 75 per cent my work on time. I do not know how to complete my work items in the estimated time. I find a fast and Agile delivery approach unpredictable and exhausting. I worry about making mistakes in my work. I am yet to learn how to prioritize my time between multiple tasks. I am confused about the company's vision and processes.*			*Once I am told the customer's needs, I figure out what needs to be done and how to do it. My work is flawless and timely. Others do not need to check my work. I understand that fast, Agile delivery provides a competitive advantage to our customers. I deliver software builds daily. I use the latest tools and techniques to speed up delivery. I deliver high-quality software.*			*I am proactive. I figure out opportunities and problems, what needs to be done and how to get it done. I propose and implement the latest technologies in my software designs. I constantly research new ways to improve delivery processes (at half the cost and half the time). I help other teams improve their delivery processes. I am working on transforming the industry with advances in delivery techniques.*				

Growth Mindsets	1	2	3	4	5	6	7	8	9	10	11	12	Current Score (1–12)	Future Score (1–12)
Adopt the latest technology	I like using familiar technologies. I am overwhelmed by changes in the software industry. It is demoralizing for me that as soon as I implement one technology, a new one shows up.			It is exhausting and painful for me to learn new technologies. I am surprised that so many of my peers worldwide have already mastered these technologies. I just do not know how I can keep up with all the technology choices. I am still searching for efficient ways to adopt the latest technologies in my projects.			People admire me as an expert on our processes and software tools. I am comfortable managing competing priorities on my projects (e.g., speed vs quality). My peers and my managers regularly recognize me for consistent, on-time and flawless delivery. I use the latest innovative technologies in my projects. I understand that by adopting new technologies as soon as they are released, we gain efficiency and simplify our work. Reducing work complexity improves team morale and provides great results to our customers.			I am a pioneer in using the latest technologies to solve team and customer problems. I use emerging technologies ahead of our company's industry peers to gain competitive advantage for the company. I contribute to transforming the industry through our code base, add-ons and approaches.				

Growth Mindsets	1	2	3	4	5	6	7	8	9	10	11	12	Current Score (1–12)	Future Score (1–12)
Team	I rely on others to complete my work. I do not understand team goals and responsibilities. Since I do not understand or agree with team goals, I am unwilling to work towards them. My supervisor has never given me any useful feedback. My team members avoid me.			I am an active member of the team. I like working with my team members. I know what is going on with them. However, I am reluctant to take responsibility for team performance. I do not have the time to explain why certain things need to be done. I am still learning how to win the respect of team members.			I model the behaviours the team should follow. I am accepted in a leadership role by my team members. I provide clear direction to my team. Colleagues like to join and stay with my team. I take an active interest in developing and mentoring my team members. I have a great team that delivers outstanding software as expected by our customers. My team and I proactively seek to raise quality standards.			I have created leaders in my team who can manage their teams effectively. My peers look up to me for motivation and advice. I share innovative approaches and knowledge with the entire industry.				

Growth Mindsets	1	2	3	4	5	6	7	8	9	10	11	12	Current Score (1–12)	Future Score (1–12)
Customer success	I implement designs and fix bugs. I am not aware of customer needs or pressures. I do not even like customers. They pressure me and create work for me.			I am constantly working to understand customer needs. I am surprised how often customers change their needs. I am frustrated with the complex designs, approaches and discussions with our customers. I hope to work on assignments where things do not change.			I am proactive and anticipate customer needs. I understand changing customer needs and incorporate the changes as fast as possible. I am solution-oriented. I bring innovative solutions to our customers. I follow through on our commitments. I am asked to present the company to our customers.			I prioritize customer success even if it negatively impacts the existing revenue streams in the short term. I help customers develop a vision (road map) to help them solve their problems and do more with less.				
	I frequently receive negative feedback from customers.			I am shocked when I find that competing teams could complete the work faster and at a lower cost. I am still trying to figure out how others can meet customer needs so easily.			I am efficient in using our customers' time and resources. My customers like working with me and frequently ask me to review their projects.			My customers have a high level of trust in my recommendations. They know that I have no hidden agendas.				

Growth Mindsets	1	2	3	4	5	6	7	8	9	10	11	12	Current Score (1–12)	Future Score (1–12)
Gratitude	I am self-made. When I struggled, no one helped me. Everyone tries to exploit me. The whole system is set up against me.			I desire to live a peaceful life full of gratitude. However, I am frustrated by current needs and demands that restrict or leave me with little time for anyone else. I am still searching for appropriate ways to be grateful. I am not sure how to be grateful to people who helped me.			Every day, I thank many people for all they did for me. I am grateful that I am healthy, I have a job and I have a place to live. I am grateful that I have a way to earn a living for my family and myself.			I am grateful for all the people I have in my life. I am happy for everything I have. I am grateful for the opportunity to share my talents, time and money with the broader society.				
Ownership	I do not have any work or financial ownership. I work as I am told to. No more, no less. New customers and company growth require additional work for my department and me.			I do not know how to accept new customers to grow the company. We already have too much work. I am frustrated that things are so complex. I am hoping to survive this project.			I take ownership of my work and get things done. Work is an important part of my life. I have an owner's mindset. I represent the company in my life (workplace and outside the workplace). I act fast (speed). I change quickly (Agile) to meet market needs. I watch company costs as if spending my own money. I am always aware of and sizing up competitive threats.			I have a Founder's Mentality. My decisions are based on the long-term interest of the company. I am proud of my company. I take ownership for outcomes for many aspects of my company. I use my extensive networks to find out how our services could be improved. I am always analysing disruptive technologies and business models that may drive us out of business.				
Total														

Appendix B

Uncover Your Mindset: Positive and Negative Behavioural Indicators

'I am not what happened to me, I am what I chose to become.'

—CARL GUSTAV JUNG

Understanding our own mindset opens the door to changing ourselves for the better. However, recognizing our mindset is often difficult. As mindsets drive most actions, it may be easier to uncover our mindsets by observing our behaviours. The table below outlines positive and negative behavioural indicators associated with certain mindsets. Comparing our habits against this table may help us identify what types of behavioural changes will improve our performance.

Mindset # 1 – Manage Oneself	
Our success depends on our daily routine and behaviours. Successful people exhibit positive behaviours consistently.	
Positive Indicators	Proud of current job, projects and career direction Seeks balance in all parts of life (career, family, health, spirituality and community) Works hard to be successful Spends time consciously and for productive purposes Arrives at work on time every day Strives to write and speak proper English by checking spelling, grammar and punctuation Manages expenses to save at least 10 per cent of income every month Manages health by eating properly Exercises regularly to stay healthy Understands that to earn more, you have to be more—i.e., you need to offer value to the world in order to receive recognition Invests in and attracts positive, growth-oriented people Resourcefully provides solutions to problems
Negative Indicators	Lacks pride in current job, but will be proud of future job Struggles to manage life. Cannot balance work versus family versus health versus spirituality versus community. Does not know that it is possible to incorporate work into other aspects of life Seeks a job that pays well and requires no work Does the minimum work one can get away with Usually late to work and provides excuses for tardiness (faulty alarm, traffic, bad weather, etc.) Makes no effort to improve English communication skills Unclear about career direction Never exercises Does not save and instead spends income unproductively, such as on depreciating assets, expensive restaurants, entertainment, etc. Uses time unproductively Does not recognize that income depends on value added, and that job hopping only works for so long Hangs out with people who are not interested in growing themselves Constantly points out problems but never provides solutions

Mindset # 2 – Manage Learning	
Successful people spend significant time every week acquiring knowledge. With rapid technological change, a disciplined approach to learning ensures that we stay competitive.	
Positive Indicators	Commits to learning goals for the next three to five years Sets quarterly goals to gain the skills required for higher-level positions Subscribes to key industry publications, newsletters, Facebook pages, Twitter feeds, etc. Regularly completes courses and certifications that are relevant to work Keeps pace with new sources of learning and takes advantage of informal growth opportunities, such as engaging with experts Reads at least one book a month Watches at least one educational video (TED.com, YouTube, etc.) or one documentary a month Shares educational resources with colleagues, family, friends and the community Converts knowledge into actionable insights for self and team Maintains awareness and understanding of key technology trends
Negative Indicators	Not committed to learning Must be forced to learn No plan for any new learning in the foreseeable future Unaware of non-traditional sources of learning Did not read any books after college Does not watch any career or industry-related movies/videos Does not use new knowledge in any useful way Not interested in learning about industry changes

Mindset # 3 – Manage Delivery	
Delivers work products such as code, reports, documents and training well. Consistently exceeds position requirements and expectations. Follows work processes and quality standards.	
Positive Indicators	Commits to excellence in all work products, whether that means delivering high-quality software or creating a training programme around the newest tools Possesses good technical knowledge of software languages, processes and customer business problems Reviews work items to provide daily status reports Delivers software builds daily Completes work as per effort estimates Follows coding standards, templates, processes and engineering best practices Follows best practices for security and privacy Work is accurate and timely Keeps work item progress current in project management software Seeks clarification on unclear guidelines and requirements Focuses and prioritizes well on key issues Seeks to improve quality of solutions Follows through on commitments
Negative Indicators	Is not concerned about the quality of deliverables. Work often includes coding mistakes, poor spacing, incorrect alignments in user interface, spelling and grammar errors Does not learn from mistakes Lacks attention to detail Does not keep knowledge current with job requirements Does not review status of projects or deliverables Does not check in code every day to ensure daily builds are delivered Does not follow standards, templates, processes and engineering best practices Does not come to the office and meetings on time. Keeps team waiting. Prioritizes poorly Blames others for mistakes Frequently forgets tasks Often finishes work late Easily distracted by phone calls, texts and WhatsApp messages Estimates effort required for tasks inaccurately, resulting in missed deadlines Has to be chased to follow up

Mindset # 4 – Use the Latest Technology	
Technology is transforming all aspects of our life. Societies, companies and individuals that take advantage of new technology first will advance first.	
Positive Indicators	Mines the latest software programs and techniques for opportunities to increase efficiency Updates software on all PCs, cell phones and other devices as soon as updates are available Simplifies the team's work by adopting and promoting the latest software and hardware Saves money by researching products and shopping online Uses cloud technology to get organized and save time
Negative Indicators	Not interested in using new technology trends to advance Acquires new technology only when the old one stops working. 'If it ain't broke, don't fix it.' Never shops online Resists use of the latest technologies Scared of cloud technology because it's unfamiliar and change is difficult

Mindset # 5 – Manage Teamwork	
We can achieve more professional success through teamwork. High-performance members build and improve great teams.	
Positive Indicators	Is a highly productive member of a team Is a role model for the team Cooperates with team members and mentors Understands development needs of team members Completes work without supervision Is respected by team members Works towards goals of the team and organization Is open to feedback and suggestions, and receives feedback with a positive attitude Explains 'why', in addition to 'what' needs to be done Provides constructive feedback to team members and mentors Trains team members to improve expertise and increase team's productivity Recruits high-calibre team members Guides team members to help them improve their performance based on their individual needs
Negative Indicators	Does not contribute to the team Disrupts team's productivity, often increasing the workload of others Sets a poor example for the team Does not cooperate with others Needs constant supervision Drags down morale Does not work towards goals of the team and organization Is not open to feedback

Mindset #6 – Manage Customer Success	
If we align our efforts with the needs of our customers, they will be more successful. If our customers are more successful, we will be more successful.	
Positive Indicators	Understands customers' problems and their organizational pressures Is trusted advisor for customers for solid recommendations Unblocks internal teams to help solve customer problems Follows up on customer questions and requests with clearly understandable answers Channels customer issues to appropriate group within the company Develops business by identifying potential opportunities to help customers Proposes, develops and explains suitable solutions to customers Develops collaborative relationships with customers Prioritizes long-term customer success over short-term revenue gains Gets positive feedback from customers Receives customer requests to be on their team Seeks feedback on how to improve delivery services Actively promotes higher service standards across the organization, such as different approaches, the latest software, best practices and newer tools Develops customer relationships at multiple levels and across departments
Negative Indicators	Does not understand customer context and their organizations Makes recommendations in which customers do not have confidence Unable and unwilling to unblock teams and move projects forward Forgets to follow up on customer requests Yet to find an opportunity to help customers beyond what is assigned Does not invest in relationships with customers Is not concerned about customer success Customers provide negative feedback Customers request that he be not a part of their team No interest in improving delivery of services

Mindset # 7 – Be Grateful	
With a gratitude mindset and behaviours, our brain changes to recognize the goodness in people and circumstances. While we may not be able to change the circumstances or people in our life immediately, we can change our responses to them.	
Positive Indicators	Expresses gratitude for all that life offers us everyday Sees the glass as half full Thanks people regularly, whether in person, by letter, or by email Maintains a gratitude diary Thinks of ways to give back to the community
Negative Indicators	Complains about everything and everyone in life Sees glass as half empty Does not thank anyone, either implicitly or explicitly Complains bitterly that everyone is unfair and unkind

Mindset # 8 – Take Ownership	
Successful people act like owners of the company. As they seek to advance the company, they advance their careers.	
Positive Indicators	At war with industry competitors that are delivering slow IT in a fast IT environment Seeks to work on behalf of underserved customers Takes responsibility for outcomes Bias towards speed and action Adopts change quickly Evaluates long-term impact of key decisions Takes personal responsibility for employee actions and how resources are used Is frugal with company money Knows that for each dollar spent, company has to bring in ten dollars Presents a positive image of the company in the workplace, with customers, while recruiting and when dealing with suppliers Always seeks new opportunities to improve the company Works to keep everything simple
Negative Indicators	Not interested in doing better than the industry norms (e.g., satisfied with slow IT mode) Slow to decide and act Does not adopt change Does not consider long-term impact of decisions Does not take responsibility for employee actions (blames others) Is wasteful with company resources Negatively talks about work, mentor, team and the company to everyone, including self Does not look for easy and simple approaches

Adapted from *How to be an Even Better Manager* by Michael Armstrong

Appendix C

Highest Educational Qualifications of Key Technology Company CEOs

Company	CEO Name	Highest Degree Earned
IBM Global Technology Services	Virginia (Ginni) Rometty	Bachelor of Science in computer science and electrical engineering from Northwestern University
HP Services	Meg Whitman	Bachelor of Arts in economics from Princeton University, MBA from Harvard University
Cognizant Technology Solutions	Francisco D'Souza	Bachelor's in Business Administration from the University of East Asia, MBA from Carnegie-Mellon University
Infosys	Vishal Sikka	Bachelor of Science in computer science from Syracuse University, PhD in computer science from Stanford University
Tech Mahindra	C.P. Gurnani	Chemical engineering degree from the National Institute of Technology, Rourkela

Tata Consultancy Services (TCS)	Rajesh Gopinathan	Bachelor of Engineering in electrical and electronics from NIT Tiruchirappally; MBA from IIM Ahmedabad
Accenture	Pierre Naterme	Master of Science in management from Ecole Supérieure des Sciences Économiques et Commerciales Business School
CapGemini	Paul Hermelin	Ecole Polytechnique in 1972 and the Ecole Nationale d'Administration (ENA) in 1978
Sogeti	Hans van Waayenburg	Technical Bachelor programme at the University of Eindhoven in the Netherlands
WIPRO Technologies	Abidali Neemuchwala	Bachelor of Engineering, National Institute of Technology, Raipur, and MTech in industrial engineering, IIT Bombay
HCL Technologies	Anant Gupta	Bachelor of Science in physics, Master of Science in engineering from the University of Liverpool, UK
Persistent Technologies	Anand Deshpande	BTech (Hons) in computer science and engineering from IIT Kharagpur, Master's and PhD in computer science from Indiana University, Bloomington
Mindtree	Krishnakumar Natarajan	Bachelor's degree in mechanical engineering from the College of Engineering, Chennai; MBA from the Xavier Institute, Jamshedpur

Appendix D

Suggested Reading

'Whether I'm at the office, at home, or on the road, I always have a stack of books I'm looking forward to reading'

—BILL GATES

Every few years, a new book is published that addresses key questions or issues faced by our company and probably the entire industry. These books may address questions in the context of broader economic conditions, sometimes about implementation of new business practices, and sometimes about advancing the company to the next stage. Some of these books are easy to read, while others take some effort.

As a manager, it is my job to curate and promote books relevant to our business. One of my key challenges is to ensure that members of the core management team are aligned with one another. And if we are reading the same book, alignment is more likely.

When I meet with key leaders, the first question we often ask each other is, 'What book are you reading these days?' There is a sense of hunger for good sources of ideas and information. Over the years, we have started a practice of gifting books to team members on their work anniversaries.

I have selected ten authors who helped me grow over the years. A lot of their work is based on empirical research and studies of people and companies. Many of these authors' sixteen-minute talks are available on Internet channels (blogs, TED and YouTube). A number of these thought leaders write in terms of 'next practices' as opposed to current benchmarks or 'best practices'. As a practising manager, I use their 'how to' approach to apply their insights to our company.

If there is one book I ask our MBA hires to read before they join our company, it is the *PMI-Agile Certified Practitioner (ACP) Exam Prep* (recommended book number five, below). This book helps guide new hires through those often-difficult first three months of work, and provides them much-needed solutions to common problems.

The following books also provide key insights, addressing business and personal concerns in a manner I have found very useful throughout my career.

Management

1. *Great by Choice*, by Jim Collins and Morten T. Hansen (New York: HarperCollins, 2011).

Jim Collins continues to have a significant impact on management thinking. Among other things, his writings allowed us to feel better about taking a long-term view of company success.

One of his earliest books, *Built to Last: Successful Habits of Visionary Companies,* helped us maintain sanity in the early stages of our company. We translated many of the concepts in his book into ideas for the software engineering world (e.g., clock building vs time telling).

His second major book, *Good to Great,* helped us get over the popular (but false) sentiment that being charismatic was a precondition for success as a leader. Collins also emphasizes the importance of disciplined thoughts and actions within the organization. By converting many of the simple ideas in the book to our management practices, we've delivered sustained growth over the last decade. Even though many examples in the book are from large Fortune 500 companies, we were able to tailor his ideas to suit a smaller company.

Every year, we review *Good to Great* diagnostic tools with our core management team to remind ourselves of our key practices.

In his latest book, *Great by Choice,* Collins provides examples of many companies that thrived despite chaos, uncertainty and bad luck. Among other things, these 10X companies were paranoid about events that might turn against them without warning at the most inconvenient moment. These ambitious 10X companies prepared themselves for productive action during both good times and bad times.

Any of these three books will provide the reader with new management perspectives.

2. *The Essential Drucker,* by Peter F. Drucker (New York: HarperCollins: 2001).

The father of modern management, Peter F. Drucker, curated sixty years of his writings and published this book in 2001 (four years before his death at age ninety-five). In this book, he has compiled his thoughts on management, on us as individuals, and on the broader society.

Drucker advises us, as individuals, to focus on our contributions (not titles), know and use our strengths (not focus on fixing weaknesses), know and use our time wisely and focus on the quality of our decisions. Every few years, a book I'm reading refers to a point Drucker has made, and all over again I'm inspired to head back to his original writing. Despite being written decades ago, his original work is very inspiring and highly relevant to addressing any and all management challenges.

More than thirty years ago, in 1985, Peter Drucker published his views on technology start-ups in *Innovation and Entrepreneurship*. In this book, he addresses many common misconceptions and mistakes that are still quite relevant to technology companies today. This could be a good place to start with Drucker's writings.

3. *The Founder's Mentality: How to Overcome the Predictable Crisis for Growth,* by Chris Zook and James Allen (Boston: Harvard Business Review Press, 2016).

Based on decades of research by leading management consulting firm Bain and Company, this book helped us increase self-awareness within our company.

As a management team, we realized that many of our business realities were normal for insurgent companies at war against their own industry. We felt reassured of our strengths (a focus on undeserved customers, lack of bureaucracy, low organizational complexity and a strong emphasis on costs). The book focuses on key challenges faced by smaller, insurgent companies as they try to grow in a sustained manner against large, established, incumbent organizations. Since the publication of this book, we have been conveying its concepts to new management recruits and existing leaders.

4. *Developing Management Skills,* by David A. Whetten and Kim S. Cameron (New Jersey: Pearson: 2015, 9th Edition)

Although this is a textbook used in management programmes, I found it very useful in learning people management skills. During our MBA coursework, most of us were required to take a basic course in organizational behaviour. Many of us treated this course as not directly relevant to our future career.

Now that we are outside of the hyper-competitive world of MBA schooling, we've read this book regularly to revisit the basics and learn how to apply them to our company. The book includes diagnostics tests and case studies that are applicable across industries and geographies.

5. *PMI-Agile Certified Practitioner (ACP) Exam Prep*, by
   Mark Griffiths (RMC Publications, 2015)

As the speed of business continues to increase, all
industries are being forced to follow Agile management
principles. Even though this book is written in the
context of the fast-changing software industry, the
approaches and techniques shared in the book are very
practical. We review this examination preparation
book regularly to train new MBA graduates who have
joined our company. Many MBA graduates with prior
industry experience find it unsettling having to unlearn
old approaches to management. I review this book
every year to remind myself of its key management
concepts.

6. *The Advantage*, by Patrick Lencioni (San Francisco:
   Jossey-Bass, 2012)

Even though one of Lencioni's earlier books, *The Five
Dysfunctions of a Team*, continues to be more popular,
I like *The Advantage* because it consolidates ideas from
many of his earlier books. As companies grow, maintaining
a strong leadership team with diverse backgrounds and
viewpoints becomes more difficult. Holding productive
business meetings is another challenge. The exercises in
this book have helped us improve our own company's
organizational health. Our leadership team is still a work
in progress, but we would be worse off today without
this book.

7. *The Checklist Manifesto: How to Get Things Right,* by Atul Gawande (New York: Henry Holt, 2009)

This simple book helped us improve the quality of our software work. As complexity has grown in all areas of our life, a simple paper checklist has helped us significantly reduce errors. In fact, I expect mistakes whenever we do not have a checklist or use an incorrect checklist. Even though Gawande provides non-business-related examples of checklists used by highly-skilled surgeons to improve patient outcomes, we have used checklists for improving software delivery that grew out of the concepts shared in this book.

8. *Lean Software Development: An Agile Toolkit,* by Mary Poppendieck and Tom Poppendieck (New Jersey: Pearson and Addison-Wesley, 2003)

The authors of this book translated ideas from Lean manufacturing practices into concepts for knowledge work, especially software development. Having spent time in the manufacturing sector that evolved into following Lean practices in the late 1980s and 1990s, I relate to the concepts in the book.

As the entire industry transforms how knowledge work is done, I use the concepts from this book to train our various teams. As I shared concepts from the book with our teams, we reduced initial employee resistance and changed our mindset towards Agile software development practices. There are additional books by the same authors, which cover additional aspects of software development.

Personal

9. *Mindset: The New Psychology of Success*, by Carol Dweck (New York: Ballantine, 2006)

This book is being used by the CEOs of leading companies to encourage employees to develop a growth mindset in approaching their professional and personal goals. With a growth mindset, our brain can foster learning and we can push our way through to accomplishing big goals. Before becoming familiar with this book, I used to focus only on our past abilities and past talents to solve problems. Over time, we have realized that it is more important to learn how to persevere when solving problems.

10. *The Power of Habit: Why We Do What We do in Life and Business*, by Charles Duhigg (New York: Random House, 2012)

Because I am always trying to improve my personal results and the performance of our organization, I had to learn about habits and their long-term importance. This book helped me analyse my own habits, what may have caused them, and how to alter them. Organizations too have habits, which shape our behaviours and have their own consequences. Before I read this book, I had no awareness about my daily actions, which were actually my habits and what caused these habits and how I could change them.

Appendix E

US Fortune 500 Churn

1976	1996	2016
AT&T	AT&T	AT&T
Chevron	Chevron	Chevron
Exxon Mobil	Exxon Mobil	Exxon Mobil
Ford Motor	Ford Motor	Ford Motor
GE	GE	GE
GM	GM	GM
Chrysler	Chrysler	Amazon.com
DuPont	DuPont	Amerisource Bergan
IBM	IBM	Apple
Mobil	Mobil	Berkshire Hathaway
Proctor & Gamble	Proctor & Gamble	Costco
Texaco	Texaco	CVS Health

Amoco	HP	HP
Atlantic Richfield	Wal-Mart	Wal-Mart
CBS	Altria Group	Fannie Mae
Conoco	Citicorp	Kroger
Gulf Oil	Kmart Holding	McKesson
ITT Industries	Prudential	UnitedHealth Group
Shell Oil	Sears Roebuck	Verizon
U.S. Steel	State Farm	Walgreens Boot Alliance

Only six of the top twenty US Fortune 500 organizations remained in the top twenty over the last forty years. In that time, many other companies appeared and disappeared from the list.

Notes

Foreword

1. The System-2 was an Intel-based minicomputer that helped launch the Indian computer market.

Preface

1. With a smaller population, South Korea transformed itself economically. Its per capita income increased from $317 (in 1971) to $13,255 (in 1996), by a factor of 42. For 2015, South Korea's per capita income is $27,221.

2. 'GDP Per Capita: China vs India', World Bank, accessed 11 April 2017, https://www.google.com/publicdata/explore?ds=d5bncppjof8f9_&met_y=ny_gdp_pcap_cd&idim=country:CHN:IND&hl=en&dl=en#!ctype=l&strail=false&bcs=d&nselm=h&met_y=ny_gdp_pcap_cd&scale_y=lin&ind_y=false&rdim=region&idim=country:CHN:IND&ifdim=region&hl=en_US&dl=en&ind=false.

1. Do You Need an MBA to Be a Great Manager?

1. Adarsh Jain, 'Out of three lakh MBA graduates every year, only 10 per cent are employable: Experts', *Economic*

Times, 13 January 2015, accessed 12 July 2017, http://economictimes.indiatimes.com/industry/services/education/out-of-three-lakh-mba-graduates-every-year-only-10-are-employable-experts/articleshow/45867352.cms.

2. Ruth Simon, 'For Newly Minted M.B.A.s, a Smaller Paycheck Awaits', *The Wall Street Journal*, 6 January 2013, accessed 12 July 2017, http://www.wsj.com/articles/SB10001424127887324296604578175764143141622.

3. Ryan Dezember and Lindsay Gellman, 'Do Buyout Kings Need MBAs?', *The Wall Street* per cent *Journal*, 4 June 2015, accessed 12 July 2017, http://www.wsj.com/articles/do-buyout-kings-need-m-b-a-s-1433349048.

4. Mintzberg, Henry. *Managers Not MBAs: A Hard Look at the Soft Practice of Managing and Management Development*, Berrett-Koehler Publishers Inc., San Francisco, 2004, p. 6.

5. For a current list of top MBA schools, *see Bloomberg Businessweek*, accessed 12 July 2017, https://www.bloomberg.com/features/2016-best-business-schools.

6. *See* Sheryl Sandberg, Quora Post: 'Did Sheryl Sandberg find her MBA Helpful . . .', accessed 12 July 2017, https://www.quora.com/Did-Sheryl-Sandberg-find-her-MBA-helpful-Did-it-lend-additional-credibility-or-other-advantages/answer/Sheryl-Sandberg.

7. Natalie Kitroeff and Patricia Clark, 'Silicon Valley Wants MBAs More Than Wall Street Does', *Bloomberg Businessweek*, 17 March 2016.

8. Drucker, Peter. *The Effective Executive*, HarperCollins, New York, 2006.

9. This interview with Mintzberg, transcript published by the *Harvard Business Review*, describes the professor's management philosophy, accessed 12 July 2017, https://hbr.org/2009/03/rethinking-the-mba.html.

2. Navigating Our Strange World of Organizations

1. *Creative Destruction Whips through Corporate America*, Innosight, Executive Summary, Winter 2012, accessed 12 July 2017, https://www.innosight.com/wp-content/uploads/2016/08/creative-destruction-whips-through-corporate-america_final2015.pdf. For a more detailed explanation, *see:* Richard N. Foster and Sarah Kaplan, *Creative Destruction: Why Companies That Are Built to Last Underperform the Market—and How to Successfully Transform Them*, Doubleday, New York, 2001.

3. Jongsoo Kim, Joon Mahn Lee, and Joonhyung Bae, 'Founder CEOs and Innovation: Evidence from S&P 500 Firms', *SSRN eLibrary*, 17 February 2016, accessed 11 April 2017, https://ssrn.com/abstract=2733456.

4. Mintzberg, Henry. *Mintzberg on Management: Inside our strange world of organisations*, Free Press, Florence, 1989, pp. 218–19.

3. Why Do We Need Managers?

1. John Kotter, 'Accelerate!' *Harvard Business Review*, November 2012, accessed 11 April 2017, https://hbr.org/2012/11/accelerate.

2. Viren Doshi, Gaurav Moda, Anshu Nahar and Jai Sinha, 'Taking the leadership leap & developing an effective executive pipeline for India's future', *strategy &* (2012), accessed 11 April 2017, http://www.strategyand.pwc.com/media/file/Strategyand_Taking-the-Leadership-Leap.pdf and ManpowerGroup '2015 Talent Shortage Survey,' *ManpowerGroup* (2015): accessed 11 April 2017, http://www.manpowergroup.com/wps/wcm/connect/db23c560-08b6-485f-9bf6-f5f38a43c76a/2015_Talent_Shortage_Survey_US-lo_res.pdf?MOD=AJPERES.

3.   Randall Beck and James Harter, 'Why Good Managers Are So Rare', *Harvard Business Review*, March 2014, accessed 11 April 2017, https://hbr.org/2014/03/why-good-managers-are-so-rare.

4.   Magretta, Joan. *What Management Is: How It Works and Why It's Everyone's Business*, HarperCollins, London, 2002.

5.   Richard P. Eibach, Justin P. Friesen, Adam Galinsky and Aaron C. Kay, 'Seeking structure in social organization: Compensatory control and the psychological advantages of hierarchy', *Journal of Personality and Social Psychology*, vol. 106, 2014, pp. 590–609.

4.   What Does a Manager Do?

1.   Ibid.

2.   Drucker, Peter. *The Essential Drucker*, HarperCollins, New York, 2001, pp. 207–08.

3.   Mintzberg, Henry. *Mintzberg on Management*, Free Press, New York, 1989, pp. 15–20.

4.   In his study of the entrepreneur's decision-making role, Mintzberg observed two patterns of behaviour in CEOs: First, many development initiatives do not involve a single decision or even a group of decisions. Rather, they involve small actions sequenced over time. CEOs prolong each project so that they can fit them bit by bit into their busy and disjointed schedules. Mintzberg speculates that it is done this way to ensure that the CEO comprehends any relevant complex issues and operational changes that may be required. Second, the CEOs Mintzberg studied supervised as many as fifty development initiatives at a time. Some projects required adoption of new processes or new software. Some required marketing campaigns related to content marketing. Others dealt with employee morale or upgradation of corporate portals to improve information

flow. The chief executives somehow kept an inventory of the corporate initiatives at various stages of development, some active while others were in limbo. Mintzberg likens them to a juggler; while several projects are active and in the air, others come down. Over time, another initiative is given an energy boost and gains importance. At various times, new projects become priorities and others are discarded.

5. This theme of handling 'unexpected events', runs through many of the books by Drucker and Sayles.

6. Pink, Daniel H. *To Sell is Human: The Surprising Truth About Moving Others*, Penguin, New York, 2012, p. 194.

7. Marcus Buckingham and Curt Coffman, *First, Break All the Rules: What the World's Greatest Managers Do Differently*, Simon & Schuster, New York, 1999, p. 63.

8. Kotter, John. *Force for Change: How Leadership Differs from Management*, Free Press, New York, 1990, p. 4.

9. Vic Gundotra, 24 August 2011, accessed 12 July 2017, https://plus.google.com/+VicGundotra/posts/gcSStkKxXTw.

10. Sayles, Leonard J. *The Working Leader: The Triumph of High Performance over Conventional Management Principles*, Simon & Schuster, New York, 1993, p. 28.

11. Ibid., p. 99.

12. *Business Dictionary*, s.v. 'Responsibility', accessed 11 April 2017, http://www.businessdictionary.com/definition/responsibility.html.

13. Ibid., 'Accountability'.

14. Ibid., 'Authority'.

15. William Oncken Jr and Donald L. Wass, 'Management Time: Who's Got the Monkey?' *Harvard Business Review* (Nov–Dec 1999). Originally published in November–December 1974 issue.

16. Harvard Business Review Press. *Delegating Work: 20 Minute Manager Series*, Harvard Business School Publishing Corporation, Boston, 2014.

5. Please Understand My Style

1. David A. Garvin, 'How Google Sold Its Engineers on Management', *Harvard Business Review*, December 2013, accessed 11 April 2017, https://hbr.org/2013/12/how-google-sold-its-engineers-on-management.
2. http://www.16personalities.com

6. Training

1. David W. Merrill and Roger H. Reid, *Personal Styles and Effective Performance*, CRC Press, Boca Raton, 1981.
2. Fortune Editors, 'The results of the 2015 Fortune 500 survey are in', *Fortune*, 4 June 2015, accessed 11 April 2017, http://fortune.com/2015/06/04/fortune-500-ceo-survey.
3. *See* Appendix E.
4. According to the Library of Economics and Liberty, Schumpeter first coined the phrase 'creative destruction' in 1942, in his book *Capitalism, Socialism, and Democracy*, published by Harper & Brothers, New York, 1942, accessed 12 July 2017, http://www.econlib.org/library/Enc/CreativeDestruction.html.
5. Peters, Tom. *Thriving on Chaos: Handbook for a Management Revolution*, HarperCollins, New York, 1987, pp. 391–94.
6. Bandura, Albert. 'Self-efficacy Mechanism in Human Agency', *American Psychologist*, vol. 37, no. 2, 1982, p. 122.
7. Donald O. Clifton and Tom Rath, *How full is your bucket?*, Gallup Press, New York, 2004.

8. As cited on the webpage, 'Passages by Albert Bandura', accessed 12 July 2017, https://www.uky.edu/~eushe2/Pajares/effquotes.html. Quote is from Bandura's 1997 book *Self-Efficacy: The Exercise of Control*, W.H. Freeman and Company, New York, p. 77.

9. The Mazur Group, accessed 23 January 2017, http://mazur.harvard.edu/research/detailspage.php?rowid=8.

10. For further information on the flipped-classroom model, see this video from the Khan Academy, accessed 12 July 2017, https://www.khanacademy.org/resources/using-technology-in-the-classroom/four-different-blended-learning-models/v/sscc-blended-flipped.

11. In February 2005, Bill Gates spoke about the 3Rs at the national education summit on high schools. Speech transcript here, accessed 12 July 2017, http://www.gatesfoundation.org/media-center/speeches/2005/02/bill-gates-2005-national-education-summit.

7. On Motivation

1. Exact figures, according to GE's website, stand at 26.8 billion in 1980 to 'nearly' 130 billion in 2000, accessed 11 April 2017, https://www.ge.com/about-us/leadership/profiles/john-f-welch-jr.

2. Harper, F.W. *Why Wages Rise*, The Foundation for Economic Education, New York, 1957.

3. Marc Andreessen, 'Why Software is Eating the World', *The Wall Street Journal*, 20 August 2011, accessed 11 April 2017, http://www.wsj.com/articles/SB10001424053111903480904576512250915629460.

4. Gallup Poll, 'Employee Engagement in U.S. Stagnant in 2015', *Gallup, Inc.*, 13 January 2016, accessed 11 April 2017, http://www.gallup.com/poll/188144/employee-engagement-stagnant-2015.aspx.

5. McGregor, Douglas. *The Human Side of Enterprise*, McGraw-Hill, New York, 1960. The annotated edition (2006) has Theory X and Theory Y chapters inside part one of the book. *The Economist* also described the concepts in brief here, accessed 12 July 2017, http://www.economist.com/node/12370445 (6 October 2008).

6. Taylor, Frederick Winslow. *The Principles of Scientific Management*, Harper & Brothers, New York, 1911. Taylor believed in using the scientific method to train and, consequently, motivate workers. Taylor's methods increased productivity. Henry Ford was an early supporter of Taylor's scientific principles.

7. Herzberg, Frederick. 'One More Time: How do You Motivate Employees?', *Harvard Business Review*, January 2003, accessed 11 April 2017, https://hbr.org/2003/01/one-more-time-how-do-you-motivate-employees.

8. Adapted from Herzberg, ibid.

9. Gallup has been measuring employee engagement since 1997 and has obtained data from over 1.8 million employees. The 2016 Gallup Q12 Meta-Analysis Report can be found here, accessed 12 July 2017, http://www.gallup.com/services/191489/q12-meta-analysis-report-2016.aspx?g_source=Q12&g_medium=search&g_campaign=tiles.

10. Pink, Daniel H. *Drive: The Surprising Truth about What Motivates Us*, Riverhead, New York, 2009.

11. The various theories of motivation can be categorized into three broadly labelled groups: content (an employee's 'internal' drive), process (the ability of the employees to 'maintain' their motivation) and outcome (how an employee responds to various 'consequences' or reactions within a workplace, e.g., a difficult caller, a thank-you email from a customer, etc.). *See* Pablo Cardona and Alvaro Espejo, 'Basics in Work Motivation,' *IESE: International Graduate School of Management*, 2004.

12. David A. Whetten and Kim S. Cameron, *Developing Management Skills*, Pearson, New Jersey, 2011.

13. Duckworth, Angela. *Grit: Passion, Perseverance, and the Science of Success*, Scribner, New York, 2016, p. 14.

14. Dweck, Carol. *Mindset: The New Psychology of Success*, Ballantine, New York, 2006, p. 6.

15. Whetten and Cameron, *Developing Management Skills*, p. 327.

16. Whetten and Cameron, *Developing Management Skills*, pp. 346–47.

8. Providing Feedback

1. Sheila Heen and Douglas Stone, *Thanks for the Feedback: The Science and Art of Receiving Feedback Well*, Viking, New York, 2014.

2. Beverly Kaye and Sharon Jordan-Evans, *Love 'Em or Lose 'Em*, Berrett-Koehler Publishers, San Francisco, 2008.

3. Armstrong, Michael. *How to be an Even Better Manager*, Kogan Page, London, 2011.

4. Unfortunately, the latest edition of Armstrong's book has removed the Positive and Negative Indicators list, so please refer to the older editions.

5. Lencioni, Patrick. *The Five Dysfunctions of a Team: A Leadership Fable*, Jossey-Bass, San Francisco, 2002.

6. Shellenbarger, Sue. 'How to Take Criticism Well', *The Wall Street Journal*, 18 June 2014, accessed 11 April 2017, http://www.wsj.com/articles/how-to-take-criticism-well-1403046866.

7. Ibid.

8. Heen and Stone. *Thanks for the Feedback*.

9. Can I Retain the Right People?

1. Beverly Kaye and Sharon Jordan-Evans, Love 'Em or Lose 'Em, Berrett-Koehler Publishers, San Francisco, 2008.

2. Adapted from Kaye and Jordan-Evans, Love 'Em or Lose 'Em. *See* more at, accessed 12 July 2017, https://www. shrm.org/resourcesandtools/tools-and-samples/hr-forms/ pages/stayinterviewquestions.aspx.

10. Why Are We So Busy?

1. Ryan Avent, 'Why Do We Work So Hard?', April–May 2016, accessed 11 April 2017, https://www.1843magazine. com/features/why-do-we-work-so-hard.

2. United States Department of Labor, 'American Time Use Survey Summary', USDL-16-1250, Washington, DC, 2016, accessed 11 April 2017, https://www.bls.gov/news. release/atus.nr0.htm.

3. Frankki Bevins and Aaron De Smet, 'Making Time Management the Organization's Priority', *McKinsey Quarterly*, January 2013, accessed 11 April 2017, http:// www.mckinsey.com/business-functions/organization/ our-insights/making-time-management-the-organizations- priority.

4. Chris Brahm, Greg Caimi and Michael C. Mankins, 'Your Scarcest Resource', *Harvard Business Review*, May 2014, accessed 11 April 2017, https://hbr.org/2014/05/your- scarcest-resource.

5. Patrick Lencioni, *Death by Meeting: A Leadership Fable About Solving the Most Painful Problem in Business*, Jossey-Bass, San Francisco, 2004.

6. 'The results of the 2015 Fortune 500 survey are in', *Fortune*, 4 June 2015, accessed 11 April 2017, http:// fortune.com/2015/06/04/fortune-500-ceo-survey.

7. Peter Drucker, *The Effective Executive*, HarperCollins, New York, 2006.

8. Stephen R. Covey, *The 7 Habits of Highly Effective People: Powerful Lessons in Personal Change*, Simon & Schuster, New York, 1989, p. 151.

9. Jack Welch and Suzy Welch, *The Real-Life MBA: Your No-BS Guide to Winning the Game, Building a Team, and Growing Your Career*, Harper Business, New York, 2015.

10. At the 2016 Code Conference, Bezos said this: 'I like to use the phrase "work-life harmony" rather than "balance". Because to me, balance implies a strict trade whereas I find that if I'm happy at work, I come home more energized, I'm a better husband, better Dad, and when come (to work) I'm a better boss, better colleague.' Video link, accessed 12 July 2017, https://www.youtube.com/watch?v=PTYFEgXaRbU.

11. Stewart D. Friedman, 'Work + Home + Community + Self: Skills for integrating every part of your life', *Harvard Business Review*, September 2014, accessed 11 April 2017, https://hbr.org/2014/09/work-home-community-self.

12. Ibid.

12. My Notes on the Business of Life

1. Edward Glaeser, *Triumph of the City: How Our Greatest Invention Makes us Richer, Smarter, Greener, Healthier, and Happier*, Macmillan, London, 2011, p. 6.

Appendix A

1. Carol Dweck, *Mindset: The New Psychology of Success*, Ballantine, New York, 2006, p. 6.